TOURISM PLANNING AND DEVELOPMENT

Tourism Planning and Development

B.S. Badan
Harish Bhatt

Commonwealth

Tourism Planning and Development

Edition : 2026

ISBN 81-311-0065-0

Published by :

COMMONWEALTH PUBLISHERS
4831/24, Prahlad Street,
Ansari Road, Darya Ganj,
New Delhi - 110002
Ph. : 23275511, 23257835
e-mail : commonwealthbooks@gmail.com

Typesetting by :
Rishu Computers
Delhi

Printed at :
Roshan Offset Printers
Delhi

PREFACE

Tourism can be defined as the act of travel for the purpose of recreation, and the provision of services for this act. It is a service industry, comprising a number of tangible and intangible components. The tangible elements include transportation systems—air, rail, road, water and now, space; hospitality services, accommodation, foods and beverages, tours, souvenirs; and related services such as banking, insurance and safety and security. The intangible elements include: rest and relaxation, culture, escape, adventure, new and different experiences.

Travel and tourism is a major industry in the world and is at the top of the league of invisible earners of foreign currency. Many sovereignties, along with their respective countries and states, depend heavily upon travel expenditures by foreigners as a source of taxation and income for the enterprises that sell services to these travellers. Consequently the development of tourism is often a strategy employed either by a non-governmental organization or a governmental agency to promote a particular region for the purpose of increasing commerce through exporting goods and services to non-locals.

During recent years the tourism industry has witnessed unprecedented growth. Increasing consumer demand for educational and participatory travel experiences has resulted in a variety of specialty niche markets such as ecotourism, cultural-heritage tourism, and agritourism. New paradigms link strategic tourism planning with sustainable development.

The leisure and tourism industry is one of the leading global economic activities, a multi-billion-dollar industry with

700 million international travellers per year around the world. Tourism is a motor for employment and income creation and, especially in poor countries, a vehicle for development. But today it is not sufficient to simply create employment without regard for the quality of jobs and the social and environmental effects of tourism in vulnerable areas. A growing number of organizations, including the tourism industry leadership, are increasingly conscious of the risks and are adopting a more responsible attitude.

The present publication provides an authoritative look at how to manage travel and tourism industry in a better way. It introduces the complexities of the tourism system so that they will be better positioned to eventually assume the managerial challenges and responsibilities in a diverse and challenging industry. The latest advancements in tourism theory and thinking, retaining the thoroughness of content, diversity of applications, regional and international issues, economic significance, tourism operators and the role of technology in the tourism industry etc. are also described elaborately. Numerous regional and global case studies and examples are included to provide an appropriately broad geographic context. This work will be highly informative and useful to students, researchers, policy makers, managers and working groups of travel and tourism industry.

B.S. Badan
Harish Bhatt

CONTENTS

1

THE IMPORTANCE OF PLANNING TOURISM

Planning tourism at all levels is essential for achieving successful tourism development and management. The experience of many tourism areas in the world has demonstrated that, on a long-term basis, the planned approach to developing tourism can bring benefits without significant problems, and maintain satisfied tourism markets. Places that have allowed tourism to develop without the benefit of planning are often suffering from environmental and social problems. These are detrimental to residents and unpleasant for many tourists, resulting in marketing difficulties and decreasing economic benefits. These uncontrolled tourism areas cannot effectively compete with planned tourist destinations elsewhere. They usually can be redeveloped, based on a planned approach, but that requires much time and financial investment.

Tourism is a rather complicated activity that overlaps several different sectors of the society and economy. Without planning, it may create unexpected and unwanted impacts. Tourism is also still a relatively new type of activity in many countries. Some governments and often the private sector have little or no experience in how to develop tourism properly. For countries that do not yet have much tourism, planning can provide the necessary guidance for its development. For those places that already have some tourism, planning is often needed to revitalise this sector and maintain its future viability.

First, tourism should be planned at the national and regional levels. At these levels, planning is concerned with tourism development policies, structure plans, facility standards, institutional factors and all the other elements necessary to develop and manage tourism. Then, within the framework of national and regional planning, more detailed plans for tourist attractions, resorts, urban, rural and other forms of tourism development can be prepared.

There are several important specific benefits of undertaking national and regional tourism planning. These advantages include:

- Establishing the overall tourism development objectives and policies–what is tourism aiming to accomplish and how can these aims be achieved.
- Developing tourism so that its natural and cultural resources are indefinitely maintained and conserved for future, as well as present, use.
- Integrating tourism into the overall development policies and patterns of the country or region, and establishing close linkages between tourism and other economic sectors.
- Providing a rational basis for decision-making by both the public and private sectors on tourism development.
- Making possible the coordinated development of all the many elements of the tourism sector. This includes inter-relating the tourist attractions, activities, facilities and services and the various and increasingly fragmented tourist markets.
- Optimising and balancing the economic, environmental and social benefits of tourism, with equitable distribution of these benefits to the society, while minimising possible problems of tourism.
- Providing a physical structure which guides the location, types and extent of tourism development of attractions, facilities, services and infrastructure.
- Establishing the guidelines and standards for preparing detailed plans of specific tourism development areas that are consistent with, and reinforce, one another, and for the appropriate design of tourist facilities.

- Laying the foundation for effective implementation of the tourism development policy and plan and continuous management of the tourism sector, by providing the necessary organisational and other institutional framework.
- Providing the framework for effective coordination of the public and private sector efforts and investment in developing tourism.
- Offering a baseline for the continuous monitoring of the progress of tourism development and keeping it on track.

The planned approach to developing tourism at the national and regional levels is now widely adopted as a principle, although implementation of the policies and plans is still weak in some places. Many countries and regions of countries have had tourism plans prepared. Other places do not yet have plans, but should consider undertaking planning in the near future. In some countries, plans had previously been prepared but these are now outdated. They need to be revised based on present day circumstances and likely future trends. Founded on accumulated experience, the approaches and techniques of tourism planning are now reasonably well understood. There is considerable assurance that, if implemented, planning will bring substantial benefits to an area.

2

APPROACHES TO TOURISM PLANNING

It is important to understand the basic approaches to planning and managing tourism development. These are described in the following sections.

Planning Tourism as an Integrated System

An underlying concept in planning tourism is that tourism should be viewed as an inter-related system of demand and supply factors. The tourism system is illustrated in Figure 2.1. The demand factors are international and domestic tourist markets and local residents who use the tourist attractions, facilities and services. The supply factors comprise tourist attractions and activities, accommodation and other tourist facilities and services. Attractions include natural, cultural and special types of features—such as theme parkes, zoos, botanic gardens and aquariums—and the activities related to these attractions. Accommodation includes hotels, motels, guest houses and other types of places where tourists stay overnight. The category of other tourist facilities and services includes tour and travel operations, restaurants, shopping, banking and money exchange, and medical and postal facilities and services. These supply factors are called the tourism product.

Other elements also relate to supply factors. In order to make the facilities and services usable, infrastructure is required. Tourism infrastructure particularly includes transportation (air, road, rail, water, etc.), water supply, electric power, sewage and solid waste disposal and telecommunications.

Demand Factors	Supply Factors
• International tourist markets	• Attractions and activities
• Domestic tourist markets	• Accommodation
• Residents' use of tourist attractions, facilities and services	• Other tourist facilities and services
	• Transportation
	• Other infrastructure
	• Institutional elements

Figure 2.1 : The tourism system.

Provision of adequate infrastructure is also important to protect the environment. It helps maintain a high level of environmental quality that is so necessary for successful tourism and desirable for residents.

The effective development, operation and management of tourism requires certain institutional elements. These elements include:

- Organisational structures, especially government tourism offices and private sector tourism associations such as hotel associations.
- Tourism-related legislation and regulations, such as standards and licensing requirements for hotels and tour and travel agencies.
- Education and training programmes, and training institutions to prepare persons to work effectively in tourism.
- Availability of financial capital to develop tourist attractions, facilities, services and infrastructure, and mechanisms to attract capital investment.
- Marketing strategies and promotion programmes to inform tourists about the country or region, and induce them to visit it, and tourist information facilities and services in the destination areas.
- Travel facilitation of immigration (including visa arrangements), customs and other facilities and services at the entry and exit points of tourists.

The institutional elements also include consideration of how to enhance and distribute the economic benefits of tourism, environmental protection measures, reducing adverse social impacts, and conservation of the cultural heritage of people living in the tourism areas.

As an inter-related system, it is important that tourism planning aim for integrated development of all these parts of the system, both the demand and supply factors and the physical and institutional elements. The system will function much more effectively and bring the desired benefits if it is planned in an integrated manner, with coordinated development of all the components of the system. Sometimes, this integrated system approach is also called the comprehensive approach to tourism planning because all the elements of tourism are considered in the planning and development process.

Just as important as planning for integration within the tourism system is planning for integration of tourism into the overall development policies, plans and patterns of a country or region. Planning for this overall integration will, for example, resolve any potential conflicts over use of certain resources of locations for various types of development. It also provides for the multi-use of expensive infrastructure to serve general community needs as well as tourism.

Emphasis is given to formulating and adopting tourism development policies and plans for an area in order to guide decision-making on development actions. The planning of tourism, however, should also be recognised as a continuous and flexible process. Within the framework of the policy and plan recommendations, there must be flexibility to allow for adapting to changing circumstances. Planning that is too rigid may not allow development to be responsive to changes. There may be advancements in transportation technology, evolution of new forms of tourism and changes in market trends. Even though allowed to be flexible, the basic objectives of the plan should not be abrogated although the specific development patterns may be changed. Sustainable development must still be maintained.

Planning for tourism development should make recommendations that are imaginative and innovative, but they must also be feasible to implement. The various techniques of implementation should be considered throughout the planning process. This approach ensures that the recommendations can be accomplished, and provides the basis for specifying the implementation techniques that should be applied. Implementation techniques can also be imaginative and not only rely on established approaches. It is common practice for a tourism plan to include specification of implementation techniques, and sometimes a separate manual on how to achieve the plan recommendations.

Planning for Sustainable Development

The underlying approach now applied to tourism planning, as well as to other types of development, is that of achieving sustainable development. The sustainable development approach implies that the natural, cultural and other resources of tourism are conserved for continuous use in the future, while still bringing benefits to the present society. The concept of sustainable development has received much emphasis internationally since the early 1980s, although tourism plans prepared even before that period often were concerned with conservation of tourism resources.

The sustainable development approach to planning tourism is acutely important because most tourism development depends on attractions and activities related to the natural environment, historic heritage and cultural patterns of areas. If these resources are degraded or destroyed, then the tourism areas cannot attract tourists and tourism will not be successful. More generally, most tourists, seek destinations that have a high level of environmental quality–they like to visit places that are attractive, clean and neither polluted nor consisted. It is also essential that residents of the tourism area should not have to suffer from a deteriorated environment and social problems.

One of the important benefits of tourism is that, if it is properly developed based on the concept of sustainability, tourism can greatly help justify and pay for conservation of an area's natural and cultural resources. Thus, tourism can be an important means of achieving conservation in areas that otherwise have limited capability to accomplish environmental protection and conservation objectives.

A basic technique in achieving sustainable development is the environmental planning approach. Environmental planning requires that all elements of the environment be carefully surveyed, analysed and considered in determining the most appropriate type and location of development. This approach would not allow, for example, intensive development in flood plain and steep hillside areas.

An important aspect of sustainable development is emphasising community-based tourism. This approach to tourism focuses on community involvement in the planning and development process, and developing the types of tourism, which generate benefits to local communities. It applies techniques to ensure that most of the benefits of tourism development accrue to local residents and not to outsiders. Maximising benefits to local residents typically results in tourism being better accepted by them and their actively supporting conservation of local tourism resources. The community-based tourism approach is applied at the local or more detailed levels of planning, but it can be set forth as a policy approach at the national and regional levels. The benefits accruing to local communities are also beneficial to the country, through the income and foreign exchange earned, employment generated and support that local communities give to national tourism development and conservation policies.

Also related to sustainable development is the concept of quality tourism. This approach is being increasingly adopted for two fundamental reasons—it can achieve successful tourism from the marketing standpoint and it brings benefits to local residents and their environment. Quality tourism does not necessarily mean expensive tourism. Rather, it refers to tourist attractions, facilities and services that offer 'good value for money', protect tourism resources, and attract the kinds of tourists who will respect the local environment and society. Quality tourism development can compete more effectively in attracting discriminating tourists. It is also more environmentally and socially self-sustaining. Achieving quality tourism is the responsibility of both the public and private sectors. This concept should be built into the tourism planning, development and management process.

Long-range and Strategic Planning

Long-range comprehensive planning is concerned with specifying goals and objectives and determining preferred future development patterns. Tourism development policies and plans should be prepared for relatively long-term periods—usually for 10 to 15 and sometimes 20 years—depending on the predictability of future events in the country or region. These may seem to be long planning periods, but it commonly requires this length of time to implement basic policy and structure plans. Even development of specific projects, such as major resorts or national park-based tourism, can require a long time.

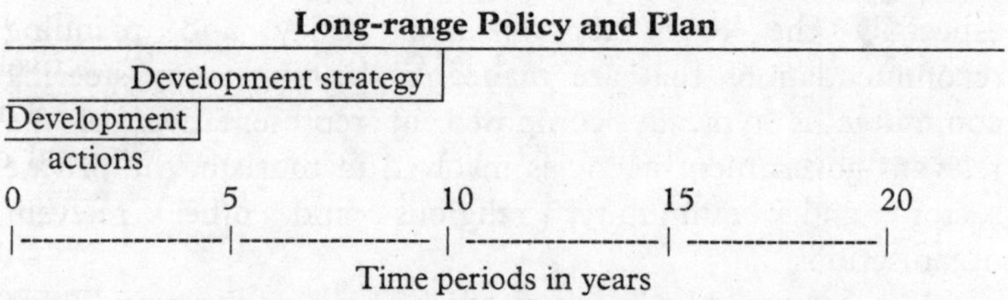

Figure 2.2: Long-range and strategic planning.

A planning approach which has received considerable attention in recent years, and is applicable to some tourism areas, is strategic planning. While the outcomes of strategic and long-range comprehensive planning may be very similar, strategic planning is somewhat different. It focuses more on identification and resolution of immediate issues. Strategic planning typically is more oriented to rapidly changing future situations and how to cope with changes organisationally. It is more action oriented and concerned with handling unexpected events.

Applied only by itself, strategic planning can be less comprehensive in its approach. By focusing on immediate issues, it may deviate from achieving such long-term objectives as sustainable development. But if used within the framework of integrated long-range plicy and planning, the strategic planning approach can be very appropriate. The relationship between long-range and strategic planning is illustrated, in a simple manner, in Figure 2.2.

Public Involvement in Planning

Planning is for the benefit of people, and they should be involved in the planning and development of tourism in their areas. Through this involvement, tourism development will reflect a consensus of what the people want. Also, if residents are involved in planning and development decisions and if they understand the benefits the tourism can bring—they will more likely support it. At the national and regional levels of preparing tourism plans, the common approach to obtaining public involvement is to appoint a steering committee. This committee offers guidance to the planning team and reviews its work, especially the draft reports and policy and planning recommendations that are made. A planning study steering committee is typically composed of representatives of the relevant government agencies involved in tourism, the private sector, and community, religious and other relevant organisations.

Also, open public hearings can be held on the plan. These hearings provide the opportunity for anybody to learn about the plan and express their opinions. Another common approach, when the plan is completed, is to organise a national or regional tourism seminar. This meeting informs participants and the general public about the importance of controlled tourism development and the recommendations of the plan. Such seminars often receive wide publicity in the communications media.

In a large country or region, the usual procedure is for the tourism plan to be prepared by the central authority with public involvement as described above. This can be termed the 'top-down' approach. Another procedure sometimes used is the 'bottom-up' approach. This involves holding meetings with local districts or communities to determine what type of development they would like to have. These local objectives and ideas are then fitted together into a national or regional plan. This approach achieves greater local public involvement in the planning process. But it is more time consuming and may lead to conflicting objectives, policies and development recommendations among the local areas. These conflicts need to be reconciled at the national and regional levels in order to form a consistent plan. It is important that the development patterns of the local areas complement and reinforce one another, but also reflect the needs and desires of local communities. Often a combination of the 'top-down' and 'bottom-up' approaches achieves the best results.

3

THE TOURISM PLANNING PROCESS

The process for preparing tourism plans at the national and regional levels—based on the sustainable, integrated and implementable approaches described in Chapter 2–can be described as a step-by-step procedure. This procedure, which is applicable to any national and regional planning situation, is illustrated in Figure 3.1 and explained in the following sections.

Study Preparation

The first step in the planning process is careful preparation of the study so that it provides the type of development guidance that is needed. Study preparation involves formulating the project terms of reference, selecting the technical team to carry out the study, appointing a steering committee, and organising the study activities.

The terms of reference (TOR) for the planning study should be carefully formulated so that the study achieves its desired results and outputs. The TOR for a national or regional plan indicates the outputs and activities that are necessary to prepare the development policy and plan. The special considerations to be made in planning–such as economic, environmental or social issues and the critical institutional elements–should be specified in the TOR. Identification of implementation techniques are also specified. The TOR format typically follows the planning process explained here, but it is tailored to the specific characteristics and needs of the planning area.

Many places already have some limited tourism development, and these existing patterns must be considered in formulating the TOR. Other countries or regions will have considerable existing tourism development, but it may be declining or not be in a form that generates optimum benefits. The TOR will therefore emphasise how to rejuvenate and improve existing development, alongwith how to provide guidance on the future expansion of tourism.

It is common for a single study to include various levels of tourism planning, such as national and regional plans alongwith detailed planning for priority development areas and projects. The planning to all these levels will need to be specified in the TOR. An advantage of including various levels of planning

Study preparation →	Determination of objectives →	Survey of all elements →	Analysis and synthesis →
Policy and plan formulation →	Formulation of other recommendations →	Implementation and monitoring	

Figure 3.1: Tourism planning process.

in one study is that there is greater continuity and consistency of the recommended development patterns. However, for detailed planning, only those areas and projects to be developed in the near future should be included in the overall study. The longer-term development areas and projects should be planned in detail later, based on circumstances prevailing at that time.

The TOR should indicate a horizon year when the plan and its targets and recommendations are to be realised. As indicated in Chapter 2, planning horizon years are typically for 10, 15 to 20 years. Development phasing or staging–usually for five-year periods–should be specified. Establishing a horizon year and staging periods provides a time framework for making projections, setting targets and phasing development.

Appendix 1 explains other aspects of preparation and organisation that are essential to carry out a successful planning study.

Determination of Objectives

Early in the planning process, the objectives of developing tourism should be determined. Deciding on objectives is very important because they state the desired results of developing tourism in the country or region. Objectives usually relate to various types of socio-economic benefits. They also specify the special considerations that must be made in tourism development, such as minimising negative environmental and socio-cultural impacts. Objectives should be determined in close consultation with the government (or steering committee) because they are basic determinants of the tourism development policies and plan.

Objectives are first established in a preliminary manner. They are later refined based on the results of the surveys and analyses and the plan formulation. Certain preliminary objectives may be found to be in conflict with one another, and they cannot all realistically be achieved. For example, one objective may state that the economic benefits of tourism should be maximised, and another objective may stipulate that environmental and socio-cultural impacts must be minimised and sustainable development maintained. It may not be possible to prepare a policy and plan that simultaneously achieves both of these objectives, at least over the long-term period. The objectives must balance economic, environmental and socio-cultural considerations.

Tourism development objectives should also reflect and reinforce any general development objectives already adopted for the country or region. This is important so that tourism is well integrated into overall development patterns. In some cases, however, it may be decided to modify the general objectives in order to achieve those tourism objectives that seem to be reasonable, and contribute to overall national and regional development.

Survey of All Elements

The survey stage of the planning process involves collecting data, both quantitative and qualitative, on all relevant aspects of tourism. These include the components of the tourism system and other factors as follows:

- Global and regional tourism patterns and trends. Regional here refers to several geographically related countries such as Africa, East and South Asia, Pacific

Islands, North and South America, Western Europe, etc. This information can be obtained from the World Tourism Organisation.

- Characteristics of existing or potential competing tourist destinations that offer similar tourism products and attract much the same tourist markets.
- Tourist arrival trends in the planning study country or region. These include the number and characteristics of tourist arrivals.
- Existing and potential tourist attractions and activities.
- Existing and already planned tourist accommodation and other tourist facilities and services.
- Existing and already planned transportation facilities and services, including both access to the country or region and the internal transportation system.
- Other types of infrastructure which are existing or already planned.
- Existing natural resource, land use and land tenure patterns. Land tenure refers to land ownership or leasing patterns.
- Existing economic and employment patterns, including employment in tourism, and economic and manpower development plans.
- Physical and social development plans–these are sometimes combined with the economic and manpower development plans listed above.
- Environmental characteristics and environmental quality. Environmental characteristics include such factors as climatic patterns and topography. Environmental quality includes the extent of air, water, noise and visual pollution, congestion, architectural interest and other factors.
- Socio-cultural patterns, especially as they relate to the effects of tourism development on the local societies and cultural patterns.
- Existing and already planned education and training programmes and training institutions designed to prepare persons to work in tourism.

- Existing government and private sector organisations in tourism, and their organisational structures and staffing.
- Present investment policies and availability of capital for investment in tourist facilities, services and infrastructure.
- Present tourism legislation and regulations.

One of the most important elements of the survey is that of tourist attractions and activities. These are what induce tourists to visit the country or region. Tourist attractions and related activities are categorised by type, and evaluated with respect to accessibility, feasibility of development, market trends of what tourists want to see and do, and other factors. They are also identified as primary attractions–those which basically attract tourists to visit the place (if the attractions are properly conserved and developed with facilities), or as secondary one–those attractions which are less important but complement the primary attractions and increase touristic interest and length of stay.

For many of these elements–such as tourist attractions and activities, accommodation, other tourist facilities and services and some types of infrastructure–field surveys are required. These surveys should include evaluation of the elements alongwith noting their characteristics. Evaluation of tourist attractions was described above. Tourist facilities and services must also be evaluated as to their suitability, quality and efficiency to serve tourists properly. Infrastructure must be assessed as to how adequately it serves tourism development. Often market surveys are conducted, with visits made to interview tour operators in the market source countries.

Other types of surveys require document research and discussion meetings with local persons. Some of the types of surveys—such as for infrastructure, natural resources, land use and land tenure patterns and environmental characteristics—are carried out generally at the national and regional levels. They are conducted more specifically in the detailed planning for tourism development areas such as resorts.

Analysis and Synthesis

Both quantitative and qualitative analysis and synthesis of the survey information must be carefully carried out. Synthesis refers to combining and integrating the various components of the analysis, in order to obtain a more comprehensive understanding of the situation. Major aspects of the analysis and synthesis are described as follows:

- The market analysis is derived from several sources. The survey of global, national and regional tourism patterns and market trends is essential input. The survey and evaluation of the tourist attractions, facilities and services in the study area is also very important. The tourism development objectives must be considered. Accessibility to the country or region from the major tourist markets areas, including cost, distance and convenience of travel, is a very important factor too. However, accessibility can often be improved if it is presently a problem. The market analysis includes establishing market targets of the number and types of tourists that potentially can be attracted, but only if the development and marketing recommendations are implemented Market targets are usually established by five-year periods, up to the horizon year of the plan.
- Several calculations can be made from the market analysis. The number and types of accommodation required are projected, and other tourist facilities and services needed are identified. Analysis of the economic impact of tourism is derived from the market targets and tourist characteristics. This includes the projection of the number and type of employees needed to work in tourism. Appendix 2 explains how accommodation needs are projected.
- Based on the projection of tourist facilities and services needed and the movement patterns of tourists, the transportation and other infrastructure facilities and services required can be determined.
- From several of the surveyed elements, the integrated analysis or synthesis of physical, economic and social

factors is prepared. This synthesis provides much of the basis for formulating the structure plan. It includes establishing carrying capacities, an essential consideration in achieving sustainable tourism development. The carrying capacity of an area is the maximum level of development or use that the area can absorb without resulting in serious environmental damage, socio-economic problems, or decline in the quality of visitor experience. Appendix 3 explains how carrying capacity is calculated.

- All the institutional elements are evaluated and analysed as a basis for formulating policy and recommendations about each of them.

An important type of synthesis is identification of major opportunities and problems or constraints for developing tourism. This provides a focus for formulating recommendations, and how to take advantage of opportunities and overcome constraints, all leading to better development of tourism.

The offerings of possible competing destinations that have similar tourism products and markets should be evaluated. There may be sufficient growth in the tourist markets to satisfy the needs for tourists in both the country or region being planned and competing destinations. But there may not be that much market growth. If the planning study area can offer some comparative advantages over competing destinations in its development of attractions, facilities and services, it will be better positioned to attract the desired numbers and types of tourists.

Policy and Plan Formulation

This step in the planning process involves formulating policy on tourism development and preparing the physical structure plan. The best approach to policy and plan formulation is first to prepare and evaluate alternative development scenarios. There is seldom a single ideal set of policies and plans, but rather optimum ones that balance costs and benefits. Alternative policies and plans are evaluated according to several factors—meeting the development objectives; optimising economic benefits; reinforcing positive and minimising negative environmental and socio-cultural impacts; and effectively competing with other tourist destinations. Based on this evolution, the final policies and plans are selected and refined.

Policy and plan formulation should be carried out in close consultation with the steering committee and other interested parties, in order to ensure that they reflect a consensus about the most appropriate future tourism development patterns.

Formulation of the Institutional Recommendations

Based on the survey, analysis and evaluation of the institutional elements, conclusions and recommendations can be made. For many types of recommendations, alternatives must be evaluated before the most suitable ones can be determined. There may be no need for changes in some of these elements, but this fact should be stated. In certain cases, alternative recommendations, all of which are acceptable, can be made. The government or private sector can later decide on which course of action to pursue, depending on future circumstances. It is also essential to involve the steering committee and other interested parties in formulating the institutional recommendations.

Implementation and Monitoring

The final step in the planning process is specifying implementation techniques. As referred to in Chapter 2, the means of implementation should be considered throughout the planning process, and especially during the formulation of the policy, plan and other recommendations. This is important so that the final plan and recommendations are realistic to achieve and implementable. During and after implementation, tourism development must be monitored to ensure that it is accomplishing the objectives and achieving the recommended policies. Monitoring will detect any problems that arise so that remedial measures can be taken before that problems become serious.

Elements of a Comprehensive Tourism Plan

An integrated and comprehensive national or regional tourism plan contains many different elements. Appendix 4 presents a checklist of the elements that should be included in a typical tourism plan. This can serve as a guide for ensuring that all the necessary elements are considered in preparing the plan.

4
FORMS OF TOURISM DEVELOPMENT

In formulating the tourism policy and plan, it is important to understand the different forms of tourism development and types of tourism related to specific travel motivations that can be considered for the country or region. The forms of tourism described in the following sections are mostly those which represent the planned development approach. Some of them have also developed spontaneously, but often with problems resulting from lack of planning and development controls, and they require planned rejuvenation.

Resorts

One of the most common forms of modern holiday tourism is some type of resort-based development. A tourist resort can be defined as a destination area that is relatively self-contained. It typically provides a wide range of tourist facilities and services including those designed for recreation and relaxation. Because of the present trend of more tourists wanting to participate in recreation, sports, cultural and other activities, resorts are now emphasising the provision of a wide variety of facilities and services. These often include major commercial and conference/ meeting facilities.

Some resorts, located where there are seasonal differences in climate (summer and winter or dry and rainy), have traditionally experienced wide seasonal variations in guest arrivals. The current trend is for these resorts to offer facilities and services for year-round use, often catering to different types of guests during the different seasons. In addition to containing their own facilities for tourist use, many resorts also serve as a base for tourists to take sightseeing trips to points of interest in the nearby area.

Resorts have their primary orientation to several types of attractions and activities—beach relaxation and recreation; marine sports in both lake and ocean coastal areas; water recreation and sports on rivers; mountain winter skiing and summer hiking and horse riding; golf and tennis sports; health facilities related to mineral springs (spas) or dry sunny climate; important archaeological and historic sites and national parks; or a combination of features. Some resorts are very large with a variety of types of accommodation, including self-catering units, and many recreation and commercial facilities. Other resorts may be composed of only one hotel but still offer a range of facilities, services and activities. 'Retreat' type resorts may be small and isolated, but they provide a high quality level of facilities and services. They cater to guests who want a quiet remote environment. Holiday villages are a type of resort.

Integrated resorts are ones which have been carefully planned as single entities, even though larger integrated resorts are usually constructed in phases over a long period of time. Most new resort areas are carefully planned to function efficiently and provide an interesting environment for tourists while not generating any serious environmental and social problems. Many unplanned resorts also exist in various parts of the world, but some of these are experiencing environmental and social problems and require redevelopment.

Town resorts combine the usual land uses and activities of a town community, but are economically focused on resort activities. They include hotels, other types of accommodation and a variety of tourist facilities and services. They contain or are located near major attraction features, such as beaches or ski facilities. Town resorts were often no initially planned as integrated developments. Many of these places are now undergoing redevelopment and applying controls in order to improve their environmental quality and economic viability.

Some recently developed planned resorts include new towns where the resort support population lives. These then function as viable resort towns.

Urban Tourism

Tourism in towns and cities is very widespread. These urban places often offer a broad range of historic and cultural attractions, shopping, restaurants and the appeal of urban vitality. Many urban attractions and amenities are primarily developed to serve residents, but their use by tourists can greatly help to support them. Additionally, urban areas may function as points of arrival and departure of tourists to the country or region, and serve as a base for tourists to take excursions to nearby areas. Hotels and other tourist facilities are an integral part of the urban fabric and serve both business and holiday travellers.

Urban tourism must also be carefully planned. Determination must be made of the location of hotels and other tourist facilities, location and development of attraction features, the additional infrastructure required for them, and perhaps institutional improvements. It is now common practice to develop or redevelop certain urban areas—such as historic districts and waterfront sites—which are oriented particularly to tourism and residents' leisure use. Major convention and sports facilities are often developed to attract more tourists.

Special Interest and Adventure Tourism

One of the rapidly expanding types of tourism is special interest and adventure tourism. This type of tourism reflects the increasing fragmentation of tourist markets. Special interest tourism refers to tourists, usually in small groups, who are travelling to learn about and experience particular features of an area. These special interest themes are often associated with the tourists' long-term avocational or professional/vocational interests.

Special interest tourism can focus on a wide range of features. Cultural themes include dance, music, drama, fine arts, handicrafts, architecture, archaeology, history and historic routes, traditional life styles, and unusual economic activities. Nature themes relate to flora, fauna, geology, scenic beauty, national parks and marine environments. Professional interests involve visits to meet people of similar professions and exchange ideas. Educational tours are a type of special interest tourism. Participatory activities are common, such as tourists working under supervision at an archaeological site excavation.

Adventure tourism involves the tourists engaging in physically and personally challenging and sometimes dangerous activities. These include safaris and trekking in remote areas, hiking, mountain climbing, river rafting and white water boating through river rapids. Hunting and fishing may be considered as an aspect of special interest and adventure tourism.

Related to special interest tourism is a form that has been variously termed alternative, responsible, appropriate and even sustainable tourism. (However, the tourism development approach used in this publication is that all forms of tourism should be planned to be responsible, appropriate and sustainable.) This form of tourism refers to small-scale, non-conventional types of development, including the following:

- *Village tourism*—small groups of tourists staying is or near traditional, often remote, villages, and learning about village life and the local environment. Facilities are owned and managed by the villagers.
- *Rural, farm or agrotourism*—tourists staying with farm families and learning about farming activities, or staying on tropical plantations and learning about plantation life and activities, or staying in fishing villages with fishermen's families and going on fishing trips.
- *Walking and cycling tours*—tourists travelling by walking or bicycling and staying in inns, hostels, private homes or bed and breakfast houses, meeting local people and learning about the culture and environment.
- *Ecotourism (a controlled form of nature tourism)*—tourists hiking or boating in natural areas, with local guides to explain about the flora, fauna and ecology. Ecotourism may also include visits to local villages and farms. This type of tourism is currently receiving much attention

because of its emphasis on environmental conservation and learning about nature.

- *Community assistance programmes*—small groups of tourists, often community organisations in their home countries, visiting an area and assisting local people with a particular development project such as building low-cost housing or constructing a village water supply.

Other Forms of Tourism

There are several other forms of tourism that are suitable in many places. These include:

- *Water transport tourism*—cruise ship travel, boating on rivers and canals and yachting, all of which are very popular in certain regions of the world. Shore-based facilities of piers, docks and marinas and related facilities and services are required for this type of tourism.
- *Residential tourism*—development of various types of housing and related community facilities and services, for use as vacation or retirement homes. This is a very common form of tourism.
- *Camping and caravan tourism*—development of camping facilities, usually near an important attraction or recreation feature, and caravan or parks for recreational vehicles located along highways or near attractions.
- *Transportation-oriented tourism*—hotels and other tourist facilities and services located near major transportation centres, especially airports for transit passengers. Airport-related tourism development is now providing meeting facilities for business travellers. Associated with road travel is the development of motels along major highways, especially in the peripheral areas of towns and cities and at major highway intersections.
- *Youth tourism*—travel by young people and students for education, sports and recreation has long been an established form of tourism and is currently being encouraged in many countries. Youth tourism requires development of inexpensive accommodation, often

hostels or dormitories. 'Elderhostel' programmes for older people undertaking educational travel and staying in hostel-type accommodation are also popular.

Not related to any particular form of tourism, but based on specialised travel motivations, are the following important types of tourism:

- *Religious tourism*—travel by pilgrims to places of religious significance, such as the Hajj to Mecca and visits to the Vatican in Rome and Varanasi in India, is very important in some countries. Religious pilgrims often require tourist-type facilities and services.
- *Ethnic tourism*—as used here, refers to persons who are visiting their own original homelands or places of their ancestral origin. Some countries are encouraging persons who have migrated overseas to visit their homelands as an important type of tourist market.
- *Nostalgic tourism*—persons visiting places where they previously had been involved in some activity. Visits by Americans and Japanese to places where they were assigned and fought in World War II is an example of nostalgic tourism. Nostalgic tourism may be important in an area for only a limited period of time.

As can be seen, many of these forms of tourism, especially those related to special interest and sightseeing activities, depend heavily on the natural and cultural resources of a tourism area. Consequently, environmental and cultural heritage conservation and interpretation is one of the major themes of contemporary tourism development. Many of the techniques that have been developed for interpretation of heritage sites are quite imaginative in educating visitors in an interesting and entertaining manner.

5

PLANNING FOR TOURISM

Tourism development is not an end in itself, but a means to an end. In other words, destinations do not develop attraction, facilities and amenities for the simple purpose of attracting and satisfying the needs of tourists. Rather, they seek to attract tourists or, more precisely, tourist spending, for the contribution that it can make to the wider economic and social development of destination areas. Indeed, it has long been recognised that international tourism can be an important means of achieving development and, as a result, many countries have embraced tourism as an integral element of their development strategies.

Similarly, domestic tourism development makes an important contribution to local economic and social regeneration. In the UK, for example, many inner city regeneration projects have been based upon tourism, the most widely cited example, perhaps, being Bradford, which established itself as an unlikely but successful destination during the 1980s. Many dookland areas, such as Bristol and Liverpool, have also developed a range of tourist facilities and attractions whilst, throughout Europe, tourism is widely considered an effective means of addressing the economic and social decline of peripheral rural areas.

In short, the fundamental role of tourism is, essentially, to 'ensure the steady acceleration of economic and social development and progress, in particular in developing countries', as well as contributing to local and regional regeneration in developed countries. In turn, this suggests that there is a need to plan tourism so that it fulfils this role effectively. That is, tourism development must be planned so that, beyond providing satisfying experiences for tourists, destinations themselves benefit economically and socially from tourism whilst the costs to the destination—the economic, environmental and socio-cultural impacts–are minimised.

However, whilst it is easy to justify the need for effective planning in tourism, the actual planning process is, for a number of reasons, rather more complex:

- Planning occurs at different levels, or 'scales' in the tourism system, from the development of specific attractions or facilities, through destination/resort planning, to regional or national plans for tourism. The objectives of planning may vary at each level. At the site level, for example, planning may focus on design issues whilst national tourism planning may be concerned with employment opportunities.
- Different types of organisations may be involved in the planning process, including businesses in the various sectors of the tourism industry, government bodies and non-profit or 'voluntary' organisations, each of which may have different objectives dependent on their role in the tourism system.
- The overall approach to planning is likely to vary according to the specific characteristics or needs of the destination or type of tourism. Rural tourism planning, for example, embraces a different set of challenges and objectives compared with, say, urban tourism development. Nevertheless, regional or national development needs should, ideally, provide the focus for tourism planning to ensure that broader developmental needs are met. This, in turn, points to the need for integration across the tourism planning spectrum.

Evidently, then, tourism planning is a complex, multi-layered process, a full consideration of which is well beyond the scope of this chapter. The purpose here, therefore, is to explore the basis of planning, its role and objectives within the tourism development process, different approaches to planning and the need for planning to be located within broader national development objectives. The first question to be addressed, however, is what *is* planning?

What is Planning?

Planning, according to Murphy, is 'concerned with anticipating and regulating change in a system, to promote orderly development so as to increase the social, economic and environmental benefits of the developmental process'. In other words, planning is a process whereby a variety of future dicisions or actions are mapped out in order to achieve desired outcomes in appropriate ways. In the context of this chapter, this means that planning is directed towards developing tourism in a manner that is appropriate to the needs of the destination community, to the capacity of the environment to absorb tourism and tourists, and to the needs of tourists themselves, optimising the desired outcomes whilst minimising the costs or negative impacts.

Implicitly, therefore, the ability to plan effectively is dependent upon the existence of goals or objectives; it is not possible to plan without having a reason for planning, a goal to aim for. Such goals might be set as part of the planning process or they may already exist as an element of broader local, regional or national policy. In either case, though, planning is guided by policy. Thus, if a destination's *policy* is to develop smaller-scale, up-market tourism, it will *plan* its accommodation and other developments, as well as its marketing and promotion activities, accordingly.

It is apparent, then, that planning is a much broader or more complex task than simply producing a plan. As Hall observes, 'planning as a process must... be distinguished from a plan', the latter representing a set of decisions or actions that are, in effect, the outcome of planning which, itself, is guided by policy. Moreover, planning does not stop once a plan has been produced. A plan must also be implemented or put into action and, once this has occurred, the results must be evaluated, reviewed and, if necessary, fed back into the policy/planning process (see Figure 5.1).

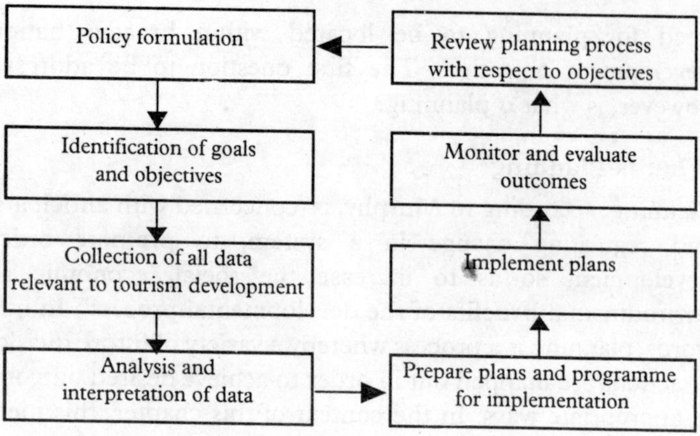

Figure 5.1: The planning process.

The model show in Figure 5.1 demonstrates a typical planning process. Though simplifying what, in practice, may be a lengthy and complex task, it nevertheless shows that planning in tourism is neither a 'one-off' event, nor simply the formulation or production of a plan. Indeed, the most important element of the planning process is, perhaps, the monitoring and evaluation of the outcomes, for tourism development not only results in a variety of environmental, economic and social consequences for the destination (both positive and negative), but also must be measured against the broader goals or objectives of developing tourism in the first place.

Thus, in short, tourism planning is a constant, cyclical process embracing policy formulation, the preparation and implementation of plans for tourism development, and the monitoring and reviewing of outcomes.

The Role of Planning in Tourism Development

Planning is an essential element of successful tourism development. In other words, experience has shown that, where tourism has been allowed to develop unconstrained by planning and control, not only to destinations suffer a variety of environmental and social problems but also, in the longer term, they may experience difficulty in continuing to attract tourists.

In short, if unplanned, tourism can destroy itself, with consequential economic consequences for the destination. Conversely, many other destinations have shown that 'the planned approach to tourism can bring benefits without significant problems, and maintain satisfied tourist markets'.

To a great extent, the nature of tourism as both an economic and social activity demands that it be planned effectively. That is, tourism is characterised by a number of 'fundamental truths' which point to the need for tourism to be planned to avoid causing social problems, environmental degradation and limited long-term benefits. McKercher's 'truths' may be summarised as follows:

- Tourism development consumes resources, creates waste and pollution and has specific infrastructure needs which may impact negatively on fragile environments.
- Tourism potentially over-consumes resources; that is, it may be developed beyond the environmental and social capacity of destinations, resulting in negative impacts on the environment and local communities.
- Tourism depends upon and competes for scarce resources. Thus, tourism may conflict with or prevent other uses of a resource.
- As a private-sector dominated industry, development decisions are likely to be based on short-term profit maximisation objectives.
- Tourism is diverse and multi-sectoral. Therefore, it is virtually impossible to control.
- Tourists are consumers who principally seek pleasurable experiences. Generally, they do not wish to 'work' at tourism.
- Tourism is entertainment, so cultural resources (festivals, shows, museums) must be adapted or 'commodified' to meet the needs of tourists.
- Tourism is consumed on-site, pointing to the inevitability of tourist-host encounters and stresses on physical infrastructure and environment.

It is evident that planning can 'solve' some, but not all, of these problems of tourism development. For example, the tourist is the customer and, therefore, as with all products and services, the tourism industry should focus on satisfying their needs rather than, as some would naively suggest, trying to modify their behaviour and attitudes. Nevertheless, planning has an important role to play in constraining or restricting the extent to which these 'truths' of tourism collectively diminish the benefits accruing from tourism development. Indeed, planning fulfils a number of significant functions:

- It provides the framework of establishing and assessing the objectives of tourism development–it is all to easy to justify tourism simply on its contribution to 'development' (see below).
- It encourages the integration of tourism development into broader development policies in the destination area.
- It ensures that, as far as possible, the resources upon which tourism depends are maintained and enhanced for both present and future use.
- It provides the framework for co-operative actions and decision-making amongst all stakeholders (i.e. private and public sector organisations and all elements of the tourism sector) involved in the development process.
- It focuses on developing and promoting tourism of an appropriate type and scale in order to optimise the economic, social and environmental benefits of tourism within the context of local needs.
- It establishes an overall 'design' for the development of a destination.
- It sets the yardsticks by which the outcomes of tourism development can be measured and evaluated against the overall objectives of such development.

There is no doubt that 'the planned approach to developing tourism at the national and regional level is now widely adopted as a principle'. Less certain, however, is the extent to which plans are implemented. In other words, although most, if not all destinations have tourism development plans, in many cases there is little evidence that those plans have been carried through to fruition. As suggested later in this chapter, this frequently results from an ineffective balance between the role of the industry (the private sector) and government (the public sector). Nevertheless, planning provides the means for controlling and directing tourism development to the benefit of the destination and, in principle, ensuring that it contributes to broader objectives. What, then, are these objectives?

The Objectives of Tourism Planning

In a general sense, the objective of tourism planning is to ensure that the desired benefits of tourism development to all stakeholders–destination communities, tourism businesses and tourists themselves–are optimised. Typically, such benefits are referred to collectively as 'development', a term which is usually taken to mean progress or improvement in people's social and economic status although, as considered below, the meaning of the term is rather more ambiguous that might be expected.

At the same time, however, the purpose of planning tourism is also to minimise the negative consequences of developing tourism. That is, it has long been recognised that the development of tourism can result in verity of impacts on destinations. These include, of course, environmental impacts, such as pollution (including so-called 'architectural pollution', epitomised, perhaps, by the concrete jungles of over-developed coastal resorts), social impacts, such as the disruption to local people's daily lives and economic impacts, such as the costs of refuse collection, policing and so on.

Thus, tourism planning has two broad sets of objectives:

- *'developmental' objectives*—those that are concerned with achieving some benefit for the destination environment and community, and
- *'management' objectives*—those that are concerned with guiding the nature, rate and scale of tourism development to minimise its negative consequences.

The specific objectives within each category will, of course, vary according to the characteristics of the destination in terms of its stage of economic and social development, its environmental diversity and robustness/fragility, the extent to which tourism has already been developed, its geographic location in relation to potential tourist markets and so on, and its broader developmental objectives. It is, therefore, difficult to highlight specific objectives of tourism planning as they are likely to vary from one destination to another.

Nevertheless, Gunn suggests that, generally, for the 'betterment of tourism there are at least the following four planning goals', three of which fall under the 'developmental objective' umbrella, and one under the 'management objective' umbrella.

(i) Enhanced visitor satisfaction—Though not, arguably, the principal objective of tourism planning, tourism 'begins with the desires of travellers to travel and ends with their satisfactions derived from such travel'. In other words, if people did not wish to be tourists, there would be no tourism industry. Thus, it is vital for a destination not only to attract tourists in the first place, but also to ensure that their needs/expectations are, as far as is possible, satisfied. Moreover, in an increasingly competitive international tourism market, it also necessary to focus continually on improving or enhancing the tourist experience as part of the planning process (hence, the need for the evaluation and review stage in planning). If this is not done, tourists may simply go elsewhere.

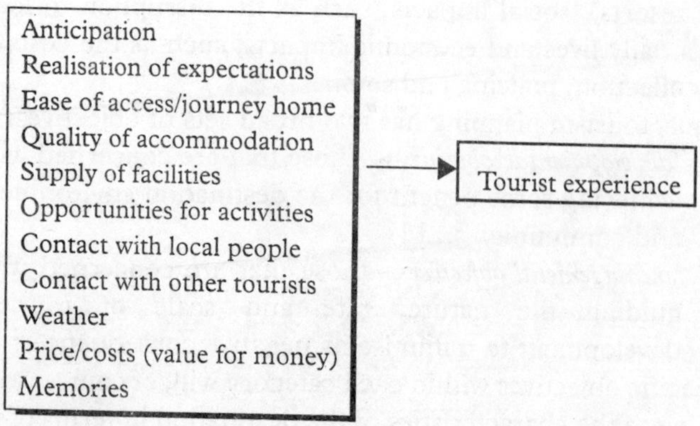

Figure 5.2: Elements of the total tourism experience.

This objective also points to the need for integrated planning in tourism. The extent to which tourists are satisfied with their holiday experience is not simply related, for example, to having good food, sunny weather and a comfortable hotel. Rather, tourists evaluate their experience of the 'total tourism product', which represents a combination of both tangible and intangible factors (see Figure 5.2). Therefore, planning must, ideally, embrace all sectors of the tourism industry at all stages of the demand process to ensure satisfying tourist experiences.

(ii) Improved economy and business success—The main purpose of developing tourism has long been, and largely remains, to achieve economic growth and development in destination areas. That is, tourism is usually developed for its potential economic benefits, including foreign exchange earnings (international tourism is an export), income to local business, employment and the 'multiplied effect'. The economic benefits of tourism are summarised in Figure 5.3.

Direct benefits	*Indirect benefits*
• Foreign exchange earnings	• Linkages throughout the economy
• Business income	- construction sector
- owners earnings	- food production sector
- employee earnings	- transport sector, etc.
• Employment	• Multiplier effect: spending from primary income, which generates
- private sector	- income
- public sector	- employment
• Government earnings	- government earnings
- Income tax from employment/ corporation	
- VAT/import duties, etc.	
- Local business taxes	

Figure 5.3: The economic benefits of tourism.

One objective of tourism planning, therefore, is to maximise these benefits by ensuring, for example, that sufficient support and incentives are provided at the national level to encourage entrepreneurs to invest in tourism, that appropriate tourist markets are attracted, that education and training are provided for employees, that other sectors of the local economy (e.g. food production, transport providers and so on) are able to benefit from tourism, and that policies are in place to encourage local ownership of tourism development.

(iii) Protected resource assets—It has long been recognised that tourism development has adverse impacts on the resources upon which it depends. This reflects the broader conflict between, on the one hand, the exploitation of natural resources to achieve development and growth and, on the other hand, the need to protect and conserve resources. Certainly, since the late 1960s, concern for the environment has become a dominant political and economic factor and there is no doubt that environmentalism, manifested in, for example, increasing membership of conservation organisations, the emergence of green political parties, and the activities of organisations such as Greenpeace and Friends of the Earth, has done much to raise global environmental awareness.

The growth of environmentalism in general has been mirrored by increasing concern for the impacts of tourism in particular. Indeed, the rapid growth in international tourism from the 1960s onwards has been matched by a no less rapid growth in calls to manage the development of tourism so that its environmental consequences are minimised. Not only does this make sound economic sense–any business has an interest in maintaining its resource base to ensure its longer-term survival – but, as a resource dependent industry, tourism depends upon a healthy, attractive environment in order to continue to attract tourists. Therefore, a fundamental 'management' objective of planning is resource protection, focusing upon the design, location and scale of facilities and infrastructure, the appropriate type of tourism (for example, small scale versus mass tourism), and targeted marketing and promotion.

(iv) Community and area integration—In addition to its environmental consequences, tourism also has an impact on local communities in destination areas. Ideally, such consequences should be positive as the primary purpose of tourism development, as observed at the beginning of the chapter, is the social and economic development of local

communities in destination areas. In other words, tourism is developed in order to improve the lives of local people and, although this is often the case, there are also many ways, of course, in which tourism has an adverse effect on locals.

Thus, a final objective of tourism planning, according to Gunn, is community and area integration. That is tourism planning should be directed towards integration tourism into the social and economic life of local communities and areas not only so that the negative impacts are minimised but also, and perhaps more importantly, so that the needs of local people and local development plans figure prominently in tourism planning.

These objectives of tourism planning are not necessarily mutually exclusive. Indeed, as discussed shortly, although different approaches to planning can be related to different objectives, the last decade or so has witnessed the virtually global acceptance and endorsement of an approach that attempts to combine and achieve all of these objectives–sustainable tourism development.

However, before going on to look at the different perspectives on planning, it is important to consider briefly what is meant by the term 'development' as the overall objective of tourism planning. That is, although tourism is usually justified on the basis of its potential contribution to the development of destination areas, until recently little attempt has been made to define what development is and, consequently to consider whether tourism is in fact an appropriate means of achieving it.

What is Development?

It is likely that, although most people refer to 'development', few would be able to define what they mean by it. This is due, in part, to the fact that it is an ambiguous term to describe both the process which a society moves through from one condition to another, and also the goal of that process. That is, the development process in any country or society may result in it achieving the state or condition of development, although even that it is not a static, final condition–Britain, for example, though a 'developed' country, is still undergoing development.

At the same time, however, the difficulty in defining development also stems from a lack of consensus over the aims or goals of development. Traditionally, it was equated with economic growth. As the national economy grows the national productive capacity (usually measured as Gross Domestic Product, or GDP) increases and, as long as national output expands at a faster rate than the population growth rate (i.e. per capita GDP is increasing), then development is said to be occurring. Certainly, throughout the 1950s and 1960s, international policies for promoting development were based on economic growth strategies and, to a great extent, tourism's contribution to development remains based on economic indicators–employment, income, foreign exchange earnings, and so on.

However, by the late 1960s it had become clear that, in many countries, economic growth was not only failing to solve wider social and political problems but was actually causing or exacerbating them. As a result, the objectives or meaning of development gradually moved beyond the goal of economic growth to embrace the broader social needs of reducing poverty, improving employment opportunities and so on. Indeed, many policy-makers rejected economic growth as the objective of development; people, rather than things, become the focus of attention. In particular, the notion of economic growth was challenged by Seers, who asserted:

> The questions to ask about a country's development are therefore: What has been happening to poverty? What has been happening to unemployment? What has been happening to inequality? If all three of these have declined from high levels, the beyond doubt this has been a period of development for the country concerned.

He later added self-reliance, or reducing dependence on other countries, as a further objective of development. In other words, for a country to be achieving development, it must be in control of its own development process and guiding it according to its own needs.

Thus, development, whilst still requiring economic growth, is a more complex and multidimensional process requiring the transformation of social and political, as well as economic, structures; it is the process whereby a whole society advances from a condition that is unsatisfactory to one that, according to that society's needs and values, better provides for the overall well-being of its members. Typically, therefore, development; as both a process and a goal, embraces a number of dimensions:

- *Economic*–the creation of wealth and the equitable access to resources and material goods;
- *Social*–health, education, employment and housing opportunities;
- *Political*–human rights, political freedom and the ability of societies to select and operate political systems that best suit their needs or structure;
- *Cultural*–protection/strengthening cultural identity and self-esteem; and
- *Environmental*–all development should occur within the ability of the environment to sustain such change and development.

As an example of these elements of development, the OECD has identified a number of goals as part of a new international development strategy (Figure 5.4).

Development goals for 2015 Shaping the 21st Century—

Economic well-being

- Reduce extreme poverty by half

Social development

- Universal primary education
- Eliminate gender disparity in education by 2005
- Reduce infant and child mortality by two-thirds
- Reduce maternal mortality by three-fourths
- Universal access to reproductive health services

Environmental sustainability and regeneration

- Implementation of a national strategy for sustainable development in every country by 2005, so as to:
- Reverse trends in the loss of environmental resources by 2015.

Figure 5.4: International development goals.
Source: OECD (1999).

The question then, of course, is: to what extent can tourism, as a specific economic sector and development option, contribute to these broad goals? Undoubtedly, tourism makes a contribution to economic growth and diversification, but less certain is its contribution to socio-cultural, political and environmental development. Nevertheless, some advance can potentially be made, particularly is the appropriate approach to tourism planning is adopted.

Approaches to Planning

Just as the objectives of tourism will vary according to the particular needs and characteristics of different destinations, so too will the approach to tourism planning vary. To an extent, this will be determined by the scale of planning.

Tourism Planning Scales

Generally, there are three levels, or scales at which tourism is planned:

(i) The site scale—Probably the most common form of tourism planning is at the site scale; that is, at the level of individual projects, developments or properties. At this level, planning is most likely to be concerned with factors relevant to the physical scale and design of the development with respect to both the environment (e.g. using appropriate materials, a design that is appropriate to the character to the area and that is on a scale that does not place excessive pressure on local resources) and to potential or desired tourist markets. Frequently, the physical design of the project will be constrained by local planning restrictions–in the English national parks, for example, all proposals are rigorously scrutinised by the relevant National Park Authority–whilst the size and type of business proposed will be subject to a variety of factors, such as location, transport services, other local attractions and services, information and marketing services, and so on. Thus, even at the site level, tourism planning cannot be divorced from a variety of wider external incluences and relationships.

(ii) The destination scale—In order to achieve local development goals, it is important to plan tourism at the destinational scale. In a sense, this represents the collective planning of all site-level developments within a broader plan for the destination as a whole, the objective usually being to provide

a critical mass of facilities and attractions sufficient to satisfy the needs of tourists. Typically, such planning will address issues such as:

- The number and variety of facilities and attractions (accommodation, restaurants, shops, etc.) to meet the needs of a number of different tourist markets;
- Limits on the scale and character of development to retain the desired 'feel' of a destination;
- Public facilities for the use of both residents and tourists (parks, museum, sports centres, etc.); and
- Efficient and attractive transport services within the destination.

Generally, destinational planning is concerned with providing the optimal tourist experience, thereby underpinning tourism's contribution to local economic and social development, whilst being sensitive to the potential social, environmental and economic impacts of tourism development on the destination.

(iii) The regional scale—At the regional (or national) scale, tourism planning is undertaken to ensure that tourism is planned and managed within the parameters of regional (or national) development policy. Thus, different destinations in the region are, in principle, planned and developed as part of a cohesive overall tourism development plan so that, for example, the problem of seasonality may can be addressed–one resort may cater principally to a summer-sun market whilst, elsewhere, business/conference tourism may be developed. At the same time, regional planning can focus on the development of transport systems that benefit all tourism development in the region whilst it is also necessary to plan at the regional or, in the case of smaller countries, such as island micro-states, to ensure that the development of the tourism sector is integrated with the planning and development of other sectors, such as industry, forestry, agriculture, housing, and so on.

Planning Approaches

Hall describes four different approaches to the planning of tourism which, to an extent, reflect increasing knowledge and awareness of the impacts of tourism and of the need for an integrated approach to planning and managing tourism development.

(i) 'Boosterism'—Boosterism is a simplistic or naïve approach to planning based on the assumption that tourism development is inherently a 'good thing', that it will inevitably bring benefits to the destination. Thus, environmental considerations are submerged by the belief that local resources should be exploited for tourism, whilst local communities are rarely involved in the planning and decision-making process. The objective of boosterism is to maximise the potential growth and, hence, economic return (in the short-term) from tourism with scant regard to longer-term consequences for the destination's environment and communities and, as Hall comments, 'may be more aptly described as a form of non-planning'. The hosting of mega-events, such as the Olympic Games, is a continuing example of boosterism.

(ii) The economic approach—The economic approach to planning regards tourism as an industry which can be used to achieve certain economic objectives (the economic benefits of tourism referred to earlier). In other worlds, it is based on the assumption that tourism is an effective means of achieving economic growth, regeneration or diversification and, therefore, the focus of tourism planning is on economic returns and the ways in which these can be optimised. As a result, greater attention is paid to economic objectives than to social and environmental issues, and planning centres on marketing and promotional activities designed to attract the type or number of tourists who will provide greatest economic return. In Cyprus, for example, the Cyprus Tourist Organisation (CTO) has long had the policy of increasing overall tourist numbers, but now focuses on attracting 'up-market' tourists in order to maximise per-head tourist spending. Arguably, the economic approach remains dominant in tourism planning, despite the popularity of sustainable tourism development (see below).

(iii) The land use approach—In comparison to the economic approach, land use-based tourism planning recognises the interdependency between tourism and the physical environment

and, as a result, primacy is given within the planning process to minimising the impact of tourism and tourists on the environment. In a general sense, land designations, such as the establishment of national parks and other forms of protected areas, are a major planning tool designed to integrate the exploitation of the environment for tourism with the overarching objective of conservation. However, more specific planning controls and visitor management techniques, such as zoning (both land-base and marine), interpretation, directional signing and marketing, are also common elements of tourism planning in environmentally sensitive areas. At the same time, Environmental Impact Assessments (EIA) are increasingly being undertaken as an integral part of tourism planning to ensure that proposed developments will not have excessive impacts on the environment.

(iv) Community tourism planning—In response to the growing recognition of the socio-cultural impacts of tourism and the need to better direct tourism planning towards satisfying the specific needs of local communities (as well as optimising the visitor experience), the concept of community-based tourism planning emerged in the 1980s as a potential means of balancing the needs of tourists with those of local people in destination areas. The community approach to planning is essentially a 'bottom-up' form of planning where the views and attitudes of local residents are incorporated into tourism plans and, ideally, where local residents also play an active role in planning and managing tourism. The purpose of this approach is to 'empower' local communities so that:

- they do not feel exploited by tourism or that their society and culture is being commodified;
- they enjoy some degree of control over the rate and nature of tourism development;
- their economic and social needs form the basic objectives of tourism planning;
- they have some control over local resource use; and
- they benefit directly from tourism development.

The extent to which community tourism planning is feasible in practice remains open to debate. Not only is it difficult to encourage widespread public participation, but local political structures may discourage the handing over of power to the community at large. At the same time, community/public involvement may lengthen the planning process, whilst certain stakeholders, such as the owners of local businesses or local landowners, may seek to dominate or impose their will on the decision-making process. As a result, as Hall observes, community involvement in tourism planning is, more usually, a form of tokenism.

Undoubtedly, there are examples in practice of all four approaches to tourism planning and, frequently, situations where a combination is adopted. The most common approach to tourism planing, however, is probably the one which attempts to combine the economic benefits of tourism (the economic approach) with environmental compatibility (the land-use approach) and community empowerment (the community approach) whilst minimising environmental degradation and social impacts. In other words, tourism planning, whether at the site, destination or regional scale, is most usually undertaken according to the principles of sustainable tourism development.

Sustainable Tourism Development

Since the mid-1980s, the concept of sustainable tourism development has become almost universally accepted as a desirable and politically appropriate approach to, and goal of, tourism development. It has achieved 'virtual global endorsement as the new (tourism) industry paradigm' and, from the local to international level, innumerable sectoral and destinational organisations within the tourism industry have produced sustainable tourism development plans and policies. At the same time, sustainable tourism development has been a dominant theme in tourism research; not only are 1990s particularly memorable for the volume of literature related to the topic but also 'defining sustainable development in the context of tourism has become something of a cottage industry.'

However, despite the widespread acceptance of and adherence to the principles of sustainable tourism development (see Figure 5.5), the extent to which it represents a universally viable or applicable approach to tourism planning • and development remains the subject of intense debate. This lack of consensus has arisen primarily from the two distinct ways in which the concept of sustainable tourism development is interpreted. According to Hunter, "those who insert the word 'tourism' between 'sustainable' and 'development' (should) ensure that, under all circumstances, the resultant principles of sustainable tourism development are the principles of sustainable development".

- Tourism should be planned and managed within environmental limits and with due regard for the long-term appropriate use of natural and human resources.
- Tourism planning, development and operation should be integrated into national and local sustainable development strategies.
- Tourism should support a wide range of local economic activities, taking environmental costs and benefits into account, but it should not be permitted to become an activity which dominates the economic base of an area.
- Local communities should be encouraged and expected to participate in the planning, development and control of tourism, with support from Central Government, to ensure the equitable distribution of the benefits of tourism.
- All organisations and individuals should respect the culture, the economy, the way of life, the environment and political structures in the destination area.
- All stakeholders within tourism (businesses, local communities and tourists themselves, should be educated about the need to develop and participate in more sustainable forms of tourism.
- Research should be undertaken throughout all stages of tourism development and operation to monitor impacts, to solve problems and to allow local people and others to respond to changes and to take advantage of opportunities.
- All agencies, organisations, businesses and individuals should work together to avoid potential conflict and to optimise the benefits to all involved in the development and management of tourism.

Figure 5.5: Principles of sustainable tourism development.

This, certainly, was the original approach to sustainable tourism development, an approach which envisaged tourism as a means of achieving or contributing to the broader sustainable development of destination areas. Inevitably, of course, this then begs the question: what is sustainable development? The fact that there exists some 70 definitions of sustainable development suggests that there is no simple answer to that question! Nevertheless, it can be seen as an approach to development that is:

- *holistic*—it must be viewed as an approach that addresses global problems of poverty, health, education, pollution, resource exploitation and degradation and other challenges of underdevelopment with global solutions.
- *equitable*—it seeks to provide equal opportunities and access to resources for present and future generations.
- *future oriented*—the focus is on future generations, and their ability to satisfy their needs.
- *environmental*—the defining element of sustainable development is that it should be within the global ecosystem's capacity to sustain development.

As such, sustainable development is an approach which seeks to achieve the broad objective of development described earlier in this chapter (i.e. social, political, cultural development) combined with environmental sustainability.

Not surprisingly, perhaps, given the nature and characteristics of tourism, sustainable tourism development has come to be seen in a much more specific, tourism-centric way, as 'tourism which is in a form which can maintain its viability in an area for an indefinite period of time'. In other words, rather than being seen as a contributor to the wider (sustainable) development of destination areas, which is, of course, the primary justification for planning and developing tourism in the first place, sustainable tourism development is, more commonly, associated with sustaining tourism itself. In other words, although the term sustainable tourism development is politically attractive, it is, in practice, little more than an adaptation of the land-use approach to planning referred to above.

This is not to say that, under specific circumstances, 'true' sustainable tourism development cannot be achieved on a local, small-scale basis. However, on a global scale a variety of factors militate against the achievement of sustainable tourism development, not least the way in which tourists themselves consume tourism. Therefore, in the context of tourism planning, it is perhaps, more realistic to plan for environmentally benign forms of tourism which, nevertheless, optimise the economic benefits to local communities.

Who Plans for Tourism?

The final issue to be addressed in this chapter is where the responsibility lies for the planning of tourism. More specifically, we have seen that tourism planning is a complex and continuous process that links policy objectives in general with the planning and implementation of tourism development is particular. This implies that, although tourism is primarily a private sector dominated industry and much planning at the site/destinational level will be undertaken by tourism businesses themselves (albeit normally within the parameters of local or national planning regulations and development objectives), there is, nevertheless, an important role that is fulfilled by government in tourism planning. Indeed, as tourism is increasingly viewed as a means of achieving regional economic regeneration or national development, it is inevitable or, indeed, essential, those governments play a role in the tourism planning process. The purpose of this section, therefore, is to consider why and how government shou!d be involved in tourism planning.

The Role of Government in Tourism Planning

In the specific context of planning, however, government policy has an inevitable impact on tourism, whether intentional or not. For example, economic policies which influence exchange rates or interest rates will impact upon tourism, as does transport policy, taxation policy, employment policy, licensing laws, and so on. Thus, in the UK, the high level of duty on fuel has undoubtedly has undoubtedly had a negative impact on international tourism to the country, whilst the introduction of the minimum wage has also had an impact in what is traditionally a lower-paid industry. At the same time, it could to be argued that government should be involved in tourism planning for the simple reason that, financially, the public purse benefits significantly from tourism. Again in the UK, the tourism industry as a whole contributes some £1.5 billion in taxation each year.

There are, however, a number of specific reasons why government should play a leading role in the planning of tourism. In particular, it is government that:

- establishes or defines the policy objectives of tourism development (for example, employment generation, economic growth, social development, inner city regeneration, etc.);
- sets out the types of tourism to be developed–domestic and/or international, mass or niche market, etc.;
- defines broader development objectives and approach – sustainable development versus 'traditional' economic growth;
- determines the extent of tourism development (i.e. a smaller contribution in a mixed economy or the principal sector of the national economy);
- controls the rate of tourism growth and development to:
    - ensure social adjustment to tourism,
    - respond to and provide for related infrastructure needs,
    - introduce policies for human resource training and development ,
    - avoid distortion in the national economy;
- introduces planning laws and regulations, establishes environmental protection measures (e.g. national park designation), and so on; and
- can influence tourism through its international policies with respect to, for example, bi-lateral air agreements or visa requirements.

Of course, not all governments will be concerned with all of these issues, whilst the extent to which governments involve themselves directly in tourism planning also varies. Much depends upon the prevailing political ideology, the stage of development of the economy as a whole and the tourism sector is particular, the importance of tourism to the economy, and a variety of other factors. However, it has been suggested that, generally, there are two forms of government involvement in tourism.

(i) Passive involvement—In many countries, in particular in the industrialised, developed nations, the involvement of government in tourism planning can generally be described as passive. That is, beyond setting broad policy objectives for tourism development and, in most cases, establishing a national tourism organisation to market and promote the country as a destination, the government is not directly involved in the planning and management of tourism at the national level. Indeed, according to Jenkins, passive involvement is limited to:

- *maindatory activities*–the introduction of legislation relating to all sectors, but which may impact on tourism, such as regulations with respect to investment incentives, the employment of foreign nationals or the minimum wage;
- *supportive actions*–these are activities, such as general training programmes, that are *not* aimed at the tourism sector in particular but may nevertheless have some supportive influence.

(ii) Active involvement—In less developed countries, government involvement in tourism planning tends to be more active, usually because the private sector lacks the necessary expertise or capital to take the lead in developing tourism. In other words, the government recognises that its active participation is necessary in the planning and development process. This takes the form of:

- *managerial activities*–the government not only sets out policies and objectives for tourism, but also establishes the necessary legislative and organisational framework to led the development of tourism. For example, it may set up a tourism development fund to provide incentives or designate tourism development areas;
- *developmental activities*–the government adopts an operational role, not only planning but investing in and running services and facilities such as hotels and travel agencies.

In the UK, the government has long adopted a 'hands-off' or passive role in tourism planning. Indeed, successive policies have been designed to further reduce public involvement in and support for tourism, with even the national and regional tourist boards being expected to finance themselves increasingly through commercial activities. However, some intervention in tourism planning at the national level will always be necessary and, given the contribution of tourism to the British economy, it is not surprising that there have long been calls for a more active role in tourism on the part of the government.

6

POLICY CONSIDERATIONS IN PLANNING

Tourism development policy establishes the basis for developing and managing tourism and is an essential element of national or regional tourism planning. The structure plan provides the physical framework for the type and location of development. This chapter describes how the policy and structure plans are formulated.

Formulating Tourism Development Policy

Tourism development policy consists of a set of statements related to various aspects of tourism development. Policy is determined based on several considerations, of which the most important is achieving the objectives of developing tourism. More generally, tourism policy should reflect the overall development policy of the country or region so that tourism is well integrated. Policy also evolves from the survey and analysis of present tourism development patterns and infrastructure, tourist attractions and activities and the tourist markets. Socio-economic and environmental factors are very important to consider.

The government should assume the lead role in a deciding tourism policy. Policy affects the entire country or region and their communities and it must balance economic, environmental and social concerns. National and regional objects should prevail over individual, group or sector interests. However, the policy should provide a framework within which the private sector and other special interests groups can effectively function.

Tourism policy can take many forms. Some of the basic issues that need to be addressed in policy formulation are as follows:

- The reasons for developing tourism should be stated in the policy. These reasons often include a combination of the following:
    - economic reasons of increasing income, providing employment, earning foreign exchange, increasing government revenues and using tourism as a catalyst for expansion of other sectors;
    - social reasons of encouraging cross-cultural exchange and introducing the country to foreigners (for international tourism) and educating persons about their own country and providing recreation opportunities (for domestic tourism);
    - using tourism to help achieve environmental and cultural conservation objectives for which resources are not otherwise available.
- The forms of tourism to be developed and related types of international and domestic tourist markets to be attracted are a basic policy consideration. The various forms of tourism were described in Chapter 4. Usually several forms of tourism are suitable for development within a single country or region, but in different areas and sometimes in different time periods. The general quality level of tourism also needs to be set forth in policy. Many destinations are now, by policy, opting for what they term quality tourism.
- Another consideration is whether tourism should be 'market-led'–developing forms of tourism that will attract a board market regardless of the impact of the development, or 'product-led' - developing forms of tourism that are most compatible with the environment and society, and targeting only those markets that are consistent with the product even though this may result in fewer economic benefits. Usually the attempt is to balance these two approaches.
- A policy consideration is the extent of development to be allowed - should tourism be limited, maintained at a

medium level, or encouraged to become a major sector of the economy. A large country or region may decide to develop different levels of tourism in different areas and at different times based on environmental, socio-cultural and infrastructure development considerations.

- The growth rate of tourism to be aimed for – slow, medium or fast – is often a policy consideration. Even though the potential exists for fast growth, for example, it may be desirable to control the growth rate for several reasons:
    - social reasons of allowing residents adequate time to adjust to tourism and learn to participate in it;
    - development reasons of balancing development of tourist facilities with development of infrastructure;
    - manpower planning reasons of allowing sufficient time to train persons to work effectively in tourism;
    - economic reasons of integrating the development of tourism with other economic sectors, and not creating distortions in the economic.
- The respective roles of the government and private sector in developing and managing tourism can be an important type of policy.
- Achieving environmental protection, cultural conservation and sustainable development are all important policy considerations.
- The general location and staging of development may be stated in the policy, and then further refined in the structure plan.

Other types of policy may, for example, relate to multi-use of tourism infrastructure, the inter-relationships between domestic and international tourism, education and training programmes, social integration of tourism, and investment and employment considerations.

Formulating the Structure Plan

The national or regional plan is composed of several elements – the primary and often secondary tourist attractions; the tourism development regions (in the national plan) and tourism development areas such as resorts (in the regional plan); the access points to the country or region; and the internal transportation linkages. Tourist excursion routes and staging of developments are also often shown on the structure plan. Preparing the structure plan is based on several considerations, including the following:

- Development objectives and policies – these are basic inputs to the structure plan, for example, the recommended forms of development.
- Type and location of the major tourist attraction features.
- Type and location of existing accommodation, and the projected accommodation and the other tourist facility needs.
- Location of existing and already planned transportation facilities, and other critical infrastructure such as water supply.
- Overall environmental, land use, tenure, resource, social and economic analysis and synthesis. This indicates various important influencing factors – suitable climate zones for tourism; location of developable and available land for tourism development; the carrying capacities of potential tourism development areas; location of resource areas that may be more important for other types of development; areas where labour supply will be available to work in tourism; and location of economically depresses areas where development needed.

Each country and region must be planned according to its particular characteristics and development policies. However, there are certain basic concepts and principles, which are generally applicable. These are based on what has proven to be functional and successful in already developed tourism areas. As is always the case in the planning process, imaginative new ideas should also be considered.

Suitable international access to a country and good regional access are essential for tourism. These access points are often termed the national and regional gateways. International airports are often the access points to countries, especially for long-haul tourists. Land border crossings and seaports also function as gateway for international travellers to some countries. Regional access may be by air, land or sea. These gateways usually have already been established before tourism was considered, and thus become a given factors around which tourism is planned. In a small country or region, a single major gateway is usually sufficient. Larger countries and regions may have more than one gateway. Multiple gateways offer the advantage of tourists entering at one point, making their tour, and existing at another point, thus saving backtracking to the entry point. Tourists are encouraged to see more of the area and there is greater flexibility in organising itineraries.

Related to the gateway concept is the principle of establishing a staging area at or near each of the gateways. Staging areas provide tourist facilities and services for overnight stays of tourists waiting for transportation to other parts of the country or region, or waiting for departure from their tour. They often contain various attaction features or can be developed with some features, including shopping facilities, which tourists can enjoy while waiting for onward transportation. These staging areas provide tourism employment and income for local residents. When the national or regional gateway is located in or near a major city, the city becomes the staging area.

Clustering of tourist attractions and activities is an important planning principle. Many attractions – such as good beaches, national parks, ski slopes and major archaeological and historic sites - have specific locations, which determine much of the planning of tourism. Other types of attractions, such as cultural performances, are more mobile. Special types of attractions, such as theme parks, can be located in many places. Clustering of attractions in particular areas can attract more tourists to each area, and induce them to stay longer. Grouping of attractions also typically makes it less expensive to provide infrastructure and more convenient for organising tours.

A clustering approach often used is to develop several secondary attractions near to a primary attraction. These secondary features may already exist in the area and only need development, or they may be mobile or special types which can be newly developed. For example, a secondary attraction of a cultural centre – for local dance and music performances, and demonstration and sale of handicrafts – can be developed near a national park or in a historic town.

Designation of tourism development regions at the national level and development areas, such as resorts, at the regional level is an important principle. This applies especially where a substantial amount of tourism development is envisaged. These development regions or areas are often termed tourism zones. Concentration of tourism development, as opposed to dispersed development, offers several advantages:

- Better opportunity for the planning of integrated development and application of development, design and environmental controls.
- More efficient provision of transportation access and other infrastructure.
- Convenience to tourists of facilities and services being in proximity.
- Capability of concentrated development to support a greater variety and more specialised facilities and services.
- Containment of any negative environmental and socio-cultural impacts in specific areas.

Tourism regions are logical geographic and planning entities. They are selected based on several considerations – containing significant tourist attractions and related activities; existing good access or potential for developing a regional gateway; an existing integrated internal transportation network, or potential for developing such a network; and suitable areas for developing integrated tourist facilities. Within the development region, it is often desirable to establish a tourism centre – this may also be staging area for the region. A tourism centre should have good access from outside the region, transportation connections to other places within the region, and offer a range of tourist facilities and services. The centre may be an existing city or town or a new resort.

Within each of the tourism development region or areas, the general type and extent of tourism should be specified. This is expressed in terms of the type and number of accommodation units. These are determined based on several factors – the development policy; the types of attractions in the region; ease of accessibility; carrying capacity; environmental and socio-cultural factors; and other considerations. Specification of accommodation provides a guide for later detailed planning of the region or area, and for decision-making on proposed development projects.

An efficient and interesting transportation facilities network and services system, whether by air, road, rail or water, is important. Transportation should provide efficient access from the national gateway to the regional gateways, and to attractions and facility development areas within the regions. The transportation network, or portions of it, also often serves as excursion routes for sightseeing tourists. An important principle of planning for development of transportation and other infrastructure is that they be as multi-purpose as possible, serving general use as well as tourism needs. In this way, overall infrastructure costs can be reduced, and tourism can help support infrastructure improvements that bring benefits to the entire economy and society.

It is common practice to designate tourist excursion routes– sometimes called tourist circuits – on the plan. These are selected to pass through scenic areas with stopovers at particularly interesting places. The stopovers, which can also be shown on the plan, should be developed with visitor facilities – restaurants, shopping and toilets. They may include such activities as local walking tours, visits to specific attraction features and cultural performances. Tour routes should be designed, to the extent possible to form loops in order to avoid backtracking over the same route on the return journey.

The tourism plan should be formulated so that it is easy to stage tourism development over a long period of time. Effectives staging requires that the various tourism regions and development areas are selected so that each one can be developed economically and efficiently as separate units when needed. Development stages are indicated for the various tourism regions and areas, usually as first, second and third stages. The stages are typically for five-year periods but can be longer. Determination of staging is based on several considerations – accessibility; when the basic infrastructure can be developed; market demands; feasibility of undertaking development of the tourist attractions and facilities; relative economic needs of the areas; and social acceptance of the people living in the tourism zones.

Selecting Development Sites

Specific tourism development sites such as for integrated resorts should be carefully selected according to certain criteria, including the following:

- Location at or near a tourist attraction feature (or features) such as a beach, marine area, lake, ski slope, and major archaeological or historic site. The development, however, should not impinge upon the immediate setting of the features, but be set away from them.
- Desirable micro-climatic conditions as related to the type of development. Local climatic conditions can vary greatly from one place to another and must be carefully investigated in selecting development sites.
- Attractive physical environment of the site and nearby area.
- Sufficient amount of available and developable land, which is economically feasible to acquire and develop and does not have a more important economic, conservation or other resource use.
- Good existing or potential access from the tourist gateway to the area and from the area to other attraction features in the region.
- Existing availability of, or feasibility of, developing infrastructure of adequate water supply, electric power, sewage and solid waste disposal and telecommunications at an acceptable cost. After transportation access, provision of an adequate water supply is often the most critical type of infrastructure.
- Suitable general area for the resort with compatible nearby land uses, with no excessive air, water or noise pollution of the site environment.

- No possibility of the resort generating problems related to the local natural environment, if the development is environmentally well planned and managed.
- Positive attitude of any nearby residents to developing tourism and their desire to work in tourism. There should be no likelihood of the tourism development generating any serious socio-cultural or economic problems for residents of the general area, if appropriate measures are applied.
- Availability of a nearby labour supply to work in tourism. If there is no nearly source of employees, there should be the possibility of attracting employees from elsewhere. If employees come from outside the area, it should be feasible to provide adequate housing and community facilities and services for them.

There may be additional criteria depending on the local circumstances and type of resort being planned. A single site may not perfectly meet all the criteria, and it may be necessary to balance site advantages and disadvantages. In the later detailed planning of the site, it is important that the nearby areas also be planned, with development controls applied to those areas. This will help avoid land use and infrastructure problems developing near to site - a common problem in many resort areas.

Reducing Seasonality

It is common for the country, region or development are to experience seasonal differences in tourist arrival. This situation leads to underuse of tour facilities and services during certain periods of the year, and often excessive demand at other times. The seasonality factor can result from either the types of tourist attractions or the characteristics of the tourist markets (or both). Therefore, the national or regional plan should incorporate ways to reduce seasonality, although it is often impossible to eliminate this factor.

Various techniques can be applied to reduce seasonality. Types of tourist attractions can be selected or developed which will attract visitors at different times of the year, and especially during the typical low season. Tourism areas can usually develop some low-season activities - such as festivals and special events, conferences, and special types of recreation facilities and activities. It is now common practice for beach resorts to develop conference tourism during the historic low season. Ski resorts often develop mountain hiking, horse riding and other recreational activities, as well as conferences and special events, during the summer season.

Marketing and pricing techniques can be used to attract tourists during the low season. These may be combined with the product development approaches described above. Discounted transportation and accommodation rates can be offered during the low period which, if well marketed, can attract tourists. A low season is often the result of the market source countries' traditional vacation periods being at certain times of the year. In this situation, marketing can be targeted to older tourists who are free to travel anytime. These tourists also often prefer the less congested destination environments that are available during the low season. Domestic tourist use of international resorts and urban tourist facilities can also be encouraged during the low season.

7

ECONOMIC, ENVIRONMENTAL AND SOCIO-CULTURAL CONSIDERATIONS

Economic, environmental and socio-cultural considerations must be well understood in order to plan, develop and manage tourism successfully. The primary reason for developing tourism in most countries and regions is for its economic benefits, although there are often other reasons, as well. In keeping with the concept of sustainable development, environmental and socio-cultural considerations are also of the utmost importance. Economic, environmental and socio-cultural costs and benefits must all be weighed together to achieve balanced development. Particular emphasis in this chapter is given to the types of impacts generated and the policies and impact control measures which should be pursued. Even though many of the control measures presented are applicable at the local level, they need to be adopted as standards, regulations and guidelines at the national and regional levels.

Measuring Economic Impacts

Several standard types of economic measurements are made in tourism. Tourism is still not usually listed as a separate sector in national economic tables but is included in the service sector. [The WTO has developed the Standard International Classification of Tourism Activities (SICTA) which has been provisionally approved by the United Nations Statistical Commission.] Therefore, it is more difficult to measure the economic contribution of tourism. But, by drawing on various information sources, tourism economists can make calculations sufficient to indicate the general extent of tourism's economic impact. The standard economic measurements are as follows:

- Income generated and contribution to Gross National or Domestic Product. This indicates the relative importance of tourism in the total economy.
- Foreign exchange earned from international tourism. This includes calculation of both the gross foreign exchange earnings - the total expenditures of foreign tourists, and net foreign exchange earnings–the foreign exchange remaining in the country after deducting the foreign exchange leakage factor. This leakage is the foreign exchange spent for imported goods and services used in tourism - food items and hotel equipment and supplies, expatriation of salaries of foreign workers and of profits of foreign-owned facilities; payments made to foreign hotel management companies; and other leakages. At the regional level, the gross and net money earned from outside the region can be calculated.
- Local employment generated by tourism. Employment is calculated by type:
    - *direct employment* – the persons who work in tourism enterprises such as hotels, restaurants, tourist shops and tour and travel agencies;
    - *indirect employment* – jobs generated in the supplying sectors such as agriculture, fisheries and manufacturing;
    - *induced employment* – additional persons supported by the spending of income made by the direct and indirect employees;
    - *construction employment* – jobs generated in the construction of tourist facilities and infrastructure (this is usually temporary but may be long-lasting in places with continuing development of tourism).
- The multiplier effect. This refers to the stimulus that an external source of income has on an economy. It is the number of rounds of spending in the local economy of

the initial tourist spending. This effect measures the way in which tourist expenditures filter through the economy and generate other economic activities.

- Contribution to government revenues. This includes hotel and other types of tourist user taxes, airport departure taxes, customs duties on imported goods used in tourism, income taxes on tourism enterprises and employees, and property taxes on tourism establishments.

Although not as quantifiable, a benefit of tourism is that it helps justify and pay for transportation facilities and services and other infrastructure that are used by the entire community. Also an important general benefit is that tourism can serve as a catalyst for expansion of other economic sectors.

If not carefully controlled, tourism can generate some economic problems. Loss of economic benefits can occur if there is a high import content of goods and services used in tourism, and if many tourist facilities are owned and managed by outsiders. This situation reduces the net income and foreign exchange earned from tourism, and may lead to resentment by residents of the tourism area. For certain types of tourism development, however, there may be few alternatives to outside ownership and management. This can be the case especially during the initial stages of development when local capital and managerial capabilities are limited. In small island economies with little local production of goods, it may be difficult to greatly reduce the import content of tourism. But the employment and income generated is still usually considered worth the investment in tourism.

Economic distortions can take place geographically if tourism is concentrated in only one or a few areas of a country or region, without corresponding development in the other places. Employment distortions may be created if tourism attracts too many employees from other economic sectors, because of its higher wages and better working conditions. Inflation of local prices of land and certain goods and services may take place in rapidly developing tourism areas. This places a financial burden on residents.

Enhancing Economic Benefits

There are several techniques that can be applied to enhance the economic benefits of tourism. These should be incorporated into the planning process so that possible problems are prevented or reduced before they occur.

Strengthening the linkages between tourism and other economic sectors is a very important technique. This reduces the import content of tourism and provides more local employment - the indirect and induced employment - and income from tourism. Opportunities often exist, for example, to increase the locally produced food items used in tourism. Also, the tourism industry should be encouraged (or required) to utilise more local items, including building materials and interior decoration, in its development and operation of hotels and other facilities.

Encouraging in-country, in-region and local ownership of tourist facilities and services is also important so that more of the profits from tourism are retained. This can be done in various ways - providing investment incentives; organising stock companies with sale of shares to the general public; and requiring joint ventures of local and foreign companies. Certain forms of tourism can be encouraged which will provide opportunities for local small business enterprises. If local capital is very limited, then a policy can be taken of initially allowing foreign ownership, but requiring purchase by local owners when capital is available.

Foreign hotel management by transnational hotel companies of large hotel properties results in a loss of some income to countries. However, it also offers the advantages of professional management and international marketing and reservation services. Whether to allow transnational management must be decided based on the circumstances of each particular country. It is also important that local tour operators be given the opportunity to handle foreign tour groups, and that local ground handling operations are not pre-empted by foreign tour operators.

Maximising local employment in tourism can be encouraged by proper training of persons to work in tourism. In some places, there may be some social resistance to service employment. It will be necessary to educate local people to understand that employment in tourism is a respected and worthwhile type of occupation. Training should be extended to the supervisory and management levels, so that these higher level positions can also eventually be filled by local staff. When a trained pool of employees exists, then tourist facility and service establishments can be required to employ local persons. For the higher level positions, replacement of foreign employees by local ones can be phased in over a period of time.

Tourist expenditures can be increased in various ways. More shopping opportunities, especially of local arts and crafts, can be provided in many places. Tourist activities can be expanded, for example, by organising more attractions and tours, which will induce tourists to stay longer. Tourism product enrichment and diversification is becoming an important aspect of expanding and upgrading tourism in many already developed tourism areas.

By developing tourism in a gradual manner, the problems of inflated prices for land and goods can often be reduced because the economy has more time to adjust to new development. This also provides local residents with more opportunity to adapt to and be trained to participate in the benefits of tourism.

Environmental Impacts

Tourism and the environment are inter-dependent. The physical (natural and man-made) environment provides many of the attractions for tourists, and the development of tourism can generate both positive and negative environmental impacts. Developing and managing tourism so that it is compatible with the environment, and does not degrade it, is a major factor in achieving sustainable development. In order to plan tourism environmentally, it is first important to understand the possible impacts of tourism on the environment.

If tourism is well planned, developed and managed, it can generate important positive environmental impacts. These include the following:

- Helps justify and pay for conservation of important natural areas and wildlife, including marine environments and development of national and regional parks and reserves, because these are major attractions for tourists. This is an especially significant benefit in countries with limited resources for undertaking environmental conservation.

- Help justify and pay for the conservation of archaeological and historic sites as attractions for tourist. Otherwise many of these sites would be allowed to deteriorate or disappear. Even entire historic districts in towns and cities are being conserved and developed for tourism.
- Helps improve the environmental quality of areas because tourists like to visit places that are attractive, clean and not polluted. Tourism provides the incentive to clean up environments through controlling air, water, noise and visual pollution, reducing congestion and upgrading overall appearance with suitable landscaping and building design. Also, well sited and designed tourist facilities themselves can contribute to the attractive appearance of both urban and rural environments. Improvement of infrastructure, especially of water supply and sewage and solid waste disposal, also contributes to improved environmental quality.
- Increases local environmental awareness when residents, and especially young people, observe tourists' interest in conservation. They then begin to realise the importance of conservation in their areas.

If tourism is not well planned, developed and managed, it can generate several types of negative environmental impacts. These include the following:

- Water pollution resulting from improper development of sewage and solid waste disposal systems for hotels and other facilities. There can be pollution of river, lake and coastal waters from sewage outfall lines, and of groundwater by seepage of waste material.
- Air pollution resulting from excessive use of internal combustion vehicles (cars, taxis, buses, motorcycles, etc.) in tourism areas. Airplanes, used by many tourists

for longer-distance travel and for local air tours generate some air (and noise) pollution.

- Noise pollution generated by a concentration of tourists and tourist vehicles.
- Visual pollution resulting from several factors - poorly designed hotels and other tourist facilities; badly planned layout of facilities; inadequate landscaping of facilities; use of large and ugly advertising signs; and obstruction of scenic views by tourism development.
- Waste disposal problems of littering the landscape by tourists, and improper disposal of waste generated by tourist facilities.
- Ecological disruption of natural areas by overuse and misuse by tourists and inappropriate tourism development. Coastal, marine, mountain and desert environments, all-important types of tourism areas, are particularly vulnerable to ecological damage.
- Damage to archaeological and historic sites by overuse or misuse by tourists and inappropriate tourism development.
- Environmental hazards and land use problems resulting from poor planning, siting and engineering of tourist attractions and facilities.

Environmental Protection Measures

Concern with environmental protection should be an integral part of the planning process. Application of the environmental planning and sustainable development approach is essential, including establishing and staying within the carrying capacities of tourism areas. Selecting the forms of tourism development that are most suitable for the environment also greatly help limit negative environmental impacts. Application of sound principles, such as concentration of facilities in certain zones with provision of adequate infrastructure, is very important in maintaining environmental protection. More generally, development of tourism on a gradual basis allows for sufficient time to monitor its environmental impacts, and make changes in the development approach if any problems have arisen.

Adopting techniques of reducing the seasonality of tourism, especially peak season use of tourism areas, is another very useful technique. Environmental problems often occur only during the peak season when overloading of the infrastructure and overuse of attractions, facilities and services take place.

In addition to these general approaches, specific environmental impact control measures should be applied. These include the following:

- Instal properly designed utility systems of water supply, electric power, sewage and solid waste disposal and drainage for tourist facilities. Conservation techniques should be applied - such as treatment and recycling of waste water and use of solar heating devices. Often these systems can be extended to serve general development in the tourism area, thus benefiting local communities.
- Develop adequate road and other transportation systems, with emphasis on development of public transit and non-polluting forms of transportation of tourists. Electric shuttle buses, for example, can be used in resorts. Proper maintenance of tourist vehicles is important.
- Provide open space, parks and suitable landscaping in tourism areas.
- Apply environmentally suitable land use and site planning principles, zoning regulations, development standards and architectural design in tourism areas. Control of advertising signs is also important.
- Carefully manage visitor flows at tourist attraction features. At fragile sites, the number of visitors may need to be limited or completely prohibited at certain times, or even year-round. For some important sites, the technique of modelling can be used - building a replica of the feature for tourists to visit, with prohibit tourists at the original site.
- Prohibit tourists to cut trees in camping and trekking areas; to collect rare plant and animal species, and to disturb the natural behavioural patterns of wild animals. Hunting and fishing should be allowed only under carefully controlled conditions.

- In marine areas, several types of controls are necessary - operations related to ship bilge cleaning and ballast dumping; use of motorised boats in environmentally sensitive areas; collection of live sea shells, coral and endangered sea life; spear fishing; disturbance of nesting turtles; use of boat anchors in coral-bottom bays; and mining of beach and coral for construction purposes. Boat piers should be properly designed so that they do not lead to erosion or other problems.
- Maintain environmental health and safety standards for the benefit of both tourists and residents.

There may be other control measures which should be applied in particular tourism areas depending on their characteristics. With respect to visitor use controls, it is important to form tourists about the controls and why they must be applied. If tourists understand why the controls are necessary, they will more likely abide by them.

Socio-cultural Impacts

Tourism can bring both benefits and problems to the local society and its cultural patterns. Although more difficult to measure than economic or environmental impacts, socio-cultural impacts are major considerations in developing tourism in any place. These impacts can be especially critical in countries that still have strongly traditional societies and economies. Although tourism can generate socieo-cultural impacts, it should be kept in mind that any type of new development brings changes. Tourism is only one source of change in a society.

If tourism is well planned, developed and managed in a socially responsible manner, it can bring several types of socio-cultural benefits. These include the following:

- Improves the living standards of people and helps pay for improvements to community facilities and services, if the economic benefits of tourism are well distributed.
- Conserves the cultural heritage of an area which otherwise might be lost as a result of general development taking place. Conservation of archaeological and historic sites was referred to under

environmental impacts. Cultural patterns of music, dance, drama, dress, arts and crafts, customs, ceremonies, life styles, traditional economic activities and architectural styles are also important attractions for tourists. If these are lost, cultural tourism will not be successful in the area. Tourism helps justify their conservation. In some places, tourism can be the impetus for revitalising cultural patterns which might be disappearing.

- Helps develop and maintain museums, theatres and other cultural facilities. These are, in part, supported by tourism but are also enjoyed by residents. Many major museums and theatres in the world receive much financial support from the admission fees paid by tourists.
- Reinforces or even renews a sense of pride by residents in their culture, when they observe tourists appreciating it. This is especially true of some traditional societies which are undergoing rapid change and losing their sense of cultural self-confidence.
- Provides the opportunity for cross-cultural exchange between tourists and residents who learn about, and come to respect, one another's cultures. This exchange can best be achieved through certain forms of tourism - educational and other types of special interest tours; village tourism; and home visit programmes whereby tourists can arrange to visit local families.

Tourism can generate some socio-cultural problems if not well planned, developed and managed. A common problem is overcrowding by tourists and loss of convenience for residents, which leads to their resentment and sense of hostility toward tourism. If there are too many tourists in an area - which can happen particularly at peak season periods - attraction and amenity features, and restaurant, shopping and transportation facilities can become so overcrowded by tourists that residents cannot easily use them. If residents are completely prohibited from access to amenity features such as hotel beaches, they may become even more resentful. Large numbers of tourists can be especially disruptive in small rural communities. Resentment can particularly arise if residents perceive that they are not receiving many economic benefits from tourism, and that tourism development is controlled by outside interests.

Some problems can lead to cultural degradation and lessening of a sense of cultural identity. Deterioration of important archaeological and historic sites can result from overuse by tourists. There can be excessive commercialisation and loss of authenticity of local customs, ceremonies, music, dance, crafts and other cultural patterns when these are inappropriately presented as tourist attractions. There can be a 'demonstration effect' of residents, especially young people, imitating the behavioural patterns and dress of tourists. This is done without understanding the different cultural backgrounds and socio-economic status of the tourists. Also, misunderstandings and conflicts may arise between tourists and residents because of different languages and customs.

Social problems of drug abuse, alcoholism, crime and prostitution may be worsened by tourism. The research conducted on these problems indicates that tourism is seldom their basic cause, but it may provide the opportunity to expand them.

Preventing Socio-cultural Problems

Some of the general policies that are applicable to economic and environmental considerations are also appropriate for socio-cultural reasons. An important general policy is to develop tourism on a gradual basis so that the society has time to adapt to it, be educated about it, and learn how to participate in its benefits. This approach also gives the government sufficient time to monitor the socio-cultural impacts of tourism, and remedy any problems before they become serious. As has been emphasised, residents should be involved in the planning and development process of tourism so that they can influence its decision-making and feel that they are part of tourism. Suitable forms of tourism must be selected that are compatible with the local societies. Also, selective marketing can attract the types of tourists who will respect the local social customs and cultural traditions.

As a policy, deliberate use of tourism as a technique of cultural conservation can greatly help in reducing its negative impacts on the culture. At the same time, many societies want to experience some positive change and participate in the benefits of modern development. The approach that they often wish to take is to be culturally selective. They want to keep the best of their traditions that give them a distinctive cultural character, but adopt the best of the changes that will make their lives more comfortable and interesting. Each society must decide on what approach is most suitable for their people when making choices about their tourism development patterns.

Several more specific socio-cultural impact control measures can be applied in tourism areas. Thee include the following:

- Maintain the authenticity of local dance, music, drama, arts, crafts and dress, even though they are somewhat adapted for presentation to tourists. This may require special training programmes being organised and quality controls being applied. However, certain types of ceremonies and rituals such as religious ones should not be modified for tourism, and tourist viewing of them must be carefully controlled.
- Preserve existing distinctive local architectural styles and encourage new development, including tourist facilities, to use local architectural motifs.
- Make certain that residents have convenient access to tourist attractions, amenity features and other facilities, and apply visitor control measures to prevent overcrowding.
- If residents cannot afford to use existing commercial tourist facilities, provide inexpensive or subsidised facilities for them to use. It is also common practice to allow residents to pay lower admission fees to attraction features than those paid by foreign tourists.
- Educate residents about tourism — its concepts, benefits and problems, the local tourism development

policy and programme, how they can personally participate in tourism, and the social patterns of tourists visiting the areas. Public awareness programmes about tourism can be organised, utilising radio, television, news papers, magazines and public meetings. Education about tourism should be included in the public and private school system.

- Inform tourists about the local society - its customs dress codes, acceptable behaviour in religious and other places, courtesies to observe in taking photographs, tipping policies, and any local problems such as crime. If tourists understand these matters, they will be more likely to respect them.
- Train employees to work in tourism effectively, including language and social sensitivity training where needed. In addition to providing better services, this will reduce any possible misunderstandings between tourists and employees.
- Apply strict controls on drugs, crime and prostitution if these are considered to be problems in the tourism areas.

Other types of controls may be appropriate in particular tourism areas.

Environmental Impact Assessment

Application of the environmental planning approach and incorporation of environmental protection measures into the planning process will prevent many environmental problems from arising. However, it is still important that an Environmental Impact Assessment (EIA) be carried out for each specific tourism development project (as well as for all types of major projects). This procedure ensures that specific projects will not generate any serious environmental problems. If it appears that a proposed project will cause problems, then it should not be approved unless it is modified to be made acceptable. The EIA procedure is established at the national and regional levels. Many countries have adopted environmental protection legislation and the EIA procedure, but others have not yet done so.

The EIA should include all types of impacts–environmental, economic and socio-cultural. Even though a project may generate substantial economic benefits, for example, it may result in unacceptable environmental or social problems. It should not, therefore, be approved without modification.

8

TOURISM DEVELOPMENT FUNDING

The financing of tourism development is an essential consideration in implementation. The type of funding needs and possible sources of financing must be understood, and an investment strategy formulated. The funding needs and approach must be specifically identified for each particular country or region. However, there are certain basic considerations that should be made, as explained in the following sections.

Funding Needs

There are three types of funding needs that should be considered in developing tourism. Funding is needed for preparation of tourism plants–the general national or regional plan; more detailed planning of tourism development areas; and planning and feasibility analyses of specific development projects. Funding the general level of planning is typically the responsibility of the government. Financing the more detailed plans and projects can be either by the government of private sector, depending on the local situation. However, the more detailed planning must still be carried out according to government planning standards, and reviewed and approved by the government. If financing is not available locally for planning, then international assistance must be sought.

Funding is required for development of the infrastructure necessary for tourism. The importance of developing adequate infrastructure has been emphasised in previous chapters. Major infrastructure is typically the responsibility of the government to finance. However, at least some of this investment, such as for utility services, can be recovered through payment of user fees. As has been emphasised, much of the infrastructure can be developed to serve general community and economic needs, as well as tourism, and thus bring substantial overall benefits to the country. Infrastructure is expensive and many countries need international assistance in financing it, especially for the foreign exchange component of the cost. Infrastructure costs within commercial development sites are usually paid by the private developers of the sites. Private developers may also be required to pay for some of the off-site infrastructure costs that benefit their sites.

Many types of major attraction features, such as national parks and museums, typically are financed by the government. However, user fees can help recover the initial investment, or at least pay for the operational and maintenance costs of these features. These attractions also serve residents of the area, as well as tourists, and their costs can be justified as providing an important public recreational or educational facility.

Human resources development, such as establishment of a hotel and tourism education centre, must also be funded, usually by the government but often with private sector involvement. A training levy may be applied as tax on tourists' hotel and restaurant expenditures to help pay for operation of a tourism education centre.

Major funding is needed for development of the commercial revenue producing tourist facilities and services including accommodation, restaurants, tour and travel agencies and shopping facilities. These are typically funded by the private sector but, in newly developing tourism areas, the government may need to be a pioneer developer until the private sector has developed the confidence to make its own investments. Development incentives may also need to be offered to induce the private sector to make investments. National tourism development banks are often organised, sometimes with some international financial support, to make loans to the private sector for investment in tourist facilities. Development corporations are also organised for implementation and operation of specific projects and enterprises. Joint venture international and local financing is a common approach to tourism project investment.

Finally, funding is required for the public management of tourism by the NTA office, including for the overall national or regional marketing of tourism. The NTA budget is typically provided by the government. However, if there is a tourism tax such as a hotel and restaurant expenditure tax, some or all of this can be allocated to the NTA budget. Thus, tourism can directly pay for its own management.

A funding mechanism sometimes used by the government is to establish a Tourism Development Fund supported by the hotel tax or other sources such as duty-free shopping facilities. This fund can be used for development, marketing, training and other purposes.

International Source of Funds

There are several types of international funding sources available for financing tourism development, as follows:

- *World Bank Group* - The IBRD (International Bank for Reconstruction and Development), although not now directly involved in tourism projects, provides major funding for infrastructure, environmental and conservation project which benefit tourism as well as serve general needs. This funding is provided in the form of long-term loans at commercial rates of interest. The IDA (International Development Association), makes loans to low-income countries at no interest rates, with ten-years grace periods and very long-term repayment schemes. The IFC (International Finance Corporation) makes loans directly to the private sector for development of revenue-producing projects, including hotels and other tourism projects. IDA loans are usually for not more than 25 per cent of the project cost, and thus serve more as a catalyst to development.
- *UNDP (United Nations Development Programme)* - The UNDP is mainly a technical assistance agency. It is an important source agency for the funding of tourism

planning and other tourism-related projects, through the WTO as the executing-agency. Many of these projects include provision of equipment as well as technical assistance. The UNCDF (United Nations Capital Development Fund) provides small-scale, capital assistance in the form of grants or long-term loans for social facilities and services and economic activities.

- *European Union* - The EU is becoming quite involved in supporting tourism projects in the many countries which constitute the ACP group under the Lome IV Convention. These projects are both technical assistance (including planning, marketing and training) and investment oriented.
- *Bilateral Sources* - Bilateral funding sources usually operate on a governmnet-to-government basis, and several of these programmes include technical assistance and investment oriented tourism projects. Many countries offer bilateral assistance, including countries in Europe, North America and the East Asia and Pacific region. Each bilateral programme has its own particular assistance policy.
- *Regional Development Banks* - The Asian Development Bank (ADB), African Development Bank (ADB), Inter-American Development Bank (IDB), and other regional development banks offer some assistance on aspects of developing tourism in their member countries. The European Development Fund has been established to provide assistance to countries in Eastern Europe.
- *Private International Capital Sources* - Many private sector companies, including those involved in tourism, are seeking to invest outside of their home countries. The type of investment often brings with is competent management resources, marketing connections and desirable international images which can benefit tourism in the countries seeking outside investment. It is important for countries to understand the nature of

these corporations and how to negotiate with them. The United Nations Centre on Transnational Corporations can offer countries technical assistance on dealing with international hotel and other tourism-related corporations, for example, on negotiating hotel management contracts.

These various funding sources are, of course, not mutually exclusive. They can be used in various combinations to meet the particular investment requirement of a country.

Tourism Investment Strategy

Each country should devise a strategy for tourism investment which best suits its circumstances and needs. Such a strategy should involve the following considerations:

- Specific tourism development projects, whether public or private investment oriented, should, wherever possible, be identified based on their being part of a tourism development plan and programme.
- The projects should additionally be identified on the basis of a thorough feasibility analysis (which may have been conducted as part of the overall development planning and programme process).
- Projects should be carefully evaluated to minimise the foreign exchange costs wherever possible.
- Domestic funding should be explored as a priority source of financing, before seeking international funding sources. The next priority should be joint domestic-international funding.
- Fiscal, legislative and administrative structures should be supportive of the project. Project development procedures should be streamlined as much as possible, while still maintaining the integrity of project review.
- When a package of investment incentives is to be offered for private sector projects, this should be selective, monitored and adjusted periodically based on current investment needs.

- Care should be taken to ensure that project management is monitored, but not to the extent where initiative is stifled.

Countries must carefully determine their priorities for the tourism sector and within the sector. Investment strategies should be realistic and targeted to achieve their stated objectives.

9

PLANNING THE INSTITUTIONAL FACTORS

Achieving successful integrated tourism development and management depends as much on effective institutional factors as it does on development policy, physical planning and impact controls. This chapter examines the major institutional factors of tourism - organisational structures, manpower planning and training, tourism legislation and regulations, and attracting investment in tourism development.

Organisational Structures for Tourism

The most appropriate types of public and private organisational structures for tourism must be adapted to the particular circumstances in each country or region. The types of structures may also be changed through time as situations change. Before deciding on organisational structures, a basic decision to be made is determining the respective roles of government and the private sector in the development and management of tourism.

The government or a statutory board typically has several responsibilities - policy, planning and development co-ordination; statistics and research; industry standards and regulations; investment incentives; some marketing services; tourism manpower planning and training, including establishing education and training standards; and provision of basic infrastructure and major public-type attractions. The private sector is responsible for the commercial development and operation of accommodation and most other tourist facilities and services, alongwith marketing of these. In newly developing tourism areas, however, the government may need to be initially involved in some commercial development in order to get tourism started.

In order to handle its functions, the national government must establish a National Tourism Administration (NTA) - a Department or Ministry of Tourism. This ministry may be single portfolio only for tourism, if this sector is currently or expected to become a major activity in the country. Or the ministry may be a mixed portfolio, combining tourism with some other related functions. If the ministry is single portfolio, this gives tourism more priority and importance in the government structure. Regional governments also often establish their own tourism organizations.

Ministry or Department of Tourism

Marketing services
- Market planning and promotion
- Operation of overseas tourism offices
- Operation of local tourist information offices

Statistics and research
- Statistical collection, compilation and reporting
- Operation of the tourism information system
- Conducting research studies

Planning and development
- Development policy and planning
- Coordination of development implementation
- Establishment and administration of facility and service standards

Education and training
- Manpower planning and programming
- Establishment and administration of training standards
- Operation of training programmes and institutions

Figure 9.1 : Model NTA structure.

The NTA is organised into various divisions and sections, often similar to that shown in Figure 9.1. Separate sections are typically organised for planning and development, statistics and research, education and training and marketing services.

Many countries have established a separate autonomous entity for marketing services, and sometimes other management functions. Assigning marketing to an autonomous body, such as a national promotion board, offers the advantage of its being able to apply flexible internal management that is more responsive to changes in market trends. Also, it allows for the possibility of coordinating with the private sector (if that is relatively well developed in the country) on joint promotion activities. However, close liaison must be maintained between the board and the NTA in order to ensure that a consistent development policy is carried out. The board must be held accountable for effective use of its funds, usually through an annual review of its programme and expenditures by the NTA.

Because tourism is a multi-sectoral activity, it is essential that maximum coordination be maintained between the NTA and other relevant government agencies and between the public and private sectors. This can best be achieved by establishing a Tourism Advisory Committee to the NTA, with representation from government agencies, the private sector and other relevant organisations.

Adequate funding and staffing are essential for effective operation of the NTA. Funding is from the government, although there may be joint public and private sector funding of some marketing activities. If there is some type of tourism tax, such as a hotel or tourist expenditure tax in the country, that can be a logical source of funding for part or all of the NTA budget. In this manner, tourism can help support its own management.

If the government needs to become involved in development of resorts or other types of tourist attractions or facilities, a commonly used approach is to organise a public development corporation. This entity is funded by the government, but functions as an independent company subject to government review. When the private sector becomes more mature in the area, the public corporation may sell its assets to private investors.

Tourism private sector organisations serve several important functions; providing a forum for discussing and resolving common problems of tourism enterprises; making coordinated recommendations to the NTA for improvements in the tourism sector, providing representation on tourism boards and committees; conducting research and training for their member enterprises; establishing and maintaining adequate facility and service standards of their members; and sponsoring special events. The private sector can be organised in various ways. There can be separate hotel, restaurant, tour and travel, and other special purpose associations, some combinations, of these or, in a small tourism area, perhaps a single tourism enterprises' association. Private sector associations are funded by membership dues.

Tourism Manpower Planning

Manpower planning is applying a systematic approach to ensure that the right people are in the right place at the right time. This is especially important in tourism, which is a service activity depending in large part for its success on the quality of personnel working in tourism. Manpower planning involves the four steps of:

- Surveying and evaluation the present utilisation of manpower in tourism and identifying any existing problems and needs.
- Projecting the future manpower needed. Projections are made for the number of personnel required in each category of employment. Then the qualifications for each category of job are determined.
- Evaluating the total human resources that will be available in the future.
- Determining training needs and formulating the education and training programme required to provide the qualified manpower.

All types of tourism employees must be considered in manpower planning. These include both public sector employers in the NTA and employees needed in private sector - hotel, catering and tour and travel operations including tour guides. Also, some training of tourism-related personnel may be required. Immigration and customs officials often need to be sensitised in how to handle tourists property. There may be need for specialised training of persons working in tourism-oriented retail shops, handicraft producers, entertainers, and others. It is important that the need for upgrading the knowledge and skills of present employees be identified. Often these persons have not been properly trained. Satisfying this need for upgrading must be incorporated into the training programme.

Evaluation of human resources refers to review of the total manpower which will be available in the country or region, and allocation of this manpower to the different economic activities including tourism. Future tourism manpower needs are projected based on application of formulas to the types and amount of expected future tourism development.

Many kinds of education and training programmes are applicable to tourism - on-the-job training; correspondence (distant learning) courses; short upgrading and specialised courses; study tours; and one-, two-, three- or four-programmes at the vocational school and university levels. In countries where tourism is being developed into a substantial sector, tourism education institutes are established. The manpower planning programme needs to be periodically reviewed and updated to meet current and projected future needs.

Tourism-related Legislation

Tourism legislation includes the basic tourism law. This law typically sets forth the policy for developing tourism and establishes the functions, structure and sources of funding of the NTA (or regional tourism office). Various specific regulations are necessary. These relate to the standards, licensing requirements and inspection procedures for hotels, tourist restaurants, tour and travel agencies, tour guides and other tourism enterprises. In some countries, a hotel classification system has been established and requires administration. These regulations are carefully prepared based on understanding the needs of the country or region. The necessary mechanisms and staff capabilities must be available to apply the regulations on a continuing basis. Procedures for administering the industry standards should be set forth in the regulations.

Certain related laws and regulations are also important for the development and management of tourism. There is need for zoning regulations to designate the regional tourism zones, and control and uses and apply development standards in specific tourism development areas. If zoning regulations already exist, it may be necessary to modify them to include tourism-type land uses such as hotel zones. Environmental protection legislation, including the EIA requirements, will be necessary if these do not already exist. Public health, sanitation, safety and fire codes, building codes, facility operation regulations, liability laws relation to guests and their belongings, labour and taxation legislation are all important for the development and operation of tourist facilities. Regulations on transportation facilities and service - control of fares, licensing of carriers, safety requirements and travel routes - also affect tourism operations.

In many countries, tourism development is based on scenic areas, nature parks and archaeological and historic places. Legislation on parks and conservation is very important to protect these resources. Conservation areas need to be legally designated and planned, with land and visitor uses carefully controlled.

Tourist consumer protection legislation is being adopted in many countries. This legislation is designed to protect tourists from being taken advantage of by unscrupulous or mismanaged tourism enterprises.

Tourism Investment Policies and Incentives

As indicated previously, the government typically must finance major infrastructure projects and public-type tourist attractions. Some or all of this investment - such as for electric power, water supply, sewage and solid waste disposal, and even attraction features - can eventually be recovered through payment of user fees. Financing of on-site infrastructure such as for hotel or resort sites is typically the responsibility of the private developer, or a public corporation if one is involved.

For private investment in hotels and other commercial facilities and services, the investment policy will depend on the local situation. If sufficient private capital resources are available, there is no problem. If capital is limited and tourism must compete with other sectors for its use, then international capital must be sought. International capital can be allowed for total financing, or there can be joint ventures organised between international and local companies. Joint ventures are obviously preferable, in order for the country to receive some of the investment profits.

Often investment incentives offered by the government are needed to attract private sector investment. Some of the common types of incentives, which can be offered singly or in combination, are as follows:

- Provision of development land, and assembly of the required amount of land, at moderate or no cost at suitable sites.
- Provision of off-site infrastructure (which is usually provided in any case), or provision of on-site infrastructure at no cost to the investor.
- Complete or partial exemption from customs duties on imported items used in the development and operation of tourist facilities and services. These may include building materials, machinery, equipment and supplies, and transportation vehicles such as tour buses.
- Complete or partial exemption from company income or property taxes for a specified number of years, and offering favourable depreciation allowances which reduce taxes.
- Provision of financial assistance - loans at regular or low interest rates; extended periods of repayments of loans; subsidies for payments made on interest of private loans; or guarantee by the government of private loans made. Outright grants of money can also be provided.
- Unrestricted repatriation of all or part of foreign capital, profits, dividends and interest, after taxes have been paid.
- Guarantees against nationalisation or appropriation of the investment.

It is important that the incentives be provided only for approved projects that conform to the development plan and programme and are suitably designed. Incentives may also be restricted to certain types of development that the government wants to encourage, for example, certain quality levels of hotels, certain types of services such as tour operations, and tourism development in remote areas. The types of incentives offered should be reviewed periodically and adjusted to current investment needs. Incentives offered during the initial stages of development may no longer be needed at a later time or should be modified to suit current needs.

In many places investment incentives are not required and the profitability of tourism development is assured. In such cases, the government may require that developers make payments, perhaps through an association, for their proportionate share of the costs of infrastructure development. Even other costs, such as for any environmental or social problems resulting from the development, can be required to be paid by the developer. These costs, for example, may include buying land and planting forest cover elsewhere to replace that which was removed from the development site, and resettlement costs of families dislocated from the site.

10

TOURISM MARKET PLANNING

Marketing of tourism for a country or region is essential. Marketing informs prospective tourists about what the area has to offer, and tries to induce them to visit it. Market planning needs to be understood as part of the overall tourism planning process, and as it related to development of the tourism product. Marketing involves several activities - establishing the marketing objectives; formulating the marketing strategy; preparing and implementing the promotion programme; and providing tourist information services. Market planning can be done for both international and domestic tourists or a combination of these.

Establishing the Marketing Objectives

In the comprehensive and integrated planning approach, the marketing objectives are represented by the market targets of the types and numbers of tourists to be attracted. As was explained in Chapter 3, market targets are set based on the markets that can likely be attracted only if the development and marketing plans are being properly implemented.

Market targets are usually established by five-year periods. The targets are expressed in terms of the approximate numbers of tourist arrivals by type, average length of stay, countries or country regions of origin, and other characteristics. The tourist groups aimed for should be closely related to the tourism product and the kinds of tourists and tourism desired. They may include, for example, general interest sightseeing or beach resort oriented tourists, various types of special interest, nature, cultural and adventure tourists, ethnic tourists and cruise ship stopover passengers. Some tourist market may be multi-destination oriented. These tourists visit the country as part of a tour of several countries. Other markets will be single destination oriented.

In already developed tourist destinations, the marketing objectives may also relate to changing the types of markets, such as aiming for higher quality or special interest markets. Such objectives must, of course, be coordinated with corresponding changes made in the tourism product of attractions, facilities and services.

Formulating the Marketing Strategy

The marketing strategy sets forth the most effective approach to be applied to achieve the marketing objectives. The strategy may include, for example:

- Whether the marketing will be general, aimed at general interest tourists, or be selective and directed to specific types of tourist markets. Primary, secondary and opportunity markets are identified.
- The general types of promotional techniques to be used and where they should be directed - to tour operators, the tourist consumer or a combination of these.
- The timing or priority scheduling of promotional efforts to certain types of markets or countries. Timing may depend on the scheduling of tourism development projects.
- The image and reality of the area to be conveyed. A newly developing tourist destination may need to create a desirable image of itself first before engaging in specific promotion.
- Any particular obstacles to overcome such as recent political instability or a natural disaster.
- Whether promotion offices should be established in the major market source countries, or local marketing representation contracted in those countries, or promotion handled directly from the home office.
- Consideration of any contingencies which may arise such as the opening of previously closed market sources.

The marketing strategy should be related to both the longer- and shorter-term objectives. By doing this, the foundation is laid to achieve the longer-term objectives but with the shorter-term ones planned more specifically. The marketing strategy should be reviewed fairly often. It can be modified, if necessary, depending on market trends and any changes in development of the tourism product.

Preparing the Promotion Programme

The promotion programme is prepared based on several considerations: the marketing strategy; knowledge of marketing distribution channels; the promotion techniques available; and the amount of the budget. This programme is usually designed for a three- to five-year period. It specifies by year the types of promotion to be undertaken and their estimated costs. Continuing costs, such as for maintenance of offices in the market source countries and local tourist information offices, are usually included in the promotion budget. The most commonly used promotional techniques are as follows:

- Preparing printed material such as brochures, posters, maps, postcards and travel agent manuals, and distributing these to travel agents, tour operators and the tourist consumers.
- Preparing audio-visual material - slide, film and video shows for use in travel seminars and other types of presentations.
- Advertising in newspapers, magazines, radio and television aimed at the tourist consumers, and in travel trade publications aimed at tour oprators.
- Attending travel trade fairs, of which there are now many held annually in Europe, North America and East Asia.
- Undertaking special promotional tips to the market countries in order to contact travel agents and tour operators.
- Inviting and hosting visits by tour operators and travel writers and photographers.
- Preparing and publishing guide and general

information books about the area, if these are not available commercially. These books can be sold to recover the costs involved.

Marketing of specialised forms of tourism, such as convention and cruise ship tourism, requires specific knowledge and promotional techniques.

Promotion of an area and its attractions and facilities should be accurate and honest. If promotion misrepresents the area and tourists are attracted by inaccurate statements made in the promotion, they may well be dissatisfied. This can lead to tourists advising their friends not to visit the area, and to unfavourable publicity in the public media of the market source countries. Under present tourist consumer protection legislation, now adopted in many countries, it can also result in legal action being taken against tour and travel operators.

Promotion should be closely coordinated between the public and private sectors. A common practice is to establish a joint promotion board for coordinating and carrying out promotional activities. This board is jointly funded by the public and private sectors. The private sector will still undertake promotional activities for their own enterprises. The government must provide an adequate budget for its share of marketing, if tourism is to be successful. At the same time, marketing should be carefully programmed so as to maximise effective use of the funds that are available. Often national air carriers can greatly assist in promotion activities, including promotion through their overseas offices, if government funding for promotion is limited.

Providing Tourist Information Services

An important function of marketing is providing information to tourists before and after they arrive at their destinations. Various types of information should be available - the general geographical, historical, and cultural background of the area the attractions, facilities and services (and their costs) that are available; transportation schedules; location of shopping, medical and postal facilities, consulates, embassies and religious institutions; and other specific information. It is also very important to inform tourists about local customs, dress and behavioural codes, tipping policy, and any security problems they should be aware of.

Tourist information offices should be established in convenient locations, and be staffed by knowledgeable personnel. Information officers should have foreign language capabilities where needed. Often, a successful approach is to develop visitor information centres. In addition to information material, visitor centres contain exhibits, offer audio-visual shows and have literature, slides and other material for sale.

11

IMPLEMENTING AND MONITORING THE PLAN

Specifying how to carry out the plan's policy and recommendations is an essential aspect of the planning process. As has already been emphasised, techniques of implementation should be considered throughout formulation of the plan. This gives greater assurance that recommendations are implementable. Specific techniques of implementation should be set forth. An increasingly common practice is to prepare an implementation manual which the government can use as a guide on implementation techniques and procedures. The major elements of implementation are explained in the following sections.

Plan Adoption and Allocation of Responsibilities

After careful review and agreement, the tourism plan should be adopted by the government as its official guide for developing tourism. Through adoption of the plan, the legal basis for its implementation is established. It then becomes more difficult to deviate greatly from the policy and plan, although some adjustments will inevitably need to be made. Also essential for effective implementation is political commitment to developing tourism on a planned basis, and strong leadership exercised in both the public and private sectors of tourism.

In the implementation approach, the first step is to decide on the respective roles of government, the private sector and special bodies such as public corporations. Whichever respective roles are decided on, close cooperation and coordination between the government and private sectors on implementation must be maintained.

Staging and Programming Development

To achieve the physical development recommendations systematically, the first stop is to determine the general staging of development. Staging is usually indicated as part of the structure plan.

Within the framework of the recommended staging, specific projects are identified for development, and then organised into an integrated development programme. This programme should include all types of development - government infrastructure, attractions and facilities, and private sector development of commercial facilities and services. It is preferable also to specify other actions that are needed for implementation - establishing certain tourism organisations; adopting tourism laws and regulations or carrying out socio-cultural and environmental programmes. Appendix 5 presents a model tourism action programme that demonstrates the approach used to prepare such a programme.

The projects and actions are shown by year, usually for a five-year period. For long-term projects, continuation of the projects over two or more years is indicated. Pre-development activities, such as setailed planning design and feasibility analysis for future projects, should be included in the programme. General cost estimates of development projects are shown, and the responsible parties for carrying out the projects or actions are specified. The responsible parties involved may include, for example, the relevant government agency, the private sector or a public corporation.

The tourism programme should be carefully coordinated with the programmes of related agencies, such as the transportation, parks and cultural departments. In order to give greater assurance of programme coordination, the tourism programme may even include a listing of projects that are the responsibility of those agencies, such as national park or museum projects. The programme must also be carefully coordinated with the overall development programme of the country or region. In fact, tourism is typically incorporated into the overall development programme.

The first stage action programme is often prepared as part of the initial tourism planning study so that it is well integrated with the planning recommendations. Alternatively, it can be prepred later after the plan has been adopted. Action programmes for the subsequent stages of development are prepared at a later time near the completion of the previous stage programme. These later stage programmes can incorporate any minor adjustments made to the plan, as well as actions and projects which could not be accomplished in the previous programme. Thus, these programmes become 'rolling plans' that are always relatively up-to-date.

A common technique for achieving efficient development programming, especially at the project development level, is critical path analysis. This involves preparing a special type of chart - a network - consisting of arrows and circles. These depict the entire development process, with an event, such as developing a hotel in a resort, being represented by a circle, and an activity, such as constructing the hotel foundation, by an arrow. The circles are connected by the arrows. Logically, an event cannot take place until all activities leading up to it have been completed. Estimated 'time to completion' values are then placed on each activity. The critical path of the network is determined by considering each event in turn, and calculating the earliest possible time in which it can occur. If an event is dependent on two or more activities, the earliest time for completion is determined by the longest activity.

The critical path is the resultant sequence of inter-connected events and activities which will require the longest time to accomplish. Adding together all the times on the critical path will give the shortest time for the project to be completed. Critical path analysis for major programmes or projects can be complicated. However, computer technology can be used to simplify preparation of the chart and for evaluating different development implementation scenarios to arrive at the most effective one.

Applying Zoning and Other Regulations

At the national and regional planning levels, zoning should be applied to designate tourism development regions or areas - the tourism zones. These zones may include other types of land uses but their zoning for tourism indicates that they are places where tourism is to be developed. The appropriate types of tourism development are also often shown for each of the tourism zones. Within the designated zones, the government can develop infrastructure suitable for tourism - tourist attractions and other public-type tourist facilities and services. Designation of the tourism zones also informs the private sector where and what type of tourism is desired, and will more likely be approved. If necessary, the government can offer incentives for private sector development in the tourism zones.

At the local level of planning, tourism-zoning regulations demarcate specific areas for different types of land uses, and the standards to be applied within each of the land uses. In a resort area, for example, the zoning will designate the accommodation, commercial, recreation and conservation zones.

Other tourism related laws and regulations were described in Chapter 9. These need to be adopted as soon as possible, in order to provide the basis for managing tourism and applying facility standards.

As a tourism area develops, it is often desirable to apply a hotel classification system, usually based on star classification levels. The advantages of a hotel classification system are that they inform tour operators, travel agents and tourists about the general quality level of the facilities so that they can better select the ones they want to use. The application of a classification system also gives incentives to the private hotel enterprises to upgrade hotels to a higher star level, where that is desirable, and provides a guide for development of new hotels. For the same reasons, classification systems can also be applied to restaurants. If needed, other types of regulations, such as those on hygiene, sanitation and building construction, should be adopted. In areas prone to earthquakes and high winds, special construction standards should be incorporated into the building code.

The government procedures for reviewing and taking action on tourism development project proposals - such as hotels, and their licensing and inspection procedures - should be clearly set forth. These procedures should be efficient and fair to enterprises making the proposals but also ensure that proper standards are met.

Applying Development Standards

Application of suitable development standards and design guidelines for tourist facilities helps ensure that tourism development is environmentally appropriate, and meets tourists' and residents' expectations. These may be applied at the national, regional or local levels of government, depending on the particular governmental situation. However, it is the central or regional government's responsibility to make certain that appropriate standards are applied at the local level. Therefore, development standards and design guidelines are usually included in national and regional plans, and are adopted as part of the plan. The types of development standards to be considered are as follows:

- *Density of development* - usually expressed in terms of number of accommodation units such as hotel rooms per acre or hectare. The density of development greatly determines its overall character.
- *Heights of buildings* - also very important in setting the character of development and environmentally integrating it. For example, in many rural resorts, buildings are not allowed to exceed the heights of trees so that they blend well into the natural environment.
- *Setbacks of buildings* - from amenity features, shorelines, roads, site boundaries and other buildings. Setbacks are important for various reasons. For example, adequate setbacks from beaches and shorelines prevent damage to buildings resulting from possible shoreline erosion, preserve the natural appearance of the shoreline, and allow sufficient space for landscaping recreation and public access to the shoreline.

- *Floor area ratio (FAR)* - the ratio, expressed in percentage, of the total area of all the floors of the building to the total site area. FARs also help determine the development character and sense of openness.
- *Coverage of the site by buildings and other structures* - expressed as a percentage of the site covered by buildings and structures. Establishing maximum site coverage ratios particularly determines the amount of open space and landscaping in the development.
- *Vehicular parking spaces and other requirements* - the amount of landscaping and open space, public access to amenity features, sign controls and under grounding of utility lines, all of which are important in making a development more attractive and functional.

These development standards are usually set forth in zoning regulations, or may be adopted separately for particular tourism development areas. The actual standards applied will, of course, vary among different types of tourism areas, depending on the desired type and character of development. It is also very important to adopt suitable engineering standards to be applied in the development of infrastructure.

Guidelines for site planning and architectural and landscaping design should be adopted. They also affect how well the development is integrated into the natural and cultural environment. These are usually prepared as guidelines, and not regulated standards, because they need to be flexible and allow for the creative imagination of the designer. Site planning refers to the exact location of buildings on the development site. Site planning guidelines should consider several factors - preventing environmental hazards of erosion, landslides and flooding; achieving proper relationships among buildings; and maintaining views from buildings and vista points. Architectural guidelines should be related to use of local traditional building styles and materials, as well as overall design attractiveness. Landscaping guidelines should consider various factors - use of local indigenous plants; appropriately designed outdoor furniture; suitable night lighting; low-cost landscape maintenance; and conservation of water in dry areas.

Site planning, architectural and landscaping guidelines are typically administered by a design review committee composed of professional persons. This committee reviews all development proposals and makes any recommendations for improvements needed to their design. The guidelines should be made available to the designers before they do their work, so that they will know what the design parameters are.

Implementing Other Programmes

Other programmes recommended by the tourism plan need to be implemented. These may include, for example, the training programme for employees in tourism, public awareness programme on tourism, and an economic programme to produce more local food items used in tourism. The promotion programme will require implementation. Environmental awareness and protection programmes often must be pursued. Park, historic conservation and cultural programmes must be carried out.

Certain critical aspects of tourism may need to be resolved. The government and private sector should be conscious of maintaining tourist health. Any special health problems, such as endemic malaria or AIDS, should be addressed and tourists informed. Travel facilitation requirements and procedures, especially immigration and customs, should be made as efficient and 'user-friendly' as possible, while still enforcing the regulations.

Monitoring and Management

Monitoring should be considered an integral part of plan implementation and management. Monitoring will detect problems in their early stages, so that remedial measures can be taken. The progress of implementation, especially of the action programme, should be continuously monitored. The number and characteristics of tourist arrivals should be monitored to see if the market targets are being maintained. Determining tourist satisfaction levels through special surveys of them is especially important. Monitoring the economic, environmental and socio-cultural impacts of tourism generally, and for specific projects, is essential. Appendix 6 presents a checklist of factors that should be monitored to determine if the plan and programme are being implemented properly and on schedule.

Even though time-based targets are established, they should be considered flexible based on changing circumstances. There are many upredictable influences on meeting targets. The overall recommendations are not necessarily invalid just because certain targets are not met exactly on schedule. During the shorter-term, it is more important to maintain a balance between the development of tourist facilities, services and infrastructure and actual market demand. By maintaining a balance, resources are not wasted. Over the long-term, efforts can be made to catch up on and achieve the various market and development targets.

One of the necessary tools for research, monitoring and the overall management of tourism is establishment of a tourism information system. This needs to be an integrated system, using computer technology. Various data are placed into the system - tourists' arrivals and their characteristics; accommodation and other tourist facilities and services; economic, environmental and social data; the results of special surveys; and any other relevant data. By building up information in the system, comparisons can be made over period of time. Any significant problems and trends can be determined, and actions taken accordingly. It is essential that data fed into the information system be reliable and accurate, or the research results will not be usable.

Review should be made periodically of whether the overall tourism development policy, plan and programme are the most effective ones to achieve the development objectives. Each country or region is unique and development approaches must be adapted to each specific place. If, through experience in applying them, certain approaches and recommendations are seen to be deficient, them different ones should be considered. Through experimentation, the most effective approaches can be determined.

Emphasis must be given to the continuous management of tourism. Tourism management relates to many considerations -

adapting to changing market and product trends; maintaining and improving the quality of facilities and services; continuously expanding the benefits of tourism socially and geographically; solving problems as they arise; and other matters. Both effective implementation of the plan and efficient management are required for the long-term success of tourism and its sustainable development.

12

PLANNING FOR TRANSPORT

Transport is acknowledged as a one of the most significant factors to have contributed to the international development of tourism. According to Gayle and Goodrich, in 1991 the international tourism industry employed 112 million people worldwide and generated over $2.5 trillion at 1989 prices. In 1996, 593 million tourists travelled abroad (World Tourism Organisation, 1997), which generated a significant demand for tourist transport. In global terms, the expansion of international tourism continues to generate an insatiable demand for overseas travel. Europe remains the most visited of all regions of the world, with half of all global tourist receipts and almost two-thirds of international arrivals in 1996. In 1996, almost 352 million arrivals and US $215.7 billion in receipts were received. Eastern and Central Europe were among the fastest growing areas to benefit from Western European tourism flows. In contrast, the East Asia-Pacific region remains the area experiencing the highest growth rates, with total arrivals increasing by 9.3 per cent in 1996 to over 87 million with receipts of US $1 billion. These two examples illustrate the scale of international tourism demand, of which a key component is the mode of transport chosen by these travellers. Despite the controversy over the extent to which tourism can be defined as both an industry and a service activity, it is widely recognised that tourism combines a broad range of economic activities and services designed to meet the need of tourists.

Transport provides the essential link between tourism origin and destination areas and facilitates the movement of holidaymakers, business travellers, people visiting friends and relatives and those undertaking educational and health tourism. Transport is also a key element of the 'tourist experience' and some commentators view it as an integral part of the tourism industry.

Transport can also form the focal point for tourist activity in the case of cruising and holidays which contain a significant component of travel (e.g. coach holidays and scenic rail journeys). Here the mode of transport forms a context and controlled environment for tourists' movement between destinations and attractions, often through the medium of a 'tour'. The integral relationship which exists between transport and tourism is demonstrated by Lamb and Davidson since

> transportation is one of the three fundamental components of tourism. The other two are the tourism product (or supply) and the tourism market (or demand). Without transportation, most forms of tourism could not exist. In some cases, the transportation experience is the tourism experience (e.g. cruises, scenic and heritage rail trips, and motorcoach, automobiles and bicycle tours).

Thus, the mode of transport tourists choose can often form an integral part of their journeys and experience, a feature often neglected in the existing research on tourism. However, the interface of transport and tourism does raise the much wider conceptual problem of what is and what is not tourism transport. While it is readily acknowledged that there are specialised, dedicated forms of tourism transport (i.e. tourist coaches, charter flights and cruise liners) there are also other forms of transport which are used by both hosts and tourists to varying extents. For example, urban buses, metro systems and scheduled flights to tourism regions are used simultaneously by tourists and local residents and in some cases this can cause competition. Where tourist use of transport modes does occur, competition with other users has wide-ranging economic, environmental, social and political implications for destination areas. The basic difficulty is that few public sector organisations have the resources or inclination to address the issue of tourist-non-tourist use of different forms of transport. Therefore, even though tourist use of transport can be conceptualised at one level, making the distinction is not necessarily feasible in practice. This remains a constant problem that pervades the tourist - transport interface. However, this should not in itself preclude the academic analysis of transport and tourism. So how has transport been viewed in existing textbooks on tourism?

Tourism Studies and Tourist Transport

The majority of influential tourism textbooks are a product of the 1980s and early 1990s, despite some notable exceptions. The rapid expansion in the number of tourism textbooks published is one indication of the emergence of the subject as a serious area of study at vocational, degree and postgraduate level throughout the world. As many national governments recognise the contribution tourism can make to GDP and national economic development, the expansion of their tourism industries has led to a consideration of the immediate and long-term human resource and training requirements. New courses have developed to fill a niche in the educational marketplace and these have generated a demand for course materials to meet the international expansion of tourism education. The range of available textbooks for tourism studies has generally been written from a North American perspective; a European perspective or an Australasian with few widely available student texts written from an Asian or less developed world perspective.

An examination of these textbooks indicates that travel and transport is a topic frequently cited in relation to its role as a facilitator of the expansion of tourism, as new technology (e.g. the railway and jet engine) and novel forms of marketing and product developments (e.g. package holidays) have contributed to the development of tourism as a mass consumer product. Collier provides an interesting insight into tourist transport, arguing that three needs need to be fulfilled:

- transporting the tourist from the generating to the host area
- transport between host destinations
- transport within host destinations.

Collier also classifies tourist transport on several bases (e.g. public or private sector transport; water/land/air transport;

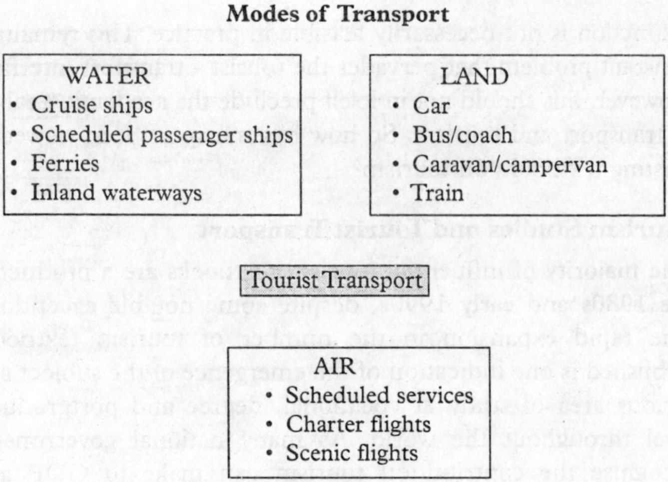

Figure. 12.1: Classification of tourist transport.

domestic and international transport and mode of transport). This classification is expanded in Figure 12.1 which outlines the main modes of transport available, and typifies the approach used in most tourism texts although the issue of scenic flights is commonly omitted (see Figure 12.2). Hall highlights the significance of transport since '. . .the evolution of tourism in Australia in inseparable from the development of new forms of transport' and '. . . a clear relationship exists between transport development and tourism growth. The development and expansion of tourist destinations are, in part, based on the need for adequate access to resort areas, their attractions and resources. Hence, the relationship between transport and tourism is usually conceptualised in most tourism textbooks in terms of accessibility.

Hobson and Uysal, however, argue that major steps in the development of tourism have been linked with advancements in transport.

> The system. . . creates the structural linkage between origins and destinations. . . [but] . . .the traditional focus on modes of travel often overlooks the underlying reason for the growth of transport communication; that is, the infrastructure that supports and sustains continued growth in the ability of people to travel.

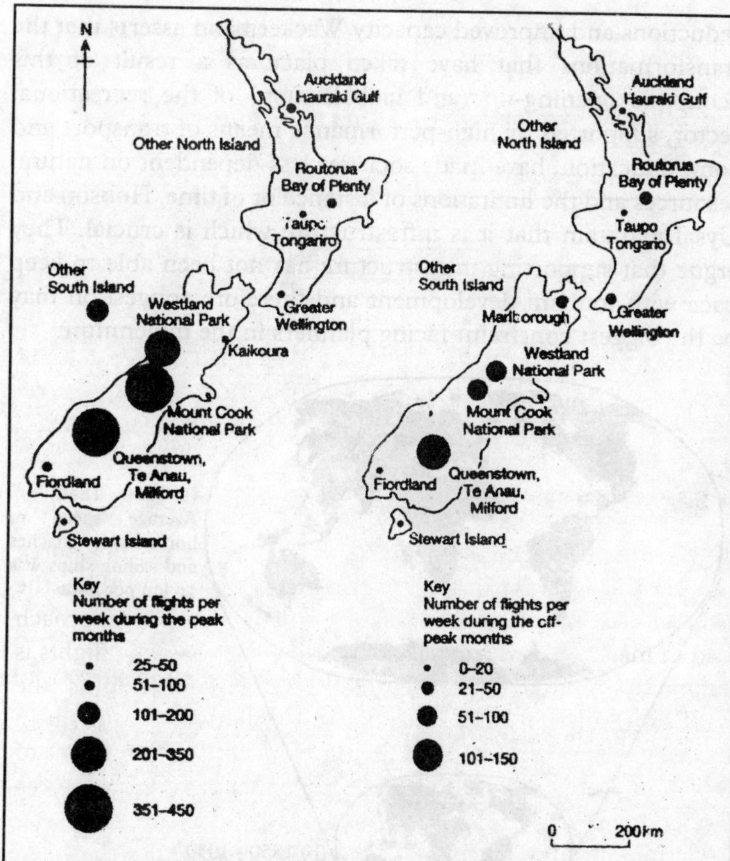

Figure 12.2: The regional distribution of scenic flights in New Zealand in 1993: peak and off-peak season.

Tolley and Turton point to the shrinking of distance by modern forms of international transport (Figure 12.3), and four major phases can be discerned in the evolution of transport technology:

- the transition from horse and windpower;
- the introduction of the steam engine;
- the development of the combustion engine;
- the use of the jet engine.

While such innovations in technology have meant that global shrinkage has occurred with reduced journey times, cost reductions and improved capacity, Wackermann asserts that the transformations that have taken place as a result of this economic opening-up (and globalisation) of the recreational sector, supported by high-performance means of transport and communication, have made societies less dependent on natural resources and the limitations of distance or of time. Hobson and Uysal maintain that it is infrastructure which is crucial. They argue that supporting infrastructure has not been able to keep pace with tourism development and therefore congestion may be the biggest constraint facing planners in the millennium.

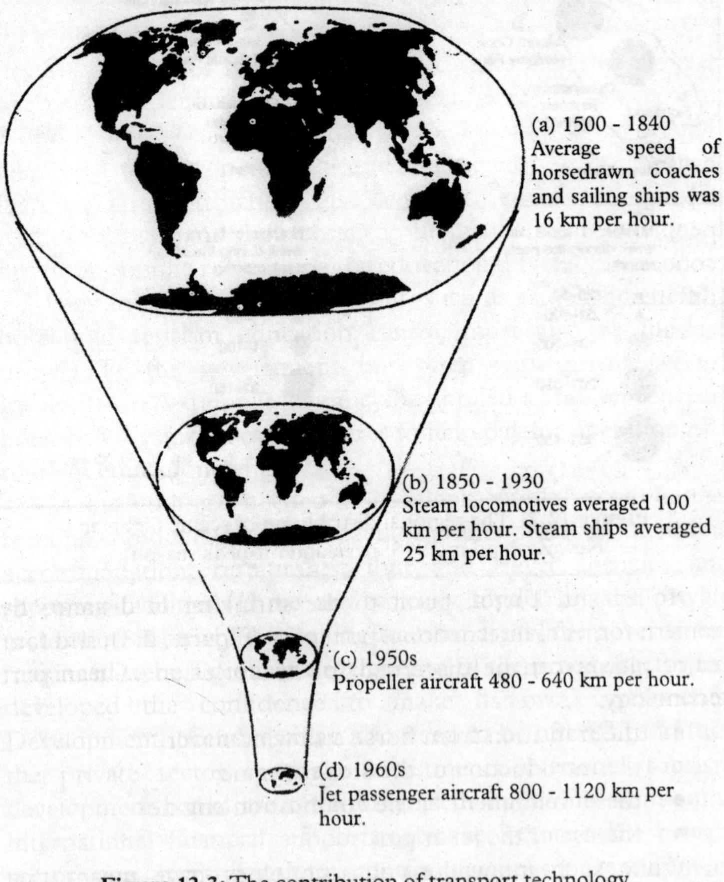

Figure 12.3: The contribution of transport technology to reductions in travel time.

A number of other textbooks have sought to develop this relationship one stage further, by discussing the historical development of tourist travel and accessibility, and the principles governing tourism's expansion within the context of different forms of tourist transport (e.g. air, road, rail and sea travel). Yet tourism studies do not have a monopoly on the analysis of transport for tourists. Textbooks on transport studies indirectly discuss the movement of tourists. Many transport studies texts are written from a disciplinary perspective such as economics while other texts focus on the operational, organisational and management issues associated with different forms of transport. However, the 'tourist' is rarely mentioned in these books as the term 'passenger' is usually substituted. In fact, a recent text on transport geography is a case in point, with the tourist also receiving only limited attention in Hoyle and Knowles. The difficulty here is that the term 'passenger' fails to distinguish between the reasons for tourist movement, implying an impersonal contractual relation ship where operators move people between areas on transport systems which are only concerned with the throughput of passengers. In reality, a different situation exists, with transport operators in the 1990s equally concerned with many of the issues facing the tourism industry - particularly customer care and the tourist's experience while travelling. Due to the choice of transport available and the competitive environment for tourist travel in free market economies, transport operators recognise the importance of ensuring that the travel experience is both pleasurable and fulfils consumers' expectations. In state-planned economies, both the demand and supply for tourist transport is regulated by the state and a different political and ideological agenda affects the availability of tourist transport compared with free market economies.

Halsall identifies the overlap between transport, tourism and recreation, arguing that in reality it is often difficult to distinguish between tourist and non-tourist use of different forms of transport, with the exceptions being dedicated forms of tourist transport such a charter flights and cruises. Former national rail operators such as British Railways (hereafter BR) did not use the term 'tourist', preferring to distinguish between 'business and leisure' travellers when identifying their potential passenger market. Thus, the tourist is not explicitly recognised as such, but is regarded as a passenger. In contrast, some tourism researchers recognise the tourist trip as an important feature to examine in its own right, although it receives only scant attention due to the smiplistic notions of the tourism - transport relationship. Consequently, the relationship between tourism and transport is rarely discussed in the context of the tourist 'experience'.

Both transport and tourism studies fail to provide an explicit and holistic framework in which to assess the transportation of tourists. For this reason, it is possible to build on the complementarity of these two areas of study to identify the concept of the 'tourist transport system' which highlights the integral role of transport in the 'tourist experience'. This also has the potential to accommodate different approaches to the analysis of tourist travel and transport. What is a 'tourist transport system'?

The Tourist Transport System: a Framework for Analysis

To understand the complexity and relationships which coexist between tourism and transport, one needs to build a framework which can synthesise the different factors and processes affecting the organisation, operation and management of activities associated with tourist travel. The objective of such a framework is to provide a means of understanding how tourists interact with transport, the processes and factors involved and their effect on the travel component of the overall 'tourist experience'. Any such framework for analysing tourist transport, needs to incorporate the tourist's use of transport services from the pre-travel booking stage through to the completion of the journey and to recognise the significance of the service component. It also needs to incorporate the different modes of transport used by tourists (e.g. air travel by scheduled or charter service, sea travel using ferries or cruise ships and land-based transport including the car, train, coach motorcaravan, motorbike and bicycle).

One methodology used by researchers to understand the nature of the tourism phenomenon is a systems approach. The main purpose of such an approach is to rationalise and simplify the real-world complexity of tourism into a number of constructs and components which highlight the interrelated nature of tourism. Since tourism studies is multidisciplinary, a systems approach can accommodate a variety of different perspectives because it does not assume a predetermined view of tourism. Instead, it enables one to understand the broader issues and factors which affect tourism, together with the interrelationships between different components in the system. According to Leiper, a system can be defined as a set of elements or parts that are connected to each other by at least one distinguishing principle. In this case, tourism is the distinguishing principle which connects the different components in the system around a common theme. Laws developed this idea a stage further by providing a systems model of the tourism industry in which the key components were the inputs, outputs and external factors conditioning the system (e.g. the external business environment, consumer preferences, political factors and economic issues). As external factors are important influences upon tourism systems, the system can be termed 'open' which means that it can easily be influenced by factors aside from the main 'inputs'. The links within the system can be examined in terms of 'flows' between components and these flows may highlight the existence of certain types of relationships between different components (Figure 12.4). For example:

- What effect does an increase in the cost of travel have on the demand for travel?

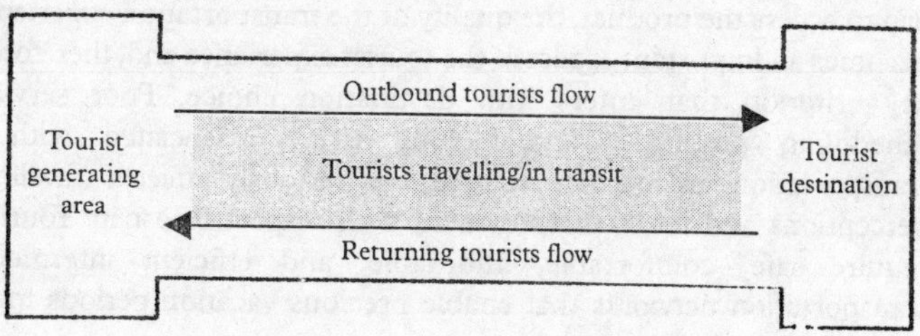

Figure 12.4: A tourism system.

- How does this have repercussions for other components in the system?
- Will it reduce the number of tourists travelling.

A systems approach has the advantage of allowing the researcher to consider the effect of such changes to the tourism system to assess the likely impact on other components.

Leiper identified the following elements of a tourism system: a tourist; a traveller-generating region; tourism destination regions; transit routes for tourists travelling between generating and destination areas, and the travel and tourism industry (e.g. accommodation, transport, the firms and organisations supplying services and products to tourists). In this analysis, transport forms an integral part of the tourism system, connecting the tourist-generating and destination regions, which is represented in terms of the volume of travel. The significance of transport in the tourism system is also apparent in the model developed by Laws, where a series of smaller sub-systems were also identified (e.g. the transport system) which can be analysed as a discrete activity in its own right while also forming an integral part of the wider 'tourism system'. Thus, a 'tourist transport' system is a framework which embodies the entire tourist experience of travelling on a particular form of transport. The analytical value of such an approach is that it enables one to understand the overall process of tourist travel from both the supplier's and purchaser's perspectives while identifying the organisations which influence and regulate tourist transport. This is aptly summarised by Lamb and Davidson who highlight the principal relationships that exist between the tourist, transport and their overall experience where

> the purchaser of the tourism product (*the tourist*) must experience the trip to access the product, the quality of the transportation experience becomes an important aspect of the tourist experience and, therefore a key criterion that enters into destination choice. Poor service, scheduling problems, and/or long delays associated with a transportation service, for example, can seriously affect a traveller's perceptions and levels of enjoyment with respect to a trip. Tourists require safe, comfortable, affordable, and efficient intermodal transportation networks that enable precious vacation periods to be enjoyed to their maximum potential.

This highlights the importance of :

- the tourist;
- the integral relationship between the transport and overall tourist experience;
- the effect of transport problems on traveller perception;
- the tourists, requirement for safe, reliable and efficient modes of transport.

To illustrate the relationship between transport and tourism, the following example of Ontario in Canada develops and reinforces many of the issues which are pursued throughout the book.

CASE STUDY: The Relationship Between Transport and Tourism: the Case of Ontario, Canada

According to Lamb and Davidson there are a number of interfaces between transport and tourism. In their pioneering study of Ontario, Canada, they provide a range of examples which highlight the multifaceted nature of tourism, transport and the relationship with government. Figure 12.5 takes a modal approach to transport (e.g. rail-, air-, bus/coach- and marine-based) and shows some of the functional roles transport infrastructure provides (e.g. linear corridors for tourism uses such as redundant rail routes). In the case of France, the state government investment in the TGV is a clear recognition of the role of intermodal transport for tourism, a feature reiterated by the OECD. Figure 12.5 is also important in emphasising how the tourism industry can harness transport linkages to develop transport-related products (e.g. scenic touring routes by car or bicycle). In the case of Canada, the Canadian province of Ontario illustrates the relationship between transport and tourism.

Ontario is arguably Canada's most prominent tourism region, since in 1991 it accounted for 36 per fent of the national tourism revenue. Nevertheless, in the early 1990s, it was losing market share at a time when the dominant American car-based holidays experienced a decline due to airline deregulation which aided the development of a more competitive domestic tourism business. Tourism Canada (now the Canadian Tourism

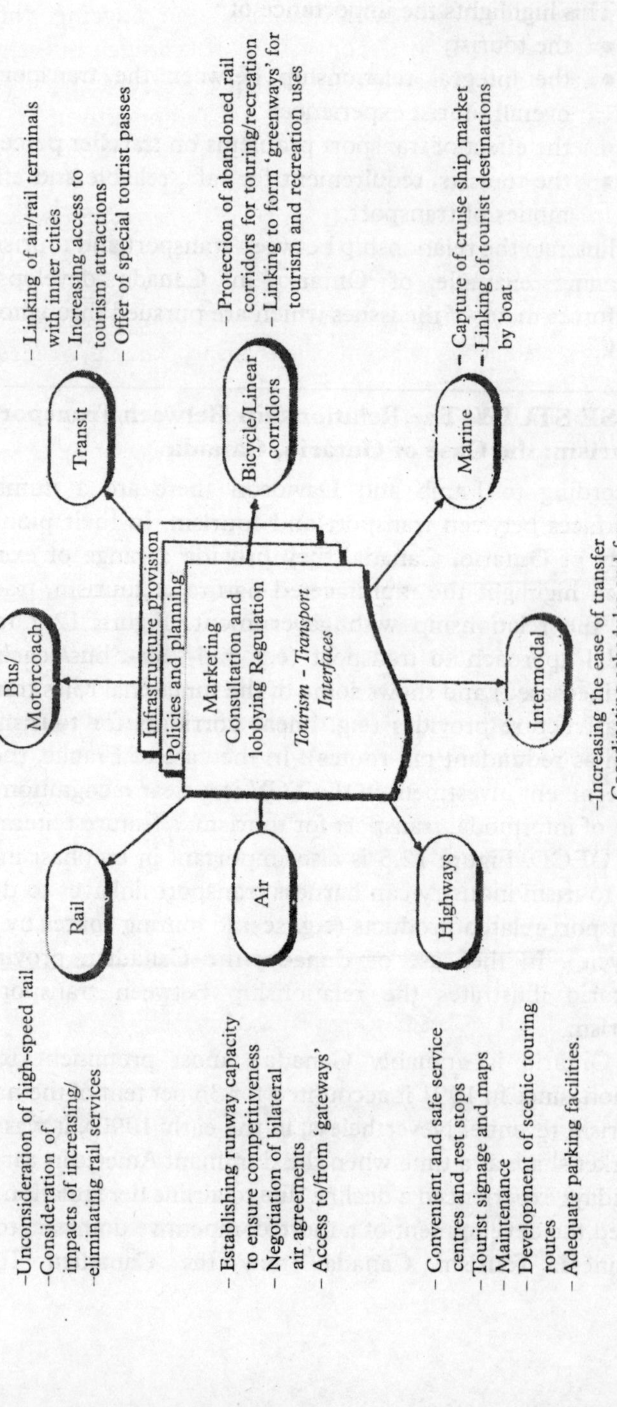

Figure 12.5: Linkages between tourism and transport.

Commission) saw poor airlinks, an ageing highway infrastructure, airport congestion, declining intercity rail services and the inability to tap into a growing cruise ship industry as key factors affecting the competitiveness of the Ontario tourism industry. This highlighted the key role of transport in the tourism industry.

In 1933, the Ontario Ministry of Tourism, in consultation with industry stakeholders, identified the following priorities for action to improve the situation including:

- Pearson International Airport in Toronto, which received 45 per cent of arrivals to Canada, needed to be upgraded.
- Ottawa, Niagara Falls, Toronto and Windsor and Sault Ste Marie were viewed as gateways for American tourists and needed to be developed as the starting point for regional tours.
- Ontario's highways, air and waterways needed improving.

A study developed by Ontario's Ministry of Transportation (Ontario Ministry of Transportation 1993) specifically focused on the transport-tourism linkages in Ontario and is relatively rare in highlighting the important integral relationships and synergies that exist. For example, Lamb and Davidson argue that in terms of air transport, the tourism industry requires:

- Good geographical coverage and frequent services from the main source areas.
- Competitive fare sturctures.
- Attractive user-friendly airport infrastructure (i.e. customs, ticketing, baggage handling and airport-related services).

Because much of the existing volume of rail traffic is intercity in character and focused in the more densely populated southern part of the province, rail transport was seen as playing a lesser role in Ontario due to the discontinuation of services and the concentration of business in high volume traffic corridors. This is complemented by scenic rail tours such as the *Agawa Canyon* route and *Polar Bear Express*. In 1989 and again in 1992, feasibility studies were undertaken to consider the viability of a

Windsor-Quebec City high speed rail corridor. Not only would the American market have access to it at Windsor and Kingston, generating visitor trips, but it would permit time savings, allowing Southern Ontario and Quebec to be visited. Other growth opportunities the project might stimulate were related to the intermodal air-links at Pearson International Airport, the coach industry and the cruise ship industry on the Great Lakes. Although this would require a subsidised rail corridor to keep rail fares competitive with air, it was seen as a viable option to revitalise Ontario's tourism industry, thereby developing a number of new products through transport innovations.

Ontario's road and highway networks also have an important bearing on tourism. According to Lamb and Davidson, Ontario possesses:

- 25,000 km of provincial highways (including four-lane highways used by tourists).
- Many two-lane highways which are more rural in character.

In fact, 80 per cent of out-of province are from the USA and car-based touring remains important for this market, despite experiencing a decline in the 1980s. The Ontario Ministry of Transport identified improving ease of access and upgrading tourism infrastructure in the gateway cities (Niagara Falls, Windsor, Sault Ste Marie and Sarnia) as vital to increase the length of stay for such visitors.

Coach tours also utilise the road network, and this segment of the transport market has seen growing popularity with the senior market. In fact, the Ontario Ministry of Transport has licensed coach operators to provide services on non-tourist routes which are less profitable in return for operating profitable tourist routes. In this sense, tourism is used to cross-subsidise non-tourist routes and is likely to increase in importance as rail travel in progressively phased out. The National Tour Association cited in Lamb and Davidson identified three characteristics of coach travellers in North America. These were:

- a growing preference for shorter trips, where tourists fly to a destination then take a coach trip;

- the greatest users of tourist coach travel are the senior market, with a median age of 66 - 70 years of age;
- comfort and convenience and ease of access to coaches are deemed important.

One important tourism relationship which is worth emphasising is that coach tours encourage overnight stays and so can stimulate spending en route. Well-developed scenic touring routes therefore need to be supported by road infrastructure, accommodation and stopping points as lookouts. In Ontario, the transport ministry oversees highway support services such as signage, tourist information centres and traffic management systems. Lamb and Davidson observe that the key issues affecting road-based tourism in Ontario include:

- *the quality of infrastructure*, since Ontario's highways are continuing to deteriorate;
- *road congestion*, especially at locations such as Lake Ontario, which may deter visiors from exploring such attractions and scenic routes;
- *signage* is seen as the highest priority for action by Ontario's tourism ministry and private sector tourism stakeholders to encourage the spontaneous visit and to facilitate the unplanned visit.

Other initiatives related to tourist transport which Lamb and Dauidson review include:

- Improving intermodal connections between Pearson International Airport and Central Toronto.
- Developing stronger linkages between Niagara Falls and Toronto rail, ferry and other transport modes.
- The development of new linear land and water corridors which integrate various forms of transport to explore the scenic regions of Ontario.

While Lamb and Davidson's invaluable study identifies the links between transport and tourism, it also highlights the need for regions or states to consider the concept of seamless transport systems for tourists. This means that the individual transport networks which exist for each mode of tourist transport need to be planned and integrated into a holistic framework. This will ensure that the tourists' experience of transport is a continuous one which is not characterised by major gaps in provision and a lack of integration. For instance, airports need to be linked to their central tourist districts so that visitors transfer from one mode of transport to another with relative ease after long flights when tiredness and disorientation can mar their experience. Recognising such linkages in terms of tourism can also yield invaluable business opportunities (e.g. the growth in airport shuttle companies) where ancillary transport operators can leverage business from the provision of convenient door-to-door services for travellers. So how does this book aim to integrate tourist travel more fully into the study of tourism?

13
TOURISM AND SOCIETY

Tourism is essentially, a social phenomenon. It is about millions of individuals who, travelling nationally or internationally, temporarily leave their own society and visit and impact upon the societies in which other people live. It is about tourists who are motivated and influenced by their own social environment, who carry with them a set of socially patterned values and expectations, and who interact with people in other places and societies which, frequently, possess a completely different set of social structures and values. In other words, tourism is about people, tourists, visiting other societies and undergoing experiences that may influence their own or their hosts' attitudes behaviour, expectations and ultimately, lifestyles.

In short, a direct relationship exists between tourism and the societies that both generate and receive tourists. The purpose of this chapter is to explore the nature and characteristics of this relationship. It introduces a number of issues and concepts that are fundamental to the understanding of the ways which societies influence, and are in turn influenced by, tourism, and it discusses the implications of the tourism-society relationship for the effective management and planning of tourism. First, however, it is necessary to determine the form of this relationship to provide a framework for the chapter.

Tourism and Society: A Two-way Relationship

The relationship between tourism and society is manifested in two ways or, more specifically, in two directions (see Figure 13.1). Firstly and, perhaps, most visibly, the development of tourism inevitably results in both positive and negative consequences for destination societies. Indeed, the rapid growth of mass, international tourism since the 1960s has been mirrored by ever increasing concern about the impacts of that growth on local people in tourism destinations, concern that was reflected in early writing on the subject. These issues are addressed in the latter part of this chapter.

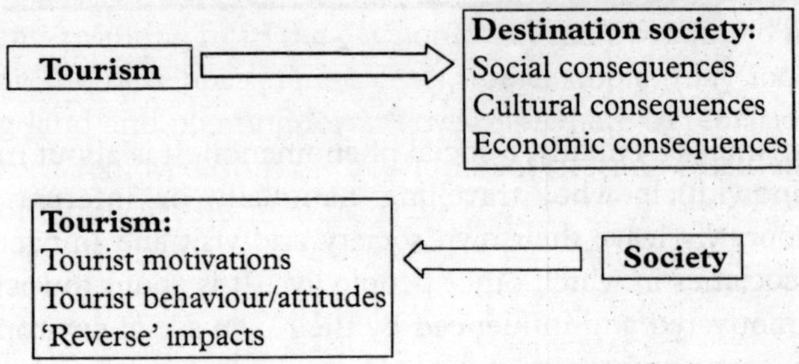

Figure 13.1 : Tourism-society relationships.

Secondly, tourism is itself influenced or impacted upon *by* society. As history shows, mass tourism has evolved as a result of transformations and developments in society; it is, in a sense, a social victory. More importantly, however, society has been, and continues to be, a powerful force in shaping the character of tourism. That is, a variety of social factors are instrumental in determining the motivation for and style of tourism, influencing how, when, where and why people participate in tourism. It is upon these factors that the first section of this chapter now focuses.

Social Influences on Tourism

Tourism is a social activity. That is, it is an activity which is undertaken by ever-increasing numbers of people, either individually or in groups and most typically for leisure or holiday purposes, and which normally involves inter action with other people, whether fellow tourists or local people in tourist destinations. It is also, however, a form of consumption. In other words, people *buy* tourism; they buy, in effect, blocks of time which are filled with a variety of services and experiences provided, for the most part, by the tourism industry.

As with many other forms of consumption, there are a variety of reasons why people choose to buy tourism as opposed to other products or services in the first place and, having done so, why they choose particular styles of tourism. Thus, although tourism is seen by many as simply a means of escape or relaxation, (the term 'holiday' being synonymous, perhaps, with having a break or resting from work), there are, in fact, a variety of underlying social factors which influence why and in what form people participate in tourism. Indeed, it has been argued that 'explaining the consumption of tourist-services cannot be separated off from the social relations within which they are embedded'. This suggests that, in order to understand the consumption of tourism and, for practical purposes, to be better able to explain and predict changes in the demand for tourism, it is important to consider those social factors which influence tourists' roles and behaviour. Here, we shall be primarily concerned with:

- extrinsic influences on tourist motivation;
- tourism as a consequence of modern society;
- tourism as an authentic experience;
- post-modern tourism and travel in 'hyper-reality'.

Extrinsic Influences on Tourist Motivation

The tourism demand process is triggered by motivation; it is person-specific motivation that translates people's needs and wants into goal-oriented behaviour and influences their tourism decision-making process. The motivational stage is, therefore, a key factor in understanding how and why people participate in tourism.

It was also noted that, just as there are many different forces and pressures that influence the motivation for tourism, there are many approaches to researching or explaining it. For the most part, however, there are two distinct perspectives on tourist motivation. Firstly, motivation is more traditionally considered in relation to the intrinsic personal or psychological needs of tourists themselves - that is, motivation is seen as a psychological concept. Secondly, there are undoubtedly a number of extrinsic, social determinants of tourist motivation. These are forces that emerge from tourists' social environment which influence or shape their needs and wants and, hence their consumption of tourism. It is these latter, extrinsic motivational factors which concern us here.

(i) Tourist typologies and motivation - A number of authors have developed typologies, or categorisations of tourist roles and behaviour as a basis for understanding the motivations of different types of tourists. Some concentrate on the intrinsic, psychographic characteristics of tourists, such as the psychocentric-allocentric continuum devised by Plog in the 1970s and referred to in many tourism texts. However, Erik Cohen developed two typologies which relate tourist behaviour to their home social environment and which are therefore of relevance here.

Both of Cohen's typologies are based on the notion of a familiarity-strangerhood continuum. He suggested that different tourists are more or less able to withstand the 'culture-shock' of travelling abroad and that, as a result, they are motivated to seek out forms of tourism that offer either novelty (i.e. the strange or new) or the familiarity of home. In other words, he proposed that tourists travel within an 'environmental bubble' which depending where they are positioned on the line between familiarity and strangerhood, they are more or less able to break out of whilst on holiday. Thus, in his first typology, he described four types of tourist:

- *The organised mass tourist* - travels on an organised package tour, stays in hotels which recreate the home environment, remains largely within the hotel complex unless on organised trips and avoids all contact with local people or culture.
- *The individual mass tourist* - similar to the organised mass tourist in that the holiday is organised and packaged, but occasionally ventures out to seek novelty by, for example, hiring a car to visit local attractions or facilities. Thus, unlike the organised mass tourist, the individual occasionally escapes from the environmental bubble.

- *The explorer* - unlike the organised or individual mass tourist, the explorer is a 'traveller' rather than a 'tourist', makes his/her own travel arrangements, avoids the 'tourist trail' and seeks out local culture. However, escape from the bubble is not total; reminders of home (a newspaper, familiar food) are needed, as is contact with fellow travellers.
- *The drifter* - at the opposite end of the familiarity-strangerhood continuum to the organised mass tourist, the drifter has no fixed itinerary, attempts to merge into local communities and customs and avoids all contact with tourists or the tourism system. The desire for novelty is greatest and escape from the environmental bubble is almost complete.

Although this typology represents a useful basis for predicting tourists' behaviour based upon their relationship with their home society, it is largely descriptive rather than analytical. That is, although it suggests *how* different people will behave as tourists, it does not explain *why*. As a result, Cohen proposed a second typology, still using the notion of the familiarity-strangerhood continuum but also introducing the idea that tourists' desired experiences will be very much dependent their experience of their home environment. That is, he argued that some people feel entirely familiar and happy with their home society; they feel they belong where they live/work and that what Cohen describes as their 'spiritual centre' is firmly rooted at home. They therefore have no need to seek reality or meaning elsewhere and their desired tourism experiences will reflect this. At the other extreme, however, are those who have no sense of belonging or no sense of place in their home environment. They feel like a stranger, or alienated, at home; their spiritual centre lies elsewhere and, as a result, they are motivated to seek out places, cultures or experiences that provide them with that sense of place or belonging which is lacking at home.

Cohen developed this concept into a five-fold typology:

- *Recreational tourist* - has no desire or need for novel experiences and, therefore, seeks out recreational, play forms of tourism.

- *Diversionary tourist* - does not feel alienated yet nevertheless seeks some diversion or change from the home environment.
- *Experiential tourist* - neither identifies with nor rejects the home environment and, therefore, is motivated to seek novelty or strangerhood as a tourist but inevitably returns home.
- *Experimental tourist* - feels very much alienated and therefore seeks reality and meaning elsewhere. However, some link with the home environment remains.
- *Existential tourist* - the opposite to the recreational tourist, the existential tourist feels no sense of belonging at home and travels to find reality, meaning and a sense of place elsewhere.

There are a number of weaknesses inherent in these and, indeed, in most typologies. In particular, they over-generalise tourist motivations; they are static, in as much as they do not allow for variable behaviour over time; they overlook many other factors that influence tourists' motivations; and, they tend to subordinate the ability of individuals to make their own decisions to the influence of their relationship with their home society. Nevertheless, they do provide a foundation for understanding that tourist motivation is influenced, in general, by the relationship of individuals with their home society and, in particular, by specific features or social factors that frame that relationship.

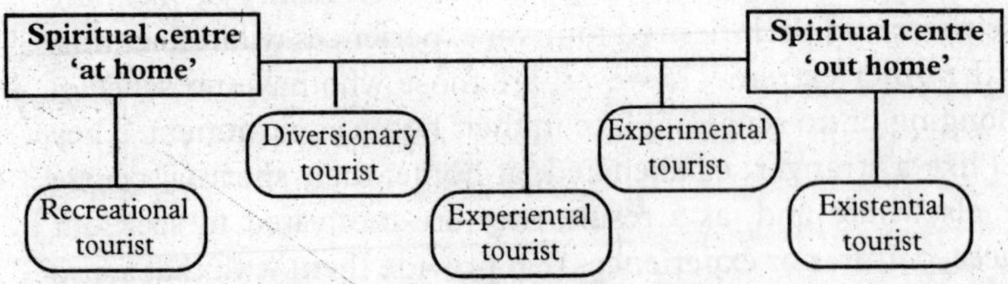

Figure 13.2: Cohen's phenomenology' of tourist experiences.

For many people, one of the most important or influential extrinsic factors that motivates them to participate in tourism is work. Indeed, tourism can be seen as the antithesis to work, the chance to escape, unwind and relax. However, as we shall now discuss, the relationship between work and tourism may be more complex than is at first apparent.

(ii) Work and tourist motivation - Tourism and work are inter-related in as much as work provides both the means (income) and the motivation for tourism. At the same time, tourism, as a form of recreation, enables people to return to work refreshed and, literally, 'recreated'. However, the relationship between work and tourism is not so straightforward as this. Different types of work are more or less stressful, challenging, stimulating or physically tiring, whilst work itself means different things to different people. To some, it may be simply a means to an end, a way of earning a living; to others it may be a way of life. In other words, different types of work, different work environments and people's differing approaches to work all combine to result in an enormous variety of personal needs and, hence, tourist motivations. As has been argued elsewhere, 'the experience of work in industrial societies. . . forms the context for the experience of leisure'.

Of course, work is not the only extrinsic motivating factor and nor does it apply to a number social groups. Nevertheless, there are three ways in which work and tourist motivation are related:

(a) Work and tourism in opposition - Alternatively described as the compensatory model, this proposes that the experiences of work and tourism are in opposition to each other. That is, the individual is motivated to seek out forms of tourism that that offer a distinct change of experience, or even lifestyle, from that found at work. Tourism thus compensates for what is lacking at work. It theory, this relationship should operate in both directions; those in monotonous, repetitive, unchallenging jobs might be expected to seek out holidays that offer excitement and that are stimulating whilst, alternatively, those who have stressful, challenging jobs might be motivated to have quieter, restful holidays where they can 'switch off'.

Interestingly, however, this model has been found to be most applicable to those in lower status jobs, where tourism compensates for deficiencies at work and, by implication, at home. Thus, people are motivated to save up for a holiday where they can indulge in a lifestyle that can normally only be dreamed of. By escaping to a fantasy life of staying in hotels and enjoying standards of service that are in direct contrast to normal, day-to-day life, tourists experience an inversion of reality; they become, as one commentator described, king or queen for a day.

The opposition/compensatory model can also be used to explain the motivation to escape the constraints imposed by work and, indeed, from social constraints in general. People at work are normally restricted by time commitments and codes of dress and behaviour, as well as by socially imposed values. Conversely, tourism offers the opportunity to indulge in 'ludic' behaviour, behaviour that represents play or freedom from the rules and regualtions of work and home society. Such behaviour may be described as simply 'letting your hair down' and not only compensates for the rigid, social structure of normal life but also prepares tourists to re-enter that structured, everyday existence.

(b) Tourism as an extension of work - In comparison to the opposition/compensation model described above, the extension theory suggests that there is little or no distinction between work and tourism. In other words, tourism complements, rather than contrasts with, work. Thus, those who are employed in challenging, stimulating jobs and who enjoy a position of responsibility are more likely to choose independent and similarly stimulating types of holiday, whereas people in regulated, routine and passive jobs will be motivated to participate in equally passive, less stimulating forms of tourism. They will choose the mass produced package holiday which, in effect, mirrors the production-line environment of the workplace. The extreme case, of course, would be where there is no distinction at all between work and tourism, where work is carried over into tourism, such as a history teacher touring historical sites.

The implication of this approach is that, as general work practices change, so too will the demand for tourism. Thus, as societies transform into post-industrial, service based economies, changes in work practices may well have an impact on tourist motivation.

(c) Neutrality between tourism and work - Unlike the previous two models, where there exists a causal relationship between the nature of work and tourist motivation, the third model proposes that work has little or no effect on the patterns of tourism demand. In other words, there is no link between the two; work becomes, in the context of tourism, simply a means to an end, a source of income to pay for tourism. This suggests that other factors will be more influential than work in determining tourist motivation, although it is probably true to say that, for the majority of tourists, work remains the dominant extrinsic motivating factor.

(iii) Social determinants of tourist motivation - Even where work and the work environment represent powerful influences on tourist motivation, a number of other extrinsic pressures may be significant determinants of tourist motivation and behaviour. Such pressure emanate from four main sources:

- *Family influences* - For many people, one of the most significant influences on their attitudes and behaviour is their family. It is the family, particularly parents, that initially provide the values and behavioural codes that frame people's social existence and, frequently, continue to do so throughout their lives. In other words, many aspects of people's behaviour, including their consumption of tourism, may be subject to the influence of their family. The VFR (Visiting Friends and Relatives) market is, of course, motivated by the desire to visit relatives or, more specifically perhaps, the need for love and affection. However, other types of tourist behaviour, such as visiting particular destinations or going on camping holidays, might be influenced by childhood experiences or family tradition.
- *Reference groups* - Just as the family is the initial source of social values and attitudes, so too may reference groups determine people's behaviour. A reference group is any group that an individual turns to as a point of reference for beliefs and attitudes, a group against which the individual can judge his or her own beliefs and behaviour. Reference groups may take various forms, such as ethnic groups, work collcagues or other social

associations, such as environmental pressure groups, and they are either normative (influencing general values) or comparative (influencing specific values). They may also be a powerful influence on tourist motivation, as in, for example, people being motivated to go on environmentally friendly, eco-tourism holidays as a result of reference to conservation organisations.

- *Social class* - Members of particular social classes tend to have similar lifestyles and values and it is likely that they will follow similar standards of behaviour. Therefore, although some would argue that traditional social class divisions are less evident or meaningful in today's post-industrial society, social class is, nevertheless, an important motivational factor. For example, different destinations may be categorised by the social class of the majority of visitors and it has been argued that, whilst the working classes traditionally prefer mass, collective forms of tourism, the middle classes seek out more solitary, individualistic or 'romantic' form of tourism.
- *Culture* - The culture of a society, its values, morals, behavioural codes as well as its more tangible identifying characteristics, such as language, dress and art forms, may be a strong influence on tourist motivation and consumption. In some cultures, tourism may be more deeply rooted or have greater significance than in others, whilst other factors, such as destination choice or types of tourism, may be culturally determined. For example, the importance of pilgrimage in Islamic culture is a powerful religious tourism motivator.
- *Social values* - As a specific category of cultural motivator various social values may be an important determinant of tourist motivation. For example, the term 'mass tourism' has increasingly been used in a derogatory sense to describe particular forms of tourism and particular destinations. That is, mass tourism, the 'degenerate offspring' of early travel, has come to be viewed as a potentially destructive force

and 'mass tourist' is, in effect, a socially defined label attached to particular types of tourist. This negative connotation of mass tourism/tourists has evolved into a social value and, although large numbers of people evidently still enjoy being mass tourists, many may be motivated to seek out forms of tourism that are more exclusive or 'better'; in a similar vein, the so-called 'good tourist' has evolved as a result of alleged widespred environmental concern, itself an emerging social value.

Tourism as a Consequence of Modern Society

So far, we have been looking at specific extrinsic factors, or particular social forces and pressures, that influence tourist motivation. In other words, we have been concerned with specific factors *within* society that motivate tourists. It is also important, however, to appreciate how overall changes in the character of society as a whole have had an impact on tourist motivation and behaviour.

It is paradoxical that, whilst modern, industrial society has provided the means of mass tourism in the form of fast, safe and economical transport systems, higher living standards, socially sanctioned leisure time (i.e. holidays, with pay, bank holidays, etc.) and the tourism industry, it has also created the need for tourism. That is, modern society not only provides the opportunity for mass participation in tourism, it also motivates people to do so. For many tourists, the annual holiday represents the chance to rest, to recover from the stresses and strains of modern life. It has become an essential ingredient in people's lifecycles; in order to survive in modern society, people must, periodically, escape from it. In a sense, therefore, society itself represents the ultimate motivation for tourism.

What, then, are the characteristics of modern society that have created this need amongst large sections of the population to escape? The answer lies in the factors that have led to a sense of alienation, a feeling of not belonging, of not having a sense of meaning or purpose in life. These factors are the work practices, activities, technological advances, expectations and social values that together constitute the modern way of life, and which create a sense of alienation in a number of ways:

- *alienation at work* - modern work practices, such as the division of labour, automation and the centralisation of various functions have separated people from the product of their labour. They are simply cogs in the system.
- *alienation from community* - greater mobility and technical advances in communication, most recently mobile phones and computer-based communication systems, have reduced the sense of community. People are more independent, live further from work or family and friends, and no longer need to communicate face-to-face.
- *alienation from nature* - urban living separates people from nature and the natural world.

In a sense, people have also become alienated from themselves. Modern society provides products to made every task easier and faster, yet technological advance diminishes human contact and reduces the need for social interaction. In a society dominated by economic growth, people's expectations and values are guided by materialism and the need for acquisition. As life gets faster, people have less time and the realities of modern life are, for many, a source of stress, disenchantment and dissatisfaction. In short, people lack a sense of meaning in modern society, they have lost their self-identity.

Of course, not all people suffer from this sense of alienation and not to the same degree. Indeed, many people undoubtedly live happy and fulfilled lives in modern society. Nevertheless, the inherent alienating characteristics of society are considered by many to be a major extrinsic tourism motivating factor and, whether to simply unwind on a beach or to search for meaning and a sense of place elsewhere, millions of people each year are motivated by their society to escape, albeit temporarily, from it.

Tourism as an Authentic Experience

One implication of the alienating characteristics of modern society discussed in the previous section is that not only are people motivated to escape temporarily from society, but also to seek out meaning and reality, or what is frequently termed 'authenticity', elsewhere. In other words, tourists are motivated by the desire for authentic experiences that compensate for the deficiencies of modern life.

The extent to which tourists do in fact seek reality or authenticity has long been debated in the literature. On the one hand, it has been suggested that all tourists are satisfied with inauthentic, staged, 'pseudo-events' and experiences and, like Cohen's organised mass tourists discussed earlier, have no need or desire to experience the reality/authenticity of destination societies and cultures. On the other hand, it has been argued that all tourists do in fact seek authenticity, that tourists are, in effect, modern day pilgrims seeking a sense of meaning and purpose in life through their touristic experiences.

In practice, most people fall between these two extremes. That is, there is no doubt that many people have no need or desire to immerse themselves in the authentic culture of destinations. For them, both modern society and the mass package tourism that reflects that modernity satisfy them completely. However, there is also no doubt that many more do seek out some form of authentic experience whilst on holiday, though not to the extent suggested by MacCannell. This then begs the question, what is an authentic tourism experience?

Strictly speaking, the term authentic means genuine or real. Therefore, an artefact in a museum, or a painting in a gallery, may be described as authentic (as opposed to fake) if it is known or recognised to as being the genuine article. In the context of tourism, however, the meaning of 'authenticity' is rather more ambiguous and it is used in two particular ways:

- *authentic destinations* - authenticity is often used to describe the works of art cuisine, dress, language, festivals and other rituals or other cultural characteristics of a destination. As long as something is produced or enacted according to local custom or tradition, then it is deemed authentic.
- *authentic travel* - authenticity is also used to describe (and sell) specific types of travel. These are usually specialist, niche forms of tourism, often involving

overland travel, and are described as authentic to distinguish them from mass market, packaged holidays or travel experiences.

In both cases, however, authenticity also connotes tradition and pre-modernity. In other words, authentic tourist destinations are perceived to be those which have not yet become, in comparison to western, industrialised societies, modern. Hence, authentic destinations are perceived to be those which are, primarily, in the less developed regions of the world. Similarly, authentic travel reflects the styles and forms of transport or travel that pre-date the modern, mass package tour, such as travelling on the Orient Express to Venice. Thus, the desire for authentic experiences is the desire to experience the pre-modern, or the past. Thus, tourism becomes, in a sense, a form of time travel.

The extent to which tourists desire, or are able, to have authentic experiences is open to debate. For example, MacCannell argues that all tourist experiences are, to a lesser or greater extent, staged and that the authentic can never be experienced. Others, conversely, suggest that the notion of authenticity is an individual experience. That is, individual tourists, based upon their personal motivations, perceptions and experience, make their own sense of each tourism setting or occurrence. The important point here, however, is that the tourism industry has recognised and is responding to widespread demands for authentic tourism experiences, as evidenced by:

- the use of authenticity as a marketing tool, where destinations or types of travel are promoted and advertised in a way that matches the perceptions of potential tourists (though not necessarily reflecting the reality or the destination), and
- the development of attractions, facilities, rituals or events that possess the aura of authenticity.

It is, therefore, paradoxical that, although tourism is primarily promoted as a means of social and economic modernisation and development, many tourist destinations will only remain attractive to tourists 'so long as they remain undeveloped and;

hence, in some way primitive'. Implicitly, tourism will then increasingly become a system of illusions or what, as we shall now see, has been described as travels in 'hyper-reality'.

Post-modern Tourism and Travel in 'Hyper-reality'

So far in this chapter we have been looking at the ways in which modern society can influence or shape the demand for tourism. In particular, we have been considering both the overall characteristics of modern society and a variety of specific social which, in one way or another contribute to the explanation of way and how people participate in tourism.

However, one other variable in the relationship between tourism and society has been overlooked, namely changes in modern society itself. In other words, whilst there can be little doubt that many tourists are motivated by the desire to escape *from* modern society and that their behaviour may be conditioned to some extent by their relationship *with* society, it has been assumed that 'modern society' is a constant, fixed factor. Certainly, a number of characteristics that have been discussed here are typical to most modern societies. However it is important to recognise that the nature of society results from a combination of economic, political, social and cultural processes which together create the framework for social life. These processes are constantly adapting and changing and so the nature, or 'condition', of modern society is also in a constant state of change. Indeed, it has been suggested by some that, as many modern societies become post-industrial with their economies becoming increasingly dependent on the tertiary, service sector they are transforming into culturally 'post-modern' societies.

It is difficult to grasp the notion that society or, more specifically, the social and cultural character of life in modern society, is undergoing an identifiable process of transformation from one condition (modern) to another (post-modern). Indeed, the entire concept of post-modernism is a controversial topic. Nevertheless, many social, cultural and economic forms in modern societies are undoubtedly undergoing change and whether or not they are inter-related and represent an all-embracing cultural transformation into what may described as post-modernism, they potentially influence the demand for tourism.

An in-depth analysis of post-modernism is, of course, beyond the scope of this chapter. Briefly, however, it is seen as representing the end of the ordered structured and defined state of (socially) modern society where strict distinctions were evident in most structures and institutions. In other words, the modernisation and industrialisation of societies resulted in most spheres of social life, including work, leisure, social class, gender roles, high and low, or popular culture, and even the past and the present, being strictly demarcated. More recently, however, there has been an evident breaking down, or de-differentiation, of many of these social structures. For example, boundaries between social class have become less distinct, societies are becoming multi-ethnic, the past, rejected by modernists in favour of scientific progress, has merged into the present as concern grows for conserving or recreating history, and there has been a fusion of popular, mass culture with high culture, such as the use of classical music to promote sporting events. In particular, it is claimed that there is a diminishing distinction between reality and representations of reality and, in the extreme, image may actually replace reality, such as in the case of computer games. Thus, post-modernism can be characterised by:

- a plurality of viewpoints and ideas;
- the fusion of distinct areas of social and cultural activity;
- lifestyles increasingly dominated by spectacle, image and visual media;
- the merging of the past into the present; and
- the breaking down of traditional social structures.

There are a number of ways in which this de-differentiation of post-modern society influences or shapes tourism. For example, the popularity of historical sites and events as tourists attractions, conveniently packaged by the so-called 'heritage industry', is evidence of the merging of the past into the present, whilst the growth of urban or industrial city tourism or the fusion of shopping and tourism activities within the context of shopping malls demonstrates how both the time and the place where people participate in tourists is less distinct.

However, the influence of post-modern culture on tourism is arguably most evident in the development and popularity of sites or attractions that are representations or images of reality and which present the tourist with 'hyper-reality'. For example, many historical attractions represent the past through a variety of interpretative techniques which artificially recreate the past as a modern spectacle, so that 'fantasy is potentially as real as history, Similarly, genuine historical artefacts are frequently placed in recreated settings, which may be a room set or an entire village, complete with the appropriate sounds and smells, in order to 'bring to life' what might be otherwise mundane or uninteresting articles. In both cases, the artificial creation is often devoid of any true analysis of the past.

The development of themed restaurants or dining areas, often within shopping malls, is a further example of post-modern tourist facilities which attempt to recreate the 'reality' of, say, dining out in Greece of Italy whilst. Similarly, inland resorts or holiday villages which are based around themed tropical swimming centres are quintessential post-modern tourist sites, being simulated environments superimposed on reality. More generally, many tourist sites and attractions have become famous as symbols or signs of a particular place or culture rather than in their own right. In other words, post-modern tourists are motivated to seek out images or representations of cultures or countries rather than to understand the true meaning of such sites. Thus, tourists visit the Taj Mahal as a sign of 'Indian-ness' or the Eiffel Tower as a sign of 'French-ness'.

In the extreme, images and recreations may be copies or simulations for which no original exists. One example of this is the successful promotion of Santa Claus as a tourist attraction in Lapland, whilst many tourists are drawn to the Peter Rabbit exhibition in the English Lake District, an attraction based entirely on the children's stories of Beatrix Potter, who lived in the region. Indeed, it was once proposed that the Lake District be promoted as 'Peter Rabbit Country', which would have been doubly ironic for a region which, for many, is a modern-day representation of an imagined rural past made famous by the poems of Wordsworth and the paintings of Turner. In short, post-modern travel in hyper-reality is tourism in constructed reality, the ultimate form of which is likely to be manifested in virtual reality or virtual travel.

The Socio-cultural Consequences of Tourism

It is, perhaps, inevitable that the development of tourism impacts upon destination societies and cultures. In fact, in some respects it would be considered unfortunate for tourism *not* to result in certain consequences for destinations, for the simple reason that tourism is usually promoted with the aim of achieving economic and social development and diversification. Therefore, social consequences of tourism in the form of higher income, greater employment opportunities improved education and healthcare facilities, infrastructural developments and an overall improvement in local communities' quality of life are largely welcomed.

At the same time, given the nature of tourism, other socio-cultural impacts are also inevitable. That is, all tourists travel to destinations, carrying with them their values, beliefs, perceptions and behavioural modes as a form of cultural baggage. Whilst on holiday they interact with members of the local, host community and this interaction brings about social consequences, whether simply as a result of the physical presence and behaviour of tourists or because of the cultural gap that exists between tourists and their hosts.

Some of these consequences may, again, be beneficial; indeed, tourism is seen by some as a vehicle to greater international harmony and understanding. Unfortunately, however, more often than not it is the negative, emotive consequences of tourism that gain most publicity or notoriety, in particular the consequences of mass tourism: 'tourism seem to be the incarnation of the materialism, philistinism and cultural homogenisation that is sweeping all before it in a converging world.' It is for this reason that the solution to the 'problem' of mass tourism is seen to lie in the development of responsible, alternative (to mass) forms of tourism.

Many of the social consequences of tourism are well known and some, such as the problems of tourism-related child prostitution or the displacement of communities to make way for tourist development, have been publicised globally. However, for our purposes here, it is first important to develop an understanding as to why and to what extent socio-cultural consequences occur. Therefore, this section of the chapter will consider:

- factors that determine the extent of socio-cultural change,
- the nature of tourist-host encounters,
- host attitudes towards tourists,
- social impacts on tourists.

The chapter will then conclude with a brief outline of the socio-cultural impacts of tourism and an introduction to the concept of sustainable tourism as a potential solution.

Factors Determining Socio-cultural Change

Although it is likely that all destinations experience social and cultural consequences of tourism development, the degree to which these consequences are felt or are manifested is dependent upon a number of factors. As a general rule, the greater the difference between the cultural and economic characteristics of the destination and those of the tourists' own society, the more significant are the social and cultural impacts likely to be. More specifically, however, the extent of tourism-induced socio-cultural change may be influenced by:

- *the types or numbers of tourists* - normally, it is considered that higher numbers of mass tourists will impact more on host societies than relatively few explorer-type tourists. However, it can also be argued that an independent traveller visiting an isolated community may have more of an impact than, say, large numbers of tourists in a purpose-built, self-contained club resort.
- *the size and development of the tourism industry* - the larger the tourism industry relative to the size of the local

community, the greater is its impact likely to be. However, the more established or mature the industry, the less likely are significant socio-cultural changes to occur.

- *the relative importance of the tourism industry* - the consequences of tourism will be felt more keenly in destinations that are highly dependent on tourism than in more mixed economies.
- *the pace of tourism development* - it has been found that socio-cultural impacts are more likely to be experienced when the development of tourism is rapid and uncontrolled.

It is also important to consider the extent to which tourism, as opposed to other pressures and influences, leads to social and cultural change in destination societies. That is, all societies are dynamic; they are in a constant state of change and no society is immune from outside influences. Tourism is undoubtedly one of these external influences but, frequently, tourism *contributes to,* but does not *cause,* social and cultural change. In other words, global information systems, the activities of multi-national corporations or the general processes of industrialisation and urbanisation potentially have a far greater impact on social structures and values yet, all too often, it is tourism that is blamed for what are seen as undesirable changes. Therefore, care must be taken to determine the precise components of social and cultural change.

The Nature of Tourist-host Encounters

As pointed out earlier, it is virtually impossible to be a tourist in isolation. Tourists inevitably come into contact with local people in destination areas and, even if such encounters are brief, such as when buying a souvenir in a shop, a variety of social processes are at work which determine the nature of that encounter. This, in turn, goes a long way to determining or explaining the potential socio-cultural consequences of tourism because, generally speaking, the more unbalanced or unequal the encounter or relationship, the more likely it is that negative impacts will occur. Thus, understanding the nature of tourist-host encounters is of fundamental importance to explaining and minimising tourism's socio-cultural consequences.

Of course, there are potentially as many types of encounter as there are tourists and hosts but, nevertheless, it is possible to make a number of observations about the nature of tourist-host encounters. In general, the greater the economic, social and cultural gap between the tourist and host, the less balanced will their encounter or relationship be. For example, the relative wealth of tourists compared to that of their hosts, particularly in less developed countries, is a fundamental difference that may lead to feelings of resentment or inferiority on the part of local people. However, differences in values and attitudes may also be significant. More specifically, four other characteristics of tourist-host encounters have been identified.

- most encounters are transitory or fleeting, the resultant relationships being shallow and superficial;
- most encounters are constrained by temporal restrictions (the two weeks of the holiday or the tourist season) and by the location or spread of tourist facilities and amenities:
- most encounters are pre-planned or lack spontaneity as hospitality becomes commercialised; and
- tourist-host encounters tend to be unbalanced, local people perhaps feeling inferior or subservient to tourists.

To this list a further characteristic may be added, namely, that many tourists travel with an apparent lack of knowledge, understanding or sensitivity to local culture or customs in destination areas. Whilst this raises broader issues about tourists' motivation and behaviour and questions of responsibility that are beyond the scope of this chapter, it represents a potential barrier to meaningful or balanced encounters and, hence, raises the potential for negative social consequences. Similarly, although it is dangerous to generalise the varied and complex social processes involved in encounters between tourists and local people, it is likely that some or all of the other characteristics will be identifiable in many such encounters. Thus, is would appear that some form of negative impact is the inevitable result of the typically unbalanced or unequal nature of inter action between tourists and hosts.

This, however, need not always be the case. It is possible for tourists to develop meaningful relationships with local people, particularly when they frequently visit one destination, and, as we shall now consider, much also depends upon the attitudes of local people towards tourists.

Host Attitudes Towards Tourists

It is widely accepted that tourists are people characterised by a range of expectations, attitudes, motivations and modes of behaviour and that these differences can result in a variety of tourism impacts and encounters with local people. It is important to recognise, however, that local communities are also made up of individuals who themselves possess an enormous variety of attitudes, values and perceptions. In other words, local people may have varying degrees of either positive or negative attitudes towards tourism and tourists, attitudes which are a vital consideration in tourism planning and management. It is essential that local communities are favourably disposed towards the development of tourism; if not, the possibility of a community backlash may arise, leading to an unwillingness to support or work in the tourism industry or, in the extreme, demonstrations of outright hostility towards tourists. Thus, the attitude of the host community is an important variable in the extent to which the socio-cultural consequences of tourism are both perceived and accepted.

Research into host attitudes towards tourists have found that, not surprisingly, positive attitudes amongst local communities are positively correlated to employment and place of residence. That is, those who are employed in the tourism industry and who live close to tourist areas are more favourable towards tourists. At the same time, research has also shown that local people often balance the benefits and costs of tourism development and that positive attitudes may be evident even where socio-cultural costs are incurred. For example, it was found that in Santa Marta, a coastal resort in Colombia, residents felt that, overall, tourism had been beneficial, particularly in terms of employment and infrastructural developments, despite higher seasonal food prices and a greater incidence of robberies and other illegal activities.

Importantly, however, the attitudes of local people can also vary according to the stage of tourism development in destination areas. That is, the perceptions of host communities and the degree of socio-cultural impact change over time and may be directly related to the stage of tourism development that a destination has reached. In a widely quoted model, Butler suggests that resorts pass through a 'life-cycle' similar to the product life-cycle theory in marketing. In the early stages of development, when there are relatively few visitors and local people offer hospitality on an informal basis, tourist-host relations are likely to be good and negative impacts minimal. However, as the resort progressively develops, attracting increasing numbers of mass tourists, tourism becomes more commercialised and local people become ambivalent or apathetic towards tourists, feelings which may in the long-run be transformed into annoyance or hostility if the resort stagnates or goes into decline. It is also at these latter stages in the life cycle of a destination that the socio-cultural consequences of tourism may be most keenly felt, when the potential benefits of tourism become outweighed by the negative and costs experienced by the local community.

In reality, few, if any, tourist destinations progress through to the decline stage, although the history of a number of traditional British seaside resorts appears to match closely Butler's model. Equally, open hostility or antagonism towards tourists is rare. That is, local communities more often than not tolerate tourists and accept the socio-cultural consequences brought about by tourism, although one exception to this is the case of the village of Agia Napa in Cyprus. Following the rapid development of the once small village into a mass tourism resort, the entire original village relocated a few kilometres away to avoid the problems and social impacts of tourism.

However, the important point is that, given the nature of tourism and the characteristics of tourist-host encounters, some degree of tourism-induced socio-cultural change or impact in destination communities is inevitable. Indeed, to expect otherwise is unrealistic because tourism, like any other business, incurs 'production' costs. Such costs are usually financial, such as investment in tourism facilities and infrastructure, but negative consequences for host communities should also represent, in effect, a debit on the tourism development balance sheet. The challenge for tourism planners and managers is then to ensure that these costs do not outweigh the benefits that tourism brings to destination areas.

Socio-cultural Impacts on Tourists

Before introducing finally the range of socio-cultural consequences of tourism that may be experienced by host communities, one issue that deserves consideration is the extent to which tourists, rather than hosts, similarly experience such consequences. That is, attention is generally focused upon the impacts or tourism on destination areas but, socially and culturally, tourism is a two-way process and, frequently, local cultures and people impact significantly on visitors.

At a basic level, such impacts occur when tourists become the victims of crime or health problems. Indeed, becoming the target of criminal activity has always been regarded as one of the risks of travel and tourism, as have health problems. More recently, however, the opening up of more distant or exotic locations to mass tourism has resulted in increasing incidence of tourists contracting serious diseases, such as malaria, whilst an increase in the number of cases of 'old' diseases, such as diphtheria, which have been virtually eradicated in Western societies, has been directly associated with the growth in tourism to previously inaccessible areas.

However, a variety of other 'reverse' socio-cultural impacts can be identified, including:

- the internationalisation of fashions and tastes in clothing, music, art forms, cuisine and so on;
- a reduction in national xenophobia resulting in a greater awareness and acceptance of different cultures;
- the verification or changing of tourists' perceptions of different places, peoples and cultures; studies have also

shown that tourists often return home with a more positive attitude towards their own society and culture; and

- the adoption by tourists, on either a temporary or permanent basis, of new cultural practices.

Little attention has been paid to these socio-cultural impacts of tourism on tourists and tourism generating societies and it is likely to be a fruitful area of research. Nevertheless, the fact remains that the majority of the social-cultural consequences of tourism are experienced by destination societies and it is no coincidence that the rapid growth in international tourism has been matched by increasing concern about the impacts of that growth. More often than not it is the negative consequences that attract most attention but, as we shall now see, tourism may also bring benefits to host societies.

Tourism's Socio-cultural Consequences: An Overview

Given the extent of concern about and research into the impacts of tourism development, it is not surprising that there is a wealth of information and case studies in the tourism literature. Therefore, the discussion here is limited to an introductory overview of the topic.

Although the effects of tourism on host societies are often collectively referred to as socio-cultural consequences or impacts, it is useful to distinguish, albeit somewhat artificially, between social and cultural consequences. Thus, social consequences can be thought of as the more immediate effects of tourism on local people and their quality of life, whereas cultural consequences are longer-term changes that occur in the context of social values, attitudes and behaviour, as well as changes in the production of cultural art forms and practices.

(i) Social consequences - The more immediate, social consequences of tourism result from both the overall development of tourism and also the more specific inter action between tourists and local people.

Firstly, tourism is primarily developed as a means of wider social and economic development. The potential beneficial social consequences are, for example, infrastructural improvements, the protection or improvement of the physical environment, and the provision of services and facilities that benefit tourists and locals alike. More specifically, tourism provides income and employment opportunities and, in the longer-term, the resources for investment in essential social services, such as education and health. In particular, the employment opportunities offered by the development of tourism have, in many societies, brought a new freedom and independence and an improved social condition for many women.

However, the extent to which these benefits accrue to destination societies is often limited. It is widely accepted, for example, that many tourism-related jobs are low grade and low paid, whilst more generally, tourism rarely fulfils its role as a vehicle to economic and social development. Furthermore, negative social impacts may occur, such as changes in community structures. It is often the case, for example, that younger people are drawn from inland rural areas to the coast or cities to work in the tourism industry. This rural-urban migration pattern often results in a population imbalance in rural areas and the polarisation of local societies between younger, more affluent groups and the older, perhaps more traditional generations.

Secondly, the physical presence of tourists, their behaviour and their interaction with local people impacts upon local communities in a variety of ways. Some of these may be immediate, such as inappropriate behaviour displays of conspicuous consumption or simply the inconvenience caused by large numbers of holiday makers, causing annoyance or resentment amongst the local population. Other consequences include:

- *the demonstration effect* - tourism introduces new or alien values or lifestyles in destination areas. Local people may attempt to emulate behaviour or styles of dress, or to strive to achieve levels or wealth, demonstrated by tourists.
- *crime* - although there is little evidence to directly link increases in crime with the development of tourism,

there is little doubt that where there are significant numbers of tourists criminal activity is also evident. This may result in increased expenditure on law enforcement, the growth in activities such as gambling and black-market operations, increased crime against residents and, potentially, a reduction in tourism as experienced by Florida in the early 1990s.

- *religion* - in tourism destinations, religious buildings, shrines and practices have become commoditised. That is, they have become an attraction and a part of the tourism product, gazed upon and 'collected' by tourists. As a result, there is frequently conflict between local communities, devout visitors and tourists as religious rituals or places of worship are disrupted by tourists.
- *prostitution* - although care must be taken in apportioning the blame on tourism, there is no doubt that, in many destinations, tourism has led to an increase in prostitution. The social impact of this can be devastating, particularly in the case of child prostitution and the spread of sexually transmitted diseases.

(ii) Cultural consequences - Over time, the culture of host societies may change and adapt either directly or indirectly as a result of tourism. Much of the literature is concerned in particular with the way in which cultural forms, such as arts and crafts or carnivals, festivals and religious events become adapted, trivialised, packaged and commoditised for consumption by tourists, and there is certainly no doubt that this occurs on a wide scale. For example, many art forms become mass produced as souvenirs (i.e. 'airport art') whilst, frequently, cultural rituals are transformed and staged for tourists, becoming devoid of all meaning to the participants. It is also true, however, that tourism also encourages the revitalisation of resurgence of interest in traditional cultural practices and there are many examples of how tourism supports the redevelopment of traditional art forms and production techniques.

Less visibly, tourism also contributes to broader, deeper cultural transformations in destination societies. These are changes that occur in a society's values, moral codes, behavioural modes and identifying characteristics, such as dress and language. As mentioned earlier, it is difficult to separate the influence of tourism from other factors which induce cultural change but, nevertheless, it is generally accepted that tourism can accelerate this process, largely through what is known as acculturation.

Acculturation is the process whereby, when two cultures come into contact (for example, through tourist-host encounters), over time they will become more like each other through a process of borrowing. By implication, if one culture is stronger or more dominant than the other, then it is more likely that this borrowing will be a one way process. The extent to which tourism contributes to the acculturation process will vary depending on a variety of factors, such as the cultural gulf between the tourist and the host and the influence of other forces yet in many instances cultural change can be directly attributable to tourism.

14

PLANNING TOURISM TRANSPORT: MULTIDISCIPLINARY PERSPECTIVES

Tourism, like transport studies, is a multidisciplinary field of study which has borrowed and refined concepts and theories from other subjects as it establishes itself as a legitimate area of academic study. This poses a number of problems for researchers when exploring the relationship between transport and tourism in the context of tourist transport systems. For example, what approaches and methods of study should one use to analyse tourist transport systems? In most cases, research is based on those social sciences disciplines with an interest in tourism and/or transport studies. This has an important bearing on the analysis of tourist transport systems because the types of question a researcher asks, and the focus of their work, are often determined by their disciplinary background. In other words, each subject area has its own range of concepts and way of viewing the world which builds upon the knowledge and research in that area.

While many subject areas have made distinctive contributions to the study of tourism no one discipline is all-embracing enough to understand the complexity of the tourist transport system. Social science subjects such as social psychology, sociology, and business and management studies have an interest in tourism and transport studies but there is a relative paucity of published research which analyses the tourist transport system.

However, for the purpose of this book, there are a number of subject areas identified for consideration since they have made a direct contribution to the analysis of tourist transport systems. These are:

- economics
- geography
- marketing
- management

Although other cognate areas such as logistics, planning, environmental science and behavioural sciences (e.g. psychology) do have a bearing, these are discussed throughout the book where their contribution is evident. However, the discussion in this chapter emphasises the main subject areas whose contribution is documented and concludes with a focus on management which tends to provide a practical setting in which the contribution of each subject area is harnessed for a practical purpose - the management of tourist transport systems and different components within the system.

It must be stressed that this chapter does not attempt to provide a comprehensive review of the literature and main areas of research on transport and tourism. A wide range of books have already been published in economics, geography and marketing which provide an insight into tourism and transport although none have developed a particular focus on transport for tourism. The approach adopted here is to outline the main principles each subject uses and to illustrate the distinctive contribution it makes to the analysis of tourist transport. This is then developed in more detail with a supporting case study. Since this is only an introductory text, readers are directed to specialised studies for a more detailed insight into particular issues.

The Economist and Tourist Transport

The economist's approach to the analysis of tourist transport is based on two distinct areas of research: transport economics and tourism economics and each area of study uses similar concepts to understand how the tourist transport system functions. For this reason, it is useful to consider what issues are examined by economists as a basis for a more detailed discussion of the concepts they use.

What is Economics?

Like many social science subjects, there is little agreement on how to define an area of study such as economics. However, according to Craven 'economics is concerned with the economy or economic system . . . [and] . . .the problem of allocating resources is a central theme of economics, because most resources are scarce'. Therefore, Craven argues that economics is the study of methods of allocating scarce resources and distributing the product of those resources, and the study of the consequences of these methods of allocation and distribution.

What is meant by scarcity and resources? The term 'scarcity' is used to illustrate the fact that most resources in society are finite and decisions have to be made on the best way to use and sustain these resources. Economists define resources in terms of:

- natural resources (e.g. the land);
- labour (e.g. human resources and entrepreneurship);
- capital (e.g. man-made aids to assist in producing goods)
- and collectively these resources constitute *the factors of production* which are used to produce commodities. These commodities can be divided into:
- goods (e.g. tangible products such as an aircraft).
- services (e.g. intangible items such as in-flight service- and the total output of all commodities in a country over a period of time, normally a year, is known as the *national product.* The creation of products and services is termed *production* and the use of these goods and services is called *consumption.* Since, in any society, the production of goods and services can only satisfy a small fraction of consumers, needs, choices have to be made in the allocation of resources to determine which goods and services to produce. They way in which goods and services are divided among people has been examined by economists in terms of the distribution of income

and the degree of equality and efficiency in their distribution. Many of these issues are dealt with under the heading of 'microeconomics' which Craven succinctly defines as:

> ...the study of individual decisions and the interactions of these decisions... [including] ...consumers' decisions on what to buy, firms' decisions on what to produce and the interactions of these decisions, which determine whether people can buy what they would like, whether firms can sell all that they produce and the profits firms made by providing and selling.

Microeconomics is therefore concerned with certain issues, namely:

- the firm,
- the consumer,
- production and selling,
- the demand for goods,
- the supply of goods.

Economists also examine a broader range of economic issues in terms of *macroeconomics* which is concerned with.

> the entire economy and interactions within it, including the population, income, total unemployment, the average rate of price increases (the inflation rate), the extent of companies' capacities to produce goods and the total amount of money in use in the country.

Therefore, macroeconomics is mainly concerned with:

- how the national economy operates,
- employment and unemployment,
- inflation,
- national production and consumption,
- the money supply in a country.

Within micro-and macro-economics, both transport and tourism economists examine different aspects of the tourist transport system which is based on the analysis of the concepts of demand and supply.

Demand

Within economics, the concern with the allocation of resources to satisfy individuals' desire to travel means that transport economists examine the *demand* for different modes of travel and the competition between such modes in relation to price, speed, convenience and reliability. Economists attempt to understand what affects people's travel behaviour and the significance of transport as something which is rarely consumed for its own sake; it is usually demanded as a means of consuming some other goods or service (i.e. commuting to work or the travel component of a holiday). According to Mill, the demand for tourist transport is also characterised by:

- its almost instantaneous and unpredictable nature, which requires operators to build overcapacity in the supply to avoid dissatisfied travellers;
- the variability in demand, ranging from *derived demand* (where tourist transport is a facilitating mechanism to achieve another objective, such as business travel) to *primary demand* which is the pursuit of travel for vacation purposes;
- non-priced items (e.g. service quality, reliability and punctuality).

Transport economists have developed mathematical models to analyse the trip-making behaviour of travellers, the factors influencing demand and why variations occur in the trip-making behaviour of consumers due to relationships between socioeconomic factors (e.g. age, income, profession and family status) and the effect of macro-economic conditions (e.g. the state of the economy). In contrast tourism economists have examined the demand for travel and tourist products, recognising the significance of demand as a driving force in the economy. This stimulates entrepreneurial activity to produce the goods and services to satisfy the demand. More specifically, tourism economists examine the *effective demand* for goods or services which is the aggregate or overall demand over a period of time. Since income has an important effect on tourism demand, economists measure the impact using a term known as the *elasticity of demand.* As Bull has shown, it is measured using a ratio calculated thus:

$$\text{Elasticity of demand} = \frac{\text{percentage change in tourism demand}}{\text{percentage change in disposable income}}$$

in relation to two equal time periods. The significance of this concept is that the demand for goods to fulfil basic needs (e.g. food, water and shelter) is relatively unchanging or *inelastic* while the demand for luxury items, such as holiday and pleasure travel, is variable or *elastic,* being subject to fluctuations in demand due to factors such as income or price. Thus, elasticity is used to express the extent to which tourists are sensitive to changes in price and service. For example, primary demand is usually more elastic than derived demand. In tourist transportation, researchers recognise the importance of price, which is acknowledged as a more complex issue than income, due to the varying impact of exchange rates, the relative prices of destinations and the high level of competition between destinations for tourists. Furthermore, the different elements which comprise the tourism product (e.g. transport, accommodation and attractions) are complementary and it is difficult to separate out one individual item as exerting a dominant effect on price since all are interrelated in terms of what is purchased and consumed.

To assess the impact of price on the demand for tourism, economists examine the *price-elasticity of demand,* where an inverse relationship exists between demand and price. For example, it is generally accepted that the greater the price, the less demand there will be for a tourism product due to the limited amount of the population's disposable income which is available to purchase the product. Price-elasticity is calculated thus:

$$\text{Price-elasticity} = \frac{\text{percentage change in quantity of tourism product demanded}}{\text{percentage change in tourism product price}}$$

Other contributory factors which influence the demand for tourism include the impact of tourist taxation, the amount of holiday entitlement available to potential tourists as well as the effects of weather, climate and cultural preferences for holiday making which are expressed in terms of seasonality. These factors also need to be viewed in the context of the economics of each specific mode of tourist transport (e.g. rail, coach, air and sea travel) to understand how demand is incorporated into the operator's supply of the services.

Supply

Economists are also interested in the *supply* of a commodity (e.g. tourist transport), which is often seen as a function of its price and the price of alternative goods. Price is often influenced by the cost of the factors of production, but in the case of tourist transport, it is difficult to identify the real cost of travel. For example, state subsidies for rail travel in Europe are used to support the supply of services in the absence of a major demand for social reasons. As a result of subsidies, the price charged may not always reflect the true cost, particularly where tourist transport providers use cross-subsidies in their operations. Cross-subsidisation implies that profits from more lucrative routes are used to support uneconomic and unviable services to maintain a route network, thereby increasing the choice of destinations. According to Bull, the supply of tourist transport can be characterised by:

- major capital requirements for passenger carriage (e.g. the cost of aircraft, passenger trains and ferries).
- government regulations and restrictions to monitor the supply which is determined by state policy.
- competitive reaction from other businesses involved in tourist transport.
- a high level of expertise required to operate and manage tourist transport enterprises.

Bull suggests that the principle questions which economists are interested in from the supply side are:

- what to produce,
- how to produce it,
- when, where and how to produce it.

From the transport operator's perspective, the main objective in supply terms is to maximise profitability from the available capacity, which is usually expressed in terms of the *load factor.* Transport companies can maximise passenger revenue by minimising costs and pricing their product or service at a competitive rate. Certain travel markets are very price-sensitive, which means that consumers may be easily persuaded to switch to another operator or mode of transport if the price rises beyond a critical level (the demand for youth travel on express coach services is a good example of a price-sensitive market). Despite price-sensitivity, airlines and other modes of transport distinguish between scheduled routes which operate a regular timetabled service and charge higher fares, and charter services operated on behalf of tour operators to carry holidaymakers who have purchased a transport-only component or package holiday from the tour operator. The price differential for scheduled and charter passengers is reflected in the passenger load factor which the scheduled airline needs to reach to achieve a profit. Scheduled routes charge a higher tariff but operate on a lower load factor compared to charter flights where a lower unit cost is charged but a higher load factor (often 90 per cent) is needed to yield a profit. Seasonality in the demand for tourist transport services may affect the load factor, and peak usage at popular times means that transport operators use premium pricing to mange the supply and maximise profit to offset losses in times of limited demand. To illustrate the importance of pricing, the following case study examines the issue in relation to air travel.

CASE STUDY : The Pricing of Air Travel

According to Hanlon the way in which airlines price their products is a complex process, with a multitude of fares available according to when one travels; whether travel is off-peak or peak; the class of travel, the length of stay at a destination and whether it includes a Saturday night in Europe. In addition, when and where the ticket is purchased influences the price, together with a host of other factors. Even though there is extensive variation in fare levels across routes, fare levels generally taper with distance so that the fare per km is lower on a long-haul route than a short-haul route. But global anomalies exist. For example, fare levels in Europe have been higher per route km than in North America, while fare levels between Europe and Asia-Pacific have been lower than between Europe and Africa. In the USA, Milman and Pope highlight the inherent problem associated with the demand for air travel. It is described as stochastic, meaning that the number of reservations and actual trips may vary, implying that airlines need to price their product in a price-sensitive manner to ensure that sales and seat prices maximise revenue for each departure. The various price strategies used include:

- *single-pricing* - where a uniform price is charged for passengers on the same flight (e.g. People Express Airlines),
- *multiple pricing* - which involves segmenting the market and offering empty seats at a lower price,
- *yield management* - involving management planning, and computer programming to optimise revenue by selecting the optimum mix of travellers,
- *leg-based pricing* - where seat allocation is used to maximise revenue on each sector of a flight,
- *origin-destination pricing models* - where complex linear programming techniques are used to compare whether a multi-leg passenger trip will generate more revenue than a single-leg trip, and to allocate seats accordingly,
- *expected marginal seat revenue* - which is explained in detail by Vasigh and Hamzee.

Because airline fares can vary and offer so many possible fare classes for one route, it raises the issue of price discrimination.

Hanlon examines the role of price discrimination, where the producer (the airline) charges different prices for various units of the same commodity where there are similar unit costs in the cost of supply. In this instance, peak and off-peak costs are not a form of discriminatory pricing because the price differential reflects the extra costs of meeting peak demand. Discriminatory pricing exists where prices differ more than costs, especially when price-cost margins vary and some customers are paying a higher differential. In many cases of price discrimination, the major factor is the difference in demand elasticity. The principal explanation advanced in the economics literature is related to the inverse elasticity rule: the firm charges more where the demand is low and less where it is high. Firms need to be able to prevent customers who have paid low prices from reselling to those who would be charged high prices.

A yield management system linked to the airline's computer reservation system employs complex algorithms combined with historical booking data to forecast the scenario which enhances revenue from the seat allocation. By restricting the availablity of lower-priced fares, airlines are able to safeguard against revenue dilution in an environment where many of the costs of airline operation are relatively fixed for each departure (see Figure 14.1). The innovative simulation model discussed by Belobaba and Wilson includes the role of passenger choice behaviour and a yield management system was employed to evaluate the impact on market shares, traffic and revenues of each competing airline in a hypothetical market situation. Simulation has to be undertaken given the commercial sensitivity of airline data and competition. A model was therefore used which included four fare options for a typical US domestic airline market (full coach fare through to a 14-day advance purchase non-refundable excursion fare priced at 40 per cent of the full fare). Historical booking data was used to forecast demand on future flights and to optimise fare class booking limits.

The simulation exercise highlighted a 'first mover' advantage, where the airline which initiates yield management

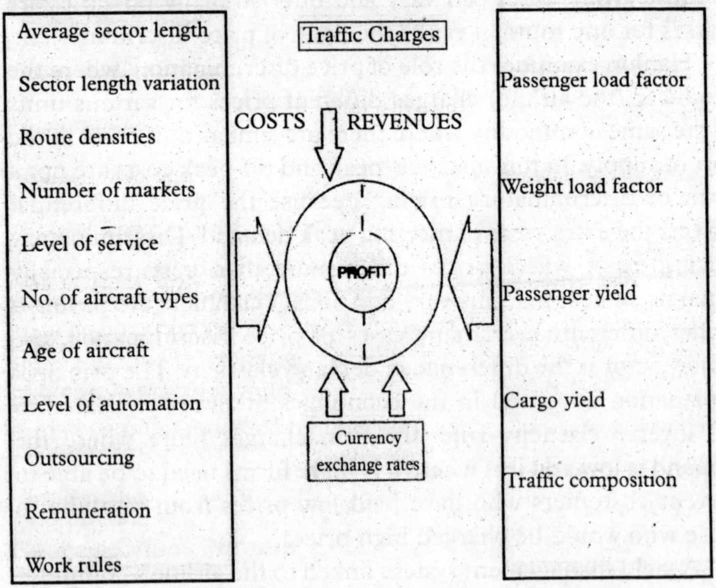

Figure 14.1: The cost factors in airline operations.

(YM) gains the competitive advantage. This results in a better fare mix of traffic and, especially, protects seats for late-booking, high fare passengers. More interesting was the finding that the airline without YM can in fact be hurt in terms of revenue by not having a YM system. The carrier with a YM system is able to dump unwanted low-fare passengers onto the flights of the carrier without YM, filling up that carrier's capacity and leaving it without adequate last-minute seat availability for the highest-fare passengers.

Airlines are able to prevent people reselling airline tickets by making them non-transferable. Airline research shows that business travellers have relatively price-inelastic demand and are not able to book far in advance. In contrast, the price-elastic traveller can book a long time in advance and be flexible, and their concern is with the benefit of travelling at a lower price. Such price discrimination provides airlines with opportunities to segment the market with price discrimination and reason for travel as major factors in the segmentation. Indeed, Belobaba and Wilson confirm that

> the practices of differential pricing and yield management, although confusing to most airline passengers, have, over the past decade, been embraced by most airlines. The incremental revenues generated by these practices contribute to the coverage of the predominately fixed operating costs of a scheduled flight departure. By offering a range of fare options at different price levels on the same flight, airlines attempt to segment the total demand for air travel according to the different sensitivities to price and the need for travel flexibility of business and leisure travellers. To ensure that low-fare leisure passengers do not consume all of the seats on high-demand flights, airlines employ yield management (YM) systems.

These yield management systems forecast the demand for flights and calculate the number of seats which should be available for sale at each fare class to miximise flight revenues. A number of studies have estimated the benefits to individual airlines, where revenue gains of 2-5 per cent occur from implementing a (YM) system. Yet the study also indicated that if another competitor implemented a YM system, both saw improvements in revenue, indicating the ability of carriers to catch up. This suggests that YM is not a zero-sum game and that

YM may force passengers to pay fares nearer to what they are prepared to pay rather than lower fares resulting from competitive pressures between the carriers. From the consumers' perspective, discriminatory pricing which is enhanced by YM is undesirable if the price is raised for some, but desirable if the price declines. However, there is a general trend in pricing airline tickets, where those most affected by discriminatory pricing (e.g. business travellers) bear higher costs. In contrast, those high costs of travel help to subsidise the costs borne by discount travellers. Of course, problems occur when the market share of the more lucrative business travel fares decline for a particular airline, reducing the cross-subsidisation that the high revenue passengers contribute to the overall profitability of its operation.

While business travellers often complain of the discriminatory pricing used to justify higher standards of service, comfort and flexibility in reservations, much of the cost is often borne by businesses as an expense rather than by individual travellers. Whether such pricing enhances or hinders competition depends upon the perspective one takes. For example, discriminatory pricing can allow airlines to experiment with fare levels. Yet it can also be viewed as a tool which companies with a dominant market position can use to weaken the competition while increasing prices in other markets. Thus, where such competition occurs, travellers who can be flexible in terms of travel arrangements for their journey, enjoy a high degree of price elasticity. As a result airlines set fares at a costs plus a low profit margin for travellers with a high degree of price elasticity.

Although this is desirable for the consumer, it assumes that competitors cannot sustain business at low profit margins if their scale of operation is not able to carry such marginal pricing. In fact, some notable examples, such as the Laker Sky Train which was engaged in a price-war on the lucrative North Atlantic routes in the 1970s, complained of one other form of pricing-predatory pricing.

Predatory pricing is where a dominant business pursues a policy of eliminating, deterring or restricting competition. This usually involves selling at below cost to destroy the competition. While Hanlon debates the rationality of such a policy, since the losses for the dominant business are much greater than for the competition, the dominant business will expect to recoup the losses once the competition is removed. In some cases, an outright takeover or merger is more rational, but predatory pricing may ease the way to takeover depending on the personalities in the organisations involved. In the USA, a paper by Areeda and Turner developed a surrogate measure of predatory pricing; it exists where the price is set below a business's short-run marginal cost. A marginal cost is generally seen as the 'addition to total cost resulting from the last unit of output. It refers to those elements of cost that can be avoided or escaped if the last unit is not produced'. Yet in air transport, the marginal cost may be low and seats are a perishable commodity which cannot be stored if supply is greater than demand. For airlines, the marginal cost is low for filling an unsold seat when the flight will depart even if the aircraft has seats left unsold. Even where low fares are sold to attract travellers to fill seats which would otherwise remain empty, these are still priced above the marginal cost. Non-price forms of predatory pricing can also be used by airlines seeking to stifle competition by increasing supply through increased frequencies so that competitors find it difficult to break into a market where supply exceeds demand. Without regulation, Computer Reservation Systems (CRSs) and Frequent Flyer Programmes (FFPs) may also disadvantage smaller airlines unable to access CRSs and offer FFPs at the same reward rate on routes facing competition. Since FFPs have been used to target customer loyalty among high-yielding passengers (e.g. first and business class), the gains may be very high, for although they may only comprise 20 per cent of passenger volumes they may contribute 50 per cent of revenue.

Discussion of the pricing of air travel illustrates that principles of economics underpin the economic behaviour of airlines. In addition, the free market economy can result in a wide range of competitive situations. In practice, there is often regulation by national and supranational organisations responsible for air travel such as the Civil Aviation Authority in London and the European Commission in Brussels. These bodies seek to adjudicate between what is acceptable and unacceptable competition and what constitutes predatory behaviour. As Hanlon rightly concludes,

> The crux of the matter is to find the dividing line between genuine revenue-enhancing yield-management techniques and practices aimed directly at undermining the economics of a competitor's operation. . . The Civil Aviation Authority approaches the problem by tracking fare developments and trends over time on a selected number of routes.

Although such monitoring can assist in the process of establishing predatory pricing, the volume of seats sold at each fare level also needs to be considered. Where predatory behaviour occurs on international routes, this falls outside the jurisdiction of national regulatory bodies and investigations can take a long time to institute. Despite the suspected existence of predatory behaviour, it is often difficult to distinguish from aggressive competitive behaviour.

Economists also have an interest in macroeconomic issues associated with the supply of tourist transport services and the structure of the market system in which companies operate. For example, economists have examined the effect of company strategy in the tourism and transport sectors in response to market competition which may affect the management, operation and provision of services to consumers. These different market conditions may range from near-perfect competition to a situation where the three following conditions may occur:

- *oligopoly* - where the control of the supply of a service is by a small number of suppliers,
- *monopoly* - where exclusive control of services is by a single supplier,
- *duopoly* - where two companies control the supply of services.

For the consumer, such activities may have a significant effect on the choice, price and degree of competition which occurs. In some cases, a monopoly situation or a variant may lead to anticompetitive practices and may not necessarily be in the public's interest, although arguments contrary to this view have also been expressed in relation to the break-up of British Rail's (BR) provision of rail services in the UK. Transport and tourism economists have also retained an interest in the macro-economic effects of tourist transport on national economies. Tourist use of transport is a major contributor to the balance of payments when examining the economic benefits of tourism. Such considerations have an important bearing on public or private sector investment decisions when examining the costs and benefits of building new tourist transport infrastructure (e.g. the construction of a new airport). Issues related to the employment-generating potential of new tourist transport infrastructure and the effect on income generation for local economies feature prominently in these investment decisions. Economists also use complex research techniques such as multiplier analysis to evaluate the secondary or indirect economic benefits of additional tourist expenditure for local areas. There is also a growing awareness among economists of the environmental costs of tourist transport.

Geography and Tourist Transport

Within geography, the study of tourist transport has largely been undertaken by transport geographers and tourism geographers. The main concern of geographers when considering tourist transport can be related to three key concepts, which characterise the study of geography:

- *space* - area, usually the earth's surface,
- *location* - the position of something within space,
- *place* - an identifiable position on the earth's surface.

Geographers are therefore interested in the spatial expression of tourist transport as a vital link between tourist-generating and tourist-receiving areas. In particular, geographers are concerned with the patterns of human activity associated with tourist travel and how different processes lead to the formation of geographical patterns of tourist travel at different scales, ranging from the world to the national (e.g. country), regional (e.g. county) and local levels (e.g. an individual place). Previous geographical research on transport has looked at its role in different regions, its impact on economic development in terms of accessibility, the effect on the environment and the role of policy making. In many of the popular transport geography textbooks there are a number of fundamental concepts which geographers use to analyse the spatial components of transport. Geographers have typically analysed travel as a response to satisfy a human desire for movement and the spatial outcome of such journeys. They have also considered the spatial variables in the transport system (e.g. location and places) and how these affect the costs and production of other social and economic activities. For the geographer, transport facilitates the process of movement which has economic and budgetary costs, while behavioural factors (e.g. perception and preferences for particular forms of transport) determine the journey in terms of the available infrastructure and routes. In analysing the transport system, geographers have considered:

- the linkages and flows within a transport system,
- the location and places connected by these linkages (usually referred to as 'centres' and 'nodes'),
- the system of catchments and relationships between places within the network.

In some respects transport tends to be viewed as a passive element by geographers in a tourism context rather than as an integral part of tourism and recreational activity. In fact, comparatively little progress has been made by researchers in this area of study since the influential studies undertaken in the 1960s and 1970s by geographers. While useful synthese such as Halsall provide bibliographies of past studies, few of the studies reviewed by Halsall were written by geographers in the 1980s and 1990s explicitly to develop an understanding of the way in which transport facilitates and in some cases conditions the type of recreational and tourism activity which occurs. Much of the research activity by geographers in the 1990s published in the *Journal of Transport Geography* has been preoccupied with air travel. The continued neglect of transport in the analysis of tourism has also been compounded by the perception of other geographers who did not concede the importance of tourism as serious areas for research until the late 1980s and 1990s. Even then, it is often relegated to a minor research are a despite the rapid growth in tourism and recreational courses in most countries.

Recent texts such as Tolley and Turton do at least highlight the need, to consider tourism in the context of transport geography. Yet even Tolley and Turton do not devote much space to the topic and few other studies have sought to place transport for recreation and tourism on the research agenda beyond the notable occasional studies by the Transport Study Group of the Institute of British Geographers. Where previous studies exist, the emphasis has been on modal forms of recreational and tourist travel (e.g. land-based transport and the use of trails, water-borne transport and heritage transport for nostalgic travel. This does not adequately develop the contribution that geographers can make to the management, planning and develop the contribution that geographers can make to the management, planning and development of transport for recreational and tourist travel.

CASE STUDY: The Geography of Tourist Transport in Ireland: Air Travel

Recent research by Horner on airport and air-route development in Ireland illustrates how the geographer can analyse tourist transport provision. Ireland is often perceived as peripheral to many of Europe's main internatinal tourism markets, and air traffic is the dominant form of transport used by inbound and outbound tourists. As Figure 14.2 shows, the main air routes and the amount of traffic carried on the routes is represented as a flow line. Each *flow* is between an origin (e.g. Ireland) and a series of destinations. The origin points or *nodes* are the airports at which visitors arrive and from which they depart. For Ireland, the main flows between:

- Dublin/London and mainland Europe.
- Belfast/Belfast City and London.
- Ireland and other places in England, Wales and Scotland.

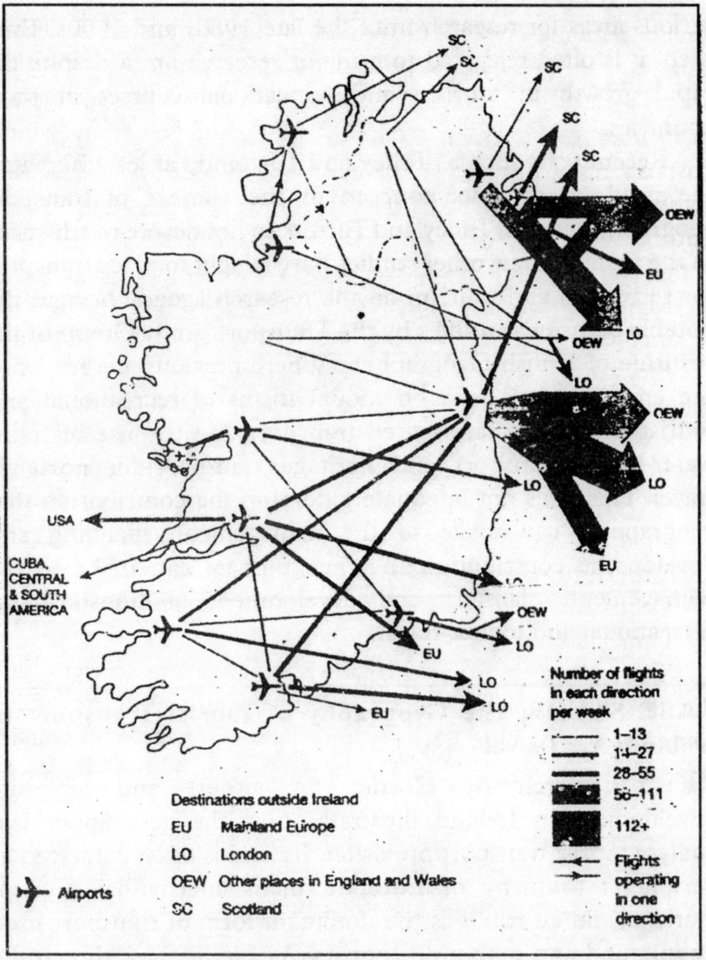

Figure 14.2: Air transport in the Republic of Ireland.

These airports are the main entry and exit points for tourists using air transport and are called *gateways*. From Figure 14.2 it is also possible to examine how the nodes are related to catchment areas the airports serve, the type and frequency of services offered and the degree of spatial organisation. Figure 14.3 shows that between 1975 and 1990 there have been changes in the degree of accessibility provided by the growth in smaller regional airports in Ireland. In 1990, most areas within Ireland were within a one-hour drive of an airport, which gives rise to a distinct pattern of airport provision. The geographer analyses this pattern in terms of the spatial hierarchy which exists in it by looking at the number and type of scheduled flights operated. Horner provided a ranking based on these two features to identify a hierarchy of airports which was a function of their airstrip size. The hierarchy comprised:

I Major airports capable of handling all sizes of aircraft, including 747 Jumbo jets (Belfast International, Dublin and Shannon).

IIa Airports able to accommodate medium-sized jets operating scheduled services (e.g. Cork, Belfast City and Knock).

IIb Similar airports without scheduled services (Baldonnel).

III Airports with scheduled services capable of accommodating small jets (Carrickfin, Co. Galway, Farranfare, Co. Kerry, Waterford, Co. Sligo).

IV Other airstrips with shorter, hard-surface landing facilities.

V Other landing areas, mainly grass.

The hierarchy of airports provides scheduled services, and the linkages and flows between the airports indicate which routes passengers use between the major gateways and smaller regional airports. This leads to a pattern of 'hubs' (gateways) and 'spokes' (smaller airports) and a distinctive spatial network. Geographers have developed methods of assessing how different nodes are connected within the network (e.g. the degree of connectivity) and how accessible different nodes are within the network. In the case of Ireland, the dominant feature is the limited amount of north-south cross-border traffic in the network. The significance of Great Britain/mainland Europe as origins and destinations for much of the traffic is based on a small number of hubs in Ireland. Aside from Dublin and Belfast, Shannon is an important node, since it is 'a mandatory stopping place for scheduled transatlantic flights originating or terminating in the Republic of Ireland'.

Transport geographers are also interested in the air transport network in Ireland in terms of how it evolved, the spatial processes which shaped the development of the network

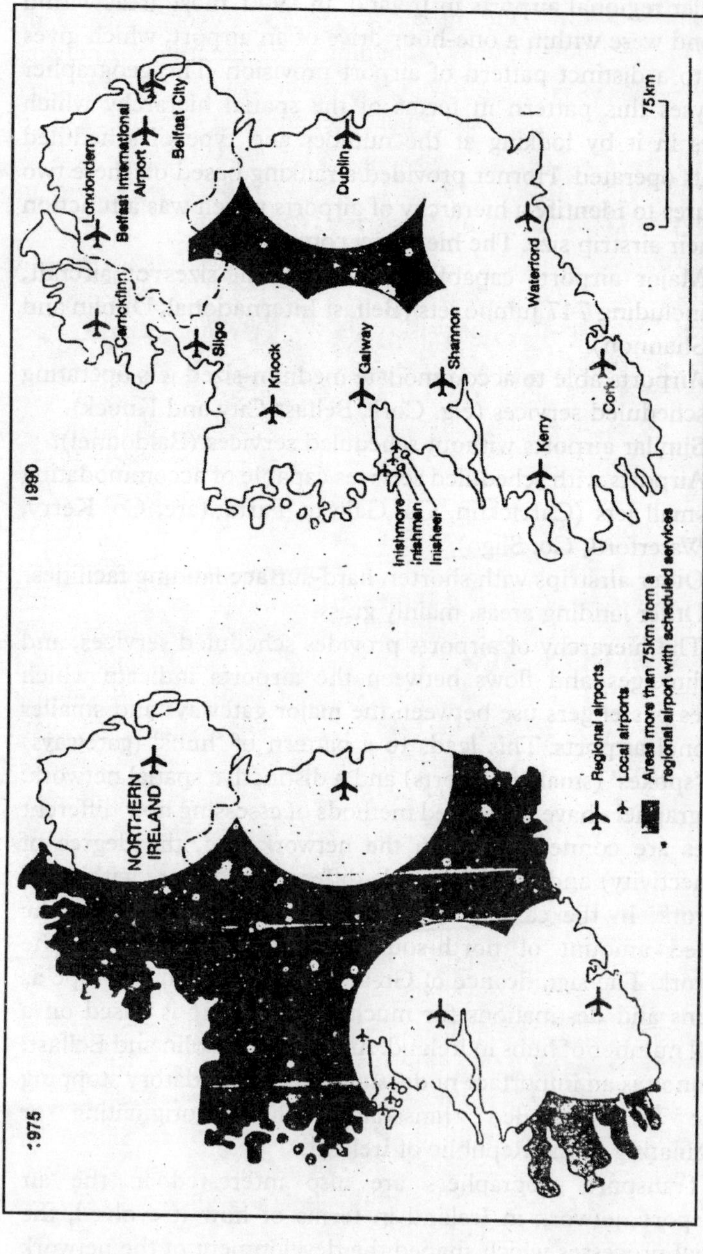

Figure 14.3: Changes in access to air travel in the Republic of Ireland, 1975 - 90.

and how geographical models and theories might be used to examine the flows and interactions in the network. Clearly, the role of government policy in shaping and regulating the network would also be of significance. How have these concepts been used by tourism geographers researching tourist use of transport?

Tourism Geography and Tourist Transport

According to Pearce, geographical research on tourism initially focused on:

- The spatial analysis of the supply and demand for tourism.
- The geography of tourist resorts.
- Tourist movements and flows.
- The analysis of the impact of tourism.
- The development of models of tourist space to understand the evolution and expression of tourism in specific locations.

Since the 1970s, tourism research has examined the patterns and processes associated with the development of international and domestic tourism. One particular skill which the geographer has contributed to the study of tourism is the ability to synthesis (i.e. sift, search and make sense of) the approaches and analysis of tourism phenomena undertaken by other disciplines. During the 1980s geographical research on tourism moved from a traditional concern with regional case studies and descriptions of tourism in particular locations, to a more systematic and analytical approach. This is reflected in the recognition of how a spatial perspective can contribute to the analysis of tourism. How have geographers viewed tourist transport?

According to Mansfeld 'the use of various modes of transport in getting to the destination has several spatial consequences' associated with the distance travelled, amount of time involved in travelling and the mode of transport used. In many case, geographers have not distinguished, or found it easy to distinguish between tourist and recreational travel. Pearce acknowledges that advances in transport technology have altered the patterns of tourist flows and made tourist travel more flexible and diffuse. Prior to the expansion of car ownership and mass air travel, the patterns of tourist travel were linear. It was constrained and confined to transport corridors (e.g. river bank railway lines) or the destinations served by sea. As the following discussion of the car shows, it has been a major catalyst in making patterns of travel more diffuse.

The Car and Tourist Travel

In the postwar period, the growth of car ownership has not only made the impact of recreational and tourist travel more flexible, it has caused overuse at accessible sites. This ease of access, fuelled by a growth in road building and the upgrading of minor roads in many developed countries has been a self-reinforcing process leading to overuse and a greater dominance in passive recreational activities. Probably the most influential study of car usage among recreationalists was Wall's study of Kingston-upon-Hull in 1969. Wall identified the two principal types of studies used to analyse recreational activity - namely site studies (of particular facilities or areas) and national studies such as the widely cited Pilot National Recreation Survey (British Travel Association and University of Keele 1967, 1969). Wall supplemented data from the national survey with a regional sample of 500 Hull car-owners in 1969. While the results are now very dated his study highlighted the importance of seasonality and timing of pleasure trips by car and the dominance of the car as a mode of transport for urban dwellers. It also highlighted the role of the journey by car as a form of recreation in itself as well as the importance of the car as more than just a means of transport. In fact, the study has a degree of similarity with other studies that followed, such as Coppock and Duffield's survey of recreation and the countryside. This focused on patterns and processes of recreational activity is Scotland and mapped and described patterns of recreational travel, especially those of caravanners. At the same time, the study noted the temdency for many recreationalists not to venture far from their car at the destination, a point reiterated by Glyptis's innovative and seminal study of recreationalists using participant observation in Hull. Wall also found that the majority of pleasure trips were day trips less than 100 km away from Hull, being spatially concentrated in a limited number of resorts along the Yorkshire coast and southerly part of the region. Other research highlighted the versatility of the car and its use to venture into the reaches of the North York Moors National Park. Other researchers' findings explained the attraction of the car to recreationalists in that it allowed them to enjoy the countryside and observe its visual characteristics rather than have physical contact with it.

More recent research by Eaton ad Holding identified the growing scale of such visits to the countryside by recreationalists in cars. In 1991, 103 million visits were made to National Parks in the UK (Countryside Commission 1992), the most popular being the Lake District and Peak District parks. In terms of car usage, car traffic was estimated to grow by 267 per cent by the year 2025 from the levels current in 1992 (Countryside Commission 1992). In fact, the greatest impact of rising car usage has been seen in the decline in public transport usage for recreational trips. Yet many National Parks seem unlikely to be able to cope with the levels of usage predicted for the year 2025, given their urban catchments and the relative accessibility by motorway and a roads in the UK. Eaton and Holding review the absence of effective policies to meet the practical problems of congestion facing many sites in the countryside in Bristain. While schemes such as the Sherpa Bus routes in Snowdonia National Park have been introduced they have not been incorporated into any wider policy objectives for transport. This combines with a failure to design public transport to suit the needs and perception of users to achieve reductions and solutions to congestion in National Parks. Thus, it is clear that the car poses a major problem, not only for urban areas and their use by commuters and recreationalists, but also in terms of the sheer growth in volume in areas not designed for large numbers of car-users. This problem is especially acute when spatially concentrated at 'honeypots' (locations which attract large numbers in a confined area) in National Parks.

The UK Tourism Society's response to the Government Task Force on Tourism and the Environment (English Tourist Board/Employment Department 1991) highlighted the impact of the car by commenting that–

> no analysis of the relationship between tourism and the environment can ignore transportation. Tourism is inconceivable without it. Throughout Europe some 40 per cent of leisure time away from home is spent travelling, and the vast majority of this is by car . . . Approaching 30 per cent of the UK's energy requirements go on transportation. . . [and] . . . this impact of traffic congestion, noise and air pollution . . . [will] . . . diminish the quality of the experience for visitors.

Various management solutions exist, such as encouraging urban areas to develop 'intervening opportunities' in the urban fringe through networks of Country Parks in the UK which are capable of absorbing large numbers of visitors seeking a countryside experience. Such parks are able to fulfil the need for local recreational demand and to reduce the impact of transport on other sites. However, car ownership in the UK developed rather later than in North America, and for this reason it is pertinent to focus on one region in North America where it has had a major influence on recreational and tourist travel - the Great Lakes area.

Chubb's study of the Great Lakes region of North America also highlighted the role of the car in cross-border travel. The region, which contains the world's largest complex of fresh water, also contains a diversity of recreational and tourism resources, including lakes, forests, large park areas, cottages and resort complexes (Figure 14.4). Recreational cottages line many of the lakes as second home development and other seasonal residences are distributed throughout the region, to which owners drive for weekend and vacation use from May to September. A range of resort areas also exist. The region also experiences a high usage of recreational vehicles such as caravans and camper vans. Table 14.1 outlines a range of tourism flows which complement the recreational travel within the region. For example, the majority of cottage owners who travel into Ontario are from the United States. The cross-border flows of car traffic produce a range of spatial forms which are

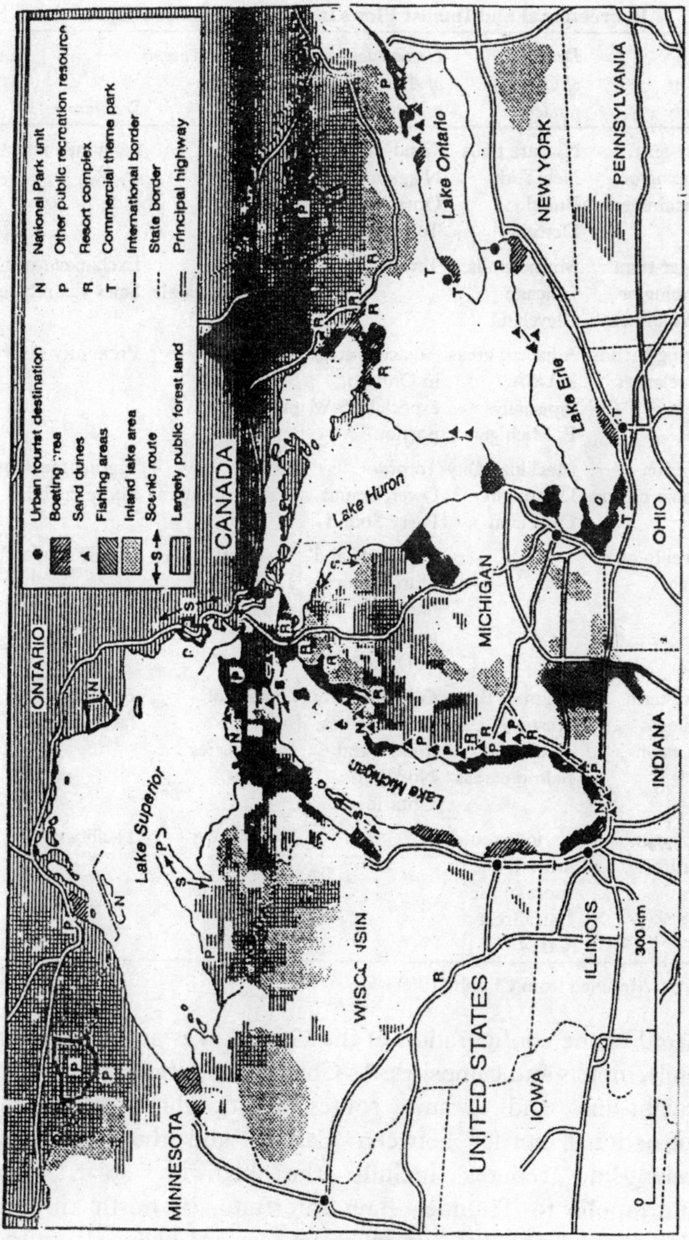

Figure 14.4: The Great Lakes region in North America.

Table 14.1
Recreational and Tourist Flows in the Great Lakes Region

Type of activity	*Destinations of Ontario residents*	*Destinations of American residents*	*Motivations* Primary	*Motivations* Secondary
Short-term shopping or entertainment	Niagara Falls New York Buffalo Detroit	Windsor Niagara Falls Ontario Toronto	Novelty Proximity Prices	Exchange rate
Longer-term shopping or entertainment	Minneapolis Chicago Cleveland	Toronto	Goods and services available Novelty	Exchange rate Sales Tax rebate
Visiting friends and relatives	Adjacent areas in USA, especially E. Michigan	Adjacent areas in Ontario, especially S.W. portion	Early history Settlement patterns	Proximity
Power or sailboat cruising	Mackinac City Detroit area Cleveland	Toronto Owen Sound Parry Sound	Proximity to sheltered waters	Marina facilities Shore facilities
Travel to own cottages		Lake Erie and Huron shore-lines Lake areas across S. Ontario	Proximity Time of acquisition	Ethnic origin
Long-term fishing excursion	Saginaw Bay Western Michigan Salmon areas	Georgian Bay interior lakes in S.E. and Northern Ontario	Chance of success Fish species Size	Environmental facilities.
Automobile touring	Various routes around one or more of the four Great Lakes		Well known Natural Commercial	Facilities

Source: Modified from Chubb (1989).

related to the configuration of the Great Lakes and location of hotels, motels and campsites. As Chubb illustrated, a number of straight-line and circuit routes exist which cross the international border between Canada and the USA. The straight-line reoutes include the highway north from Minneapolis to Thunder Bay; Interstate 75 north through Michigan, along Lake Superior; the Niagara Falls - Toronto -

Georgian Bay route. The circuit routes which incorporate a touring component and cross the border include the Lake Ontario route (800 km) which is the shortest; the Lake Erie route (1,000 km) which includes Niagara Falls; and the Lake Superior and Lake Huron routes, each of which is approximately 1,600 km in length. Therefore, it is clear that while the car has an overwhelming influence on the choice of recreation and tourism, it is also used for passive recreation, especially day trips. Likewise, in North America, distance is not so much of an inhibiting factor for recreational and tourist travel as the example of the Great Lakes implies. Distances and greater and the car is a fundamental catalyst in the region's development of a recreational and tourism infrastructure to serve the needs of visitors and recreationalists from within Ontario and from the USA.

Both air transport and car travel have provided new opportunities for more flexible patterns of travel though, as Sealy, suggests, air travel and the expansion of international tourism are largely a nodal transport system depending upon the airports (the nodes) and the flights (the flows) serving them. In the case of the Mediterranean, Pearce indicates that the expansion of charter airlines has provide a closer link between the tourism markets and potential destinations, and the increase in the geographical range of charter aircraft (i.e. increased flying time) and reduced costs of air travel have led to an expansion in the scale and distribution of tourism in the Mediterranean.

One further concept which tourism geographers have examined in the patterns of tourist transport - namely the tour. A tour is a tourist-oriented form of travel and Pearce examines the patterns and flows of tourist traffic in terms of preferred routes of travel. In the case of New Zealand, Forer and Pearce examine the tour itineraries of coach operators to provide information on the patterns of travel and circuits of coach tours. They found that on the North Island of New Zealand, a series of linear tours existed between the major gateways - Auckland and Wellington, with tourists visiting popular resorts and attractions en route. On the South Island, a more complex series of looped tours existed. Many of these often originated and ended at Christchurch (the second largest gateway) as tourists explored the diverse range of landscapes and scenic locations associated with National Parks such as Mount Cook, Westland and Fiordland. Pearce and Elliot developed a statistical technique - the Trip Index - to examine the extent to which places visited by tourists were major destinations or just a stopover. The Trip Index was calculated thus:

$$\text{Trip Index} = \frac{\text{Nights spent at the destination}}{\text{Total number of nights spent on the Trip}} \times 100$$

A Trip Index of 100 means that the entire trip was spent at one destination and a value of zero would mean that no overnight stay was made on the entire journey.

Other features which the tourism geographer has examined in terms of tourist transport include the use of the private car and public transport. Pearce also notes the importance of transit services from airports to city centres, as well as tourist use of transport to tour sites in major cities such as the London Underground system. In fact, the Docklands Light Railway which connects Central London to London Docklands has also become a popular form of tourist transport in its won right. Thus, geographers have undertaken research on tourist transport systems at different spatial scales in 'terms of mode, routes and types of operation (e.g. scheduled/non-scheduled)' and the spatial patterns, processes and networks which facilitate tourist travel, thereby making destinations more accessible. To illustrate how geographers can produce a sysnthesis of different disciplinary perspectives (e.g. environmental science) and the application to tourist transport, a case study follows on recreational boating. The case study highlights how the coexistence of recreational and tourist use of a particular form of tourist transport - boating - can generate a range of problems which require solutions that can be addressed from a management perspective (which is discussed later in the chapter).

CASE STUDY: Tourist and Recreational Boating on the Norfolk Broads

The Norfolk Broads (hereafter the Broads) is a wetland region in East Anglia (Figure 14.5) which was created in the medieval period through a series of flooded peat diggings. The region

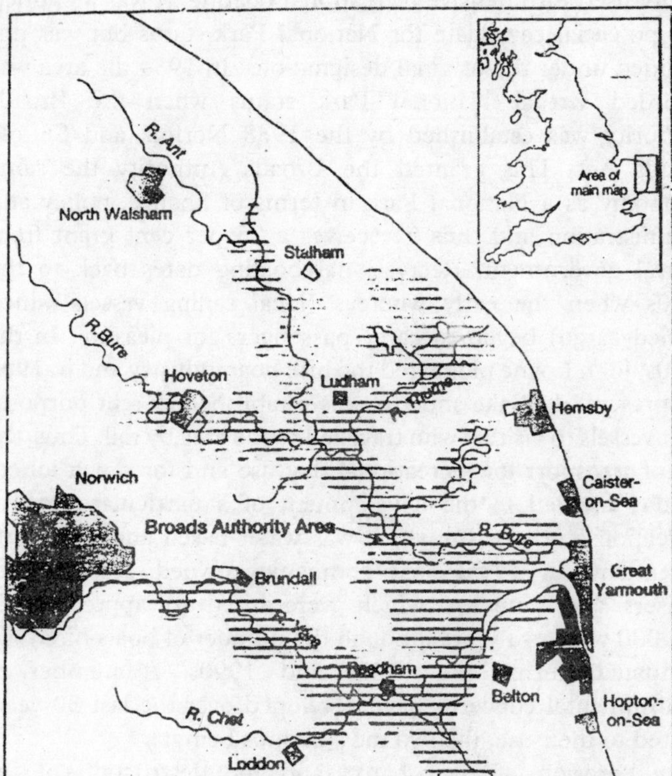

Figure 14.5: The Norfolk Broads region.

comprises a wetland are focused on a number of rivers such as the Bure, the Yare and the Waveney and their tributaries in the eastern part of Norfolk and northern part of Suffolk. Although the region, with 200 km of tidal rivers and 3,640 ha of water space, is not large compared to the previous example of the Great Lakes region in North America, it is an area of natural beauty used for intensive recreational boating. It was identified as a potential candidate for National Park status but was not included under the original designations. In 1989 the area was accorded virtual National Park status when the Broads Authority was established by the 1988 Norfolk and Suffolk Broads Act. This granted the Broads Authority the same autonomy as a National Park in terms of finance, policy and administration and thus it receives a 75 per cent grant from central government. Recreational boating dates back to the 1870s when the early whereas (local sailing vessels which carried cargo) began to carry passengers for pleasure. In the 1880s, John Loyne pioneered the hire boat industry and in 1908 the present H. Blake and Co. was established to rent purpose-built vessels to visitors who travelled to the area by rail. Thus, the use of transport for recreational day use and for much longer holiday use led to the development of a particular form of recreation and tourism which was water-based and transport-dependent. In 1995, boat companies owned 1,481 motor cruisers and launches which were hired to approximately 200,000 visitors a year, although the number of boats hired has fluctuated during the 1980s and 1990s. A number of environmental concerns have developed over the last 30 years related to their use, the two most serious being:

- erosion of river banks and the destruction of the protective reed fingers, which have implications for all river bank users and farmers,
- enrichment of the nutrient content of the water with nitrates and phosphates. This has contributed to the process known as eutrophication, which leads to an excessive growth in a limited number of plant species and the extinction of the diverse range of flora and fauna.

The Norfolk Broads in a recreational resource under pressure. Given the region's proximity to the urban centres in South East England, the Midlands and towns in East Anglia, access to this series of interconnected linear parks has undoubtedly contributed to these pressures. In essence, there are two competing arguments for and against the continued growth and development of recreational boating in the Broads. On the one hand, there is the physical environmental debate which emphasises the damage motor boats cause to the local ecosystem through their wash turbidity, as their propellers cause a suction effect on the river bed. This also impacts upon reed beds and causes abrasion on the river banks as well as polluting the water through petrol and oil emissions. However, boats alone are not the main cause of environmental damage as agricultural fertilisers and domestic sewage are also a major contributor to overenrichment and species extinction problems. Anglers may also be equally to blame for damage to river banks. Yet the problem with the hire boat industry is that it is spatially concentrated (see Table 14.2) and heavy usage occurs at weekends in the northern parts of the river system (e.g. Thurne Mouth and the middle reaches of the rive Bure at Horming and Wroxham/Hoveton and to a lesser degree the lower reaches of the river Ant). This places intense pressure upon attractions within that region, especially during the very short summer season. For example, a Broads Authority boat movement census in 1994 highlighted that on one peak Sunday in August, there were 6,296 craft movements recorded at 14 census points. In contrast, the upper reaches of many rivers are protected by their relative inaccessibility and in a few cases, by low bridges.

In contrast to the environmental arguments, there are powerful economic arguments for continuing to promote the development of recreational boating. The hire boat industry is estimated to contribute £25 million to the local economy and generates approximately £9,000 for the economy for each boat rented (Broads Authority 1997). In 1991, a survey of boatyards by the Broads Authority found that in the 105 yards responding, boating employed 1,622 people: 884 full-time, 148 part-time, 590 on a seasonal basis. Furthermore, recreational and tourist

Table 14.2
Hire Craft Operators on the Broads

Location	*Number of operators*	*Motor cruisers*	*Day launches*	*Sailing cruisers or day craft*
River Waveney				
Burgh St Peter	1	-	2	-
Burgh Castle	1	-	1	-
St Olaves	2	9	2	-
Somerleyton	1	8	-	15
Beccles	4	42	17	-
Oulton Broad	5	23	16	-
Total	14	82	38	15
River Chet				
Loddon	5	46	3	-
River Yare				
Reedham	2	24	-	-
Brandall	12	190	2	-
Thorpe	5	113	7	-
Total	19	327	9	0
River Bure				
Acle	4	86	10	-
S. Walsham	1	9	2	-
Upton	1	-	-	16
Horning	7	128	32	19
Wroxham/Hoveton	14	209	124	13
Belaugh	1	74	-	-
Total	28	506	168	48
River Thurne				
Ludham	2	11	-	17
Potter Heigham	3	124	69	1
Martham	2	19	7	29
Hickling	1	9	6	2
Total	8	163	82	49
River Ant				
Ludham Bridge	1	-	7	1
Sutton	1	12	-	-
Stalham	4	357	6	2
Wayford	2	6	9	-
Total	8	375	22	3

Source: Broads Authority (1997) based on the Broads Authority *Register of Bouts 1995.*

spending indirectly contributes to 5,000 - 5,500 jobs in the hospitality sector, local tourist attractions as well as in the local marine industry. Even though boating has been in recession within the area in the 1990s, boatyard diversification to develop facilities for the needs of visitors (e.g. the construction of accommodation) has also posed planning problems for the Broads Authority since such diversification changes the traditional image of the area.

Given these two competing arguments over recreational boating, it is pertinent to ask who is responsible for decision-making and planning for boating in this region. Much of the decision-making is fragmented across a number of public and private sector bodies, each with particular powers, responsibilities and visions relating to boating. These include:

- National government working through the Countryside Commission has debated the issue of the most appropriate administrative structure for the region, which led to the Broads Authority being established. Yet other government departments such as the Ministry for Agriculture, Food and Fisheries has a very different view of the region's function from the Countryside Commission, which is not recreational or conservationist in focus.
- The Broads Authority and regulate planning proposals for new boatyards and extensions to existing ones. It can also develop new waterside facilities such as public moorings in accordance with its overall management plan (Broads Authority 1997).
- The Great Yarmouth Port and Haven Commissioners are responsible for all navigation on the Broads and rivers. They license boats and have imposed speed restrictions, enforced by river inspectors. The can also regulate river traffic charges.
- The East Anglian Tourist Board and its parent body, the English Tourist Board, can promote the region to visitors together with local districts. Each body has a degree of choice over the image it chooses to portray

and the markets it targets, and could even advocate alternative tourist activities in the region.

- The hire boat companies and their marketing agencies have undertaken publicity campaigns to try and influence the behaviour of visitors and to encourage a grater consciousness of the natural environment. Boat companies could restrict the number of vessels hired at particular places, and at certain times if they felt it was in their long-term interest.
- A variety of other bodies have responsibilities, such as the regional water authority (Anglian Water), while the National Rivers Authority has powers over water quality and land drainage. There are also a large number of pressure groups which have a strong lobby function such as the National Farmers Union, the Nature Conservancy Council and the Local Broads Society. Although no one group has direct influence over the hire boat industry, they can exert pressure on decision makers in other bodies to influence planning outcomes.

This case illustrates that it is not so much the volume of boats but rather the intensity of use in time and space as well as the behaviour of users which conflicts with the natural environment. For this reason, it is worthwhile focusing on the possible solutions to the recreational problems which this form of transport poses. There is no all-embracing solution which will deal with the conflicts. Coexistence with the fragile ecosystem is therefore a major challenge for recreation management. Environmental deterioration is not a problem that can be solved quickly, but the Broads Authority has a management plan for the area which is viewed as a long-term vision for the Broads. It is a workable strategy and takes into account the fact that although a general decline in recreational boating holidays occurred in the late 1980s and early 1990s, demand is likely to develop again in the new millenium. Furthermore, the 1981 Wildlife and Countryside Act has also highlighted the problem of reconciling agricultural and commercial practices with environmental conservation. Since any from of management for the Broads needs to be accompanied by objectives which inform the strategic direction, sustainability is a prime concern for the region (Broads Authority 1997). The Broads Authority has developed a number of policies to address the issue of coexistence of the recreational boating industry with the authority's underlying objective, which is to foster sustainable management and development. Each of these policies not only requires coordination of the various agencies involved with the hire boat industry, but also an ongoing dialogue with all parties affected by the Broads management plan. By fostering an ongoing partnership between public and private sector groups, the management plan will remain a workable strategy for the future and ensure the boating industry is an integral but managed element of tourism and recreational activities available in the region. The case study also illustrates that there is a growing concern over management of the impacts of recreational boating and that sustainable policies and practices are developed in relation to recreational and tourism transport systems.

Marketing and Tourist Transport

When one considers the contribution of economics and geography to the analysis of tourist transport, it is evident that a wide range of research papers and books exist. In the case of marketing, the number of studies focused on tourist transport is limited because there is a tendency for marketing to be more visible and results-oriented than based on the academic analysis of good practice. Promotional material and advertising campaigns constitute a major investment in time, money and creative thinking, with companies reluctant to highlight good practice which might undermine their future business potential. According to Horner and Swarbrooke the diversity of transport modes used in tourism (e.g. air, rail, water, road and off-road transport) makes it difficult to generalise about transport and marketing. This is further complicated by the private, public and voluntary sector organisations involved in transport for tourism which all have different marketing objectives. In addition, a conceptual problem exists: sometimes transport may be sold as a self-contained product, sometimes as part of a large composite product (e.g. and inclusive tour). In order to understand how marketing is integral to the analysis of tourist transport, it is, therefore, useful to examine the principles used in marketing and the activities undertaken by marketers.

What is Marketing?

According to Kotler and Armstrong, marketing is a process whereby individuals and groups obtain the type of products or goods they value. These goods are created and exchanged through a social and managerial process which requires a detailed understanding of consumers and their wants and desires so that the product or service is effectively delivered to the client or purchaser. Within tourism studies, there has been a growing interest in marketing compared with transport studies, which has tended to employ marketers when required to deal with such issues. More recently, new marketing-for-tourism texts have begun to incorporate material on marketing transport services, although this usually tends to focus on airlines. In transport studies, marketing has assumed less importance than operational and organisational issues, but their is a growing awareness that 'transport operators are seeking to augment their basic product with add-on services that generate more income but also satisfy more of the consumers' needs'. Gilbert considers the growth and establishment of marketing within tourism and the critical role of a consumer orientation among transport providers. For example, British Airways explained its financial turnaround from a loss of £544 million in 1981/82 to a profit of £272 million in 1983/84 in terms of a greater marketing orientation based on recognising customer needs and attempting to satisfying them. In this respect, marketing has a fundamental role to play in analysing tourist transport. Within marketing, three key areas exist:

- strategic planning,
- marketing research,
- the marketing mix.

Strategic Planning

Within any business or company, there is a need to provide some degree of order or structure to its activities and to think ahead. This is essential if companies are to be able to respond to the competitive business environment in which organisations operate. For this reason, a formal planning process in necessary which is known as *strategic planning.* According to Kotler and Armstrong, strategic planning can be defined as 'the process of developing and maintaining a strategic fit between the organisation's goals and capabilities and its changing marketing opportunities.

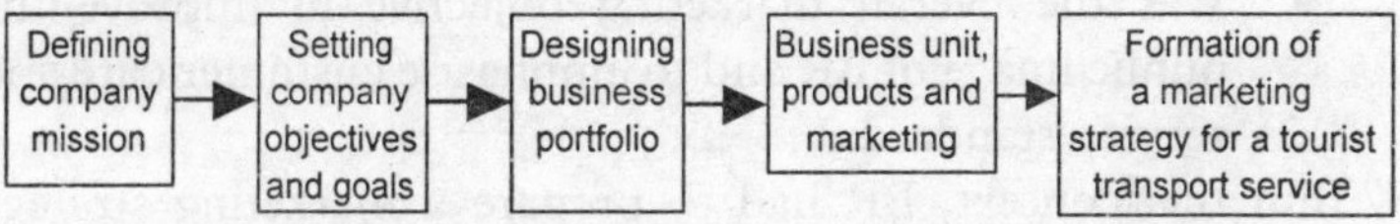

Figure 14.6: Strategic planning for tourist transport.

Bussiness need to be aware of their position in the wider business environment and how they will respond to competition and new business opportunities within an organised framework. To illustrate how strategic planning operates and its significance to tourist transport, it is useful to focus on the structured approach devised by Kotler and Armstrong. As Figure 14.6 shows, the first stage is the definition of an organisation's purpose, which requires a company to consider:

- What business is it in?
- Who are its customers?
- What services do its customers require?

Following the definition of purpose, a company may incorporate these principles into a *mission statement.* This provides a focus for the company activities, as can be seen in the case, of BR's *Passenger's Charter,* which identified the following aims as part of its mission for customer service:

- A safe, punctual and reliable train service,
- Clean stations and clean trains,
- Friendly and efficient service,
- Clear and up-to-date information,
- A fair and satisfactory response if things go wrong.

Although a mission statement may be used for public relations purposes, as in the case of BR, it is necessary to set objectives and goals. For example, the BR *Passenger's Charter* required the organisation to consider:

- What were its business objectives?
- Was it seeking to improve its market share of tourist travel by rail?
- Was the overriding business concern to improve the financial turnover and profitability?
- If so, what marketing objectives would need to be set to achieve these goals?
- Was the overall marketing objective to improve the public image of BR and to emphasise customer care and service standards?

Within this context, BR had to prepare a marketing strategy which acknowledged its business and marketing objectives and identified the resource requirements to achieve internal targets (e.g. achieving a greater market share of tourist travel) as well as the implications for research, sales and promotion and how this translates into an overall benefit for BR in a given timescale, such as a one-year or five-year period.

Obviously the *Passenger's Charter* was only one aspect of strategic planning for BR's passenger services in 1992, but it does emphasise how important marketing and strategic planning are in launching such a new business initiative. The next stage following the setting of objectives and goals is termed the *business portfolio.* Here the company analyses its own products or services in terms of its own business expertise and how competitor's products and services may affect them. This is frequently undertaken as a SWOT analysis, which considers:

- the Strengths,
- the Weaknesses,
- the Opportunities,
- the Threats.

of its products and services in the business environment.

For those operators who may wish to develop a strategy which incorporates an element of organisational growth and expansion, a number of options exist. As Horner and

Swarbrooke show, these can be divided into:

- *Marketing consortia* - where a group of operators cooperate to create and develop a product such as the Euro Domino joint railway ticket, permitting rail travel on different European railways.
- *Strategic alliances* - where different businesses agree to cooperate in various ways. This has varied by sector in the tourism industry, but may involve marketing agreements of technical cooperation. However, in the airline industry, Gallacher and Odell observed that 280 alliances existed among 136 airlines, 60 per cent of which were formed after 1992. Hanlon outlined the nature of such alliances among airline companies, which included joint sales and marketing; joint purchasing and insurance; joint passenger and cargo flights; code sharing; block spacing; links between frequent flyer programmes; management contracts; and joint ventures in catering, ground handling and aircraft maintenance. The strategic value of such alliances as they can result in 'horizontal alliances . . . [involving] . . . firms selling the same product . . . vertical alliances . . . [being] . . . those with suppliers distributors or buyers. And external alliances . . . with potential entrants or with the producers. . . in other industries'. The main concern for governments is that the transport industry may be overconcentrated among a limited number of companies or consortia that could eventually lead to market domination and higher prices. For example, Youssef and Hansen's study of the Swissair and SAS alliance indicated that on the main hub routes - Copenhagen, Stockholm and Oslo to Geneva - competition was severely reduced. Consequently, the alliance had yielded higher profits for the airlines on the hub-to-hub routes.
- *Acquisition* - which is the purchase of equity in other operations such as the Scandinavian company Stena's acquisition of European ferry operations, especially in the UK.

- *Joint ventures* - where operators seek to create new carriers.
- *Franchising* - where major operators use their market presence and brand image to extend their influence further by licensing franchisees to operate routes using their corporate logo and codes (e.g. the British Airways agreement with Maersk, Air UK, Manx Airlines and Loganair); see Table 14.3.
- *Ancillary activities* - the development of which adds value to the operator or organisation's core business. For example, many European ferry operators now offer inclusive tour operations (e.g. P&O European Ferries).

Table 14.3
British Airways Franchise Airline Agreements, 1997

Airline	*Number of destinations served*	*Airline base*	*Date franchise began*
British Mediterranean	6	Heathrow Airport	February 1997
British Regional Airlines	37	Isle of Man	January 1995
Brymon Airways[1]	13	Plymouth and Bristol Airports	August 1993
City Flyer Express	14	Gatwick Airport	July 1993
Cornair	12	South Africa	October 1996
GB Airways	17	Gatwick Airport	February 1995
Loganair	16	Glasgow Airport	July 1994
Maersk Air	9	Birmingham Airport	August 1993
Sun Air	9	Billund Airport	August 1996

1. Brymon Airways was acquired by British Airways in August 1993.
Source: Modified from K. O'Toole (1998) 'Widening the Franchise', *Flight International* 25-31 March, 1998, p. 35.

Marketing Research

This process is one which is often seen as synonymous with market research but as the following definition by Seibert implies, in reality it is a much broader concept as marketing research is an organised process associated with the gathering, processing, analysis, storage and dissemination of information to facilitate and improve decision-making'. It incorporates various forms of research undertaken by organisations to understand their customers, markets and business efficiency. The actual research methods used to investigate different aspects of a company's business ultimately determine the type of research undertaken. The main types of research can be summarised into six categories (see Table 14.4). A number of good introductions to marketing reserch are available and more recent books on tourism research are recommended as preliminary reading on this topic. Marketing research allows the company to keep in touch with its customers to monitor needs and tastes which are constantly changing in time and space. However, the actual implementation of marketing for tourist transport ultimately depends on the 'marketing mix'.

The Marketing Mix

The marketing mix is 'the mixture of controllable marketing variables that the firm [or company] uses to pursue the sought level of sales in the target market' . This means that for a given tourist transport organisation such as an airline, there are four main marketing variables which it needs to harness to achieve the goals identified in the marketing strategy formulated through the strategic planning process. These variables are:

- *Product formulation* - the ability of a company to adapt to the needs of its customers in terms of the services it provides. These are constantly being adapted to changes in consumer markets.
- *Price* - the economic concept used to adjust the supply of a service to meet the demand, taking account of sales targets and turnover.
- *Promotion* - the manner in which a company seeks to improve customets' knowledge of the services it sells so that those people who are made aware may be turned into actual purchasers. To achieve promotional aims, advertising, public relations, sales and brochure production functions are undertaken. Not surprisingly, promotion often consumes the largest proportion of marketing budgets. For transport operators, the

Table 14.4
Categories of Marketing Research

Research category	*Used in*	*Typical marketing use*
1. Market analysis and forecasting	Marketing planning	Measurement and projections of market volumes, shares and revenue by relevant categories of market segments and product types.
2. Consumer research	Segmentation and positioning	(a) Quantitative measurement of consumer profiles, awareness, attitudes and purchasing behaviour including consumer audits. (b) Qualitative assessments of consumer needs, perceptions and aspirations
3. Products and price studies	Product formulation presentation and pricing	Measurement and consumer testing of amended and new product formulations, and price sensitivity studies.
4. Promotions and sales research	Efficiency of communications	Measurement of consumer reaction to alternative concepts and media usage; response to various forms of sales promotion, and sales force efectiveness.
5. Distribution research	Efficiency of distribution network	Distributor awarencess of products, stocking and display of brochures, and effectiveness of merchandising, including retail audits and occupancy studies.
6. Evaluation and performance monitoring studies	Overall control of marketing results	Measurement of customer satisfaction overall, and by product elements, including measurement through marketing tests and experiments.

Source: Middleton (1988 : 109).

timetable is widely used as a communication tool, while brochures and information leaflets are produced to publicise products. Some of the other promotional tools used to increase sales include promotional fares, frequent flyer programmes and 'piggy-back promotions . . . where purchasing one type of product gives consumers and opportunity to enjoy a special deal in relation to another product' such as the Sainsbury - British Airways promotion in the early 1990s.

- *Place* - the location at which prospective customers may be induced to purchase a service – the point of sale (e.g. a travel agent).

As marketing variables, production, price, promotion and place are normally called the four P's. These are incorporated into the marketing process in relation to the known competition and the impact of market conditions. Thus, the marketing process involves the continuous evaluation of how a business operates internally and externally and it can be summarised as 'the management process which identifies, anticipates and supplies customers' [see the section of this chapter on management studies] requirements efficiently and profitably (UK Institute of Marketing). To illustrate the importance of marketing, particularly promotion, the following case study of Queensland Rail in Australia emphasises how a product in decline can be revitalised and repacked for the tourist.

CASE STUDY: Marketing Tourist Transport - Queensland Rail

In the state of Queensland in Australia, the rail services were state-owned in 1997. The railway company Queensland Rail has sought to inject a new lease of life into its loss-making, long-distance passenger services by repackaging its services to meet a niche demand among tourists. Research by Dann explained the resurgence of interest in rail travel as a function of nostalgia among tourists, as feature also emphasised in the context of heritage tourism by Swarbrooke. Furthermore, Prideaux cites the research by Taylor which identified the speed, comfort, amenities and sociability of train travel as appealing for tourists.

Although long-distance passenger services commenced in 1885 in Queensland, with luxury services being added in the

1930s (e.g. the *Sunshine Express)*, followed by air-conditioned carriages in the 1950s (e.g. the *Sunlander* operating between Brisbane and Cairns in 1953), the postwar period saw a decline in rail travel. Road transport, notably the rise of the private car, and the expansion of air travel led to a decline in services. The extensive network of passenger services contracted as routes were reduced, lines closed and services cancelled. Although rail sought to introduce innovations to stem the flow of traffic (e.g. car-carrying wagons), its decline mirrored the future of rail in many other countries up to the 1980s. This led to a downward spiral of declining passenger numbers and declining services. In addition, Prideaux pointed to:

- The slow nature of train travel (e.g. in 1997 travel by air between Brisbane and Cairns took 2½ hours compared to 32 hours by the *Sunlander*).
- Services are infrequent, with the *Sunlander* operating six times a week in 1964 and three times a week in 1997.
- Passenger carriages were designed for longevity and recent fashions and tastes are not reflected in 1950s rolling stock.
- The train is inflexible compared to the car, with its convenience and wide availability.
- Concessionary fares for retirement pensioners have not yielded a great deal of revenue and generated intense competition in the peak season, also impacting upon the image of the railway.
- Lack of investment in new rolling stock and new technology, until the introduction of the *Spirit of Capricorn* in 1989 and upgraded track in the 1990s. The introduction of a tilt-technology on the *Spirit of Capricorn* in 1997 (similar to the ill-fated British Rail Advanced Passenger Train in the 1970s and 1980s) will reduce the journey time for Brisbane to Rockhampton from 9 hours 25 minutes to 7 hours.
- An absence of promotion due to public sector principles that did not emphasise commercial practices until the late 1990s.
- A perceived lack of reliability in keeping to the published schedules.

- Rail travel was expensive and not price-competitive with air travel.
- Competition from long-distance coaches, following the deregulation of the sector in 1985. Price and departure flexibility among coach operators combined with mass media advertising and their attractive multi-sector price structures for tourist travel, severely dented rail's market share.

While Queensland Rail sought to address some of these issues in the 1990s, the loss of traditional clientele meant the search for new markets after the state government's corporation of Queensland Rail in 1995. This followed the reorganisation of long-distance rail services in the late 1980s into a new group – Traveltrain. Tourism was seen as an area for expansion, with two services – Sunshine Rail Experience and Kuranda Scenic Railway, which departs from Cairns and traverses scenic gorges and travels through virgin rainforest and the jungle village of Kuranda. By 1994, 500,000 passengers a year were travelling on the Kuranda Scenic Railway, making it Australia's sixteenth-largest tourist attraction that same year, which exceeded visits to the Great Barrier Reef.

Following the success of the *Queenslander* tourist train in 1986, the *Spirit of the Outback* and the *Spirit of the Tropics* were introduced in 1993 to help offeset losses in other long-distance services. In 1995, the *Savannahlander* was brought in and subsequently won tourism awards. The extent of services in 1996 is outlined in Table 14.5 which is to be complemented by the introduction of the Great South Pacific Express in 1998, a joint venture with the Venice-Simplon Orient Express, estimated to cost A$34 million. But how has Queensland Rail been able to turn an ailing railway company into a successful tourist venture?

One of the tools used by Queensland Rail was the development of promotional themes to sell individual services, where a number of market segments were carefully nurtured. According to Prideaux, these included:

- Long-distance rail services (e.g. the *Sunlander)* using traditional routes developed in the nineteenth century with free travel of pensioner concessionaires, which

Table 14.5
Queensland Rail Traveltrains 1996

Name	*Date of introduction*	*Length of service (km)*	*Time of journey*	Cost (A$) 1996 *Economy*	Cost (A$) 1996 *Sleeper*	*Facilities*	*Service per week*	*Types of service*
The Queenslander (Brisbane/Cairns)	1986	1,681	31 hours	N/A	489	Restaurant, lounge car, roomettes	1	Tourist
Sunlander (Brisbane/Cairns)	1953	1,681	32 hours	159	243	Dining car, club car	3	Tourist/ scheduled passengers
Kuranda Scenic Railway (Cairns/Kuranda)	1891	35	1.3 hours	23	N/A	Commentary	26	Tourist
Spirit of the Tropics (Brisbane/Cairns)	1994	1,681	32 hours	135	129	Disco, dining car	2	Tourist/ youth
Inlander (Townsville/Cairns)	1954	977	19 hours	125	192	Dining car	2	Passenger
Westlander (Brisbane/Charleville)	1954	777	16 hours	107	172	Club car, dining car	2	Passenger
Spirit of the Outback (Brisbane/Longreach)	1993	1,325	24 hours	158	226	Club car, dining car	2	Tourist
Savannahlander (Mt. Surprise/Forsayth)	1994	121	5 hours	35	N/A	Commentary	2	Tourist
Gulflander (Normanton/Croydon)	1891	152	4 hours	35	N/A	Commentary	2	Tourist
Spirit of Capricorn Brisbane/Rockhampton	1989	639	9.5 hours	67	N/A	Light refreshments	9	Commuter
Sunshine Rail Experience	1962	1,681	6 days	1,199	N/A	Club car	19 per year	Rail tour

Source: Pridenux (1997).

contributed to revenue losses, have been upgraded and new traffic sought since pensioner concessions could be curtailed in a climate of public sector retrenchment In 1995, the *Sunlander* under went a A$2.8 million refit with themed carriages and public entertainment areas. This was accompanied by a reimaging of these services to convey a restful travel experience full of discovery and attractions.

- Luxury on wheels, such as the *Queenslander* tourist train introduced in 1986 which will be complemented by the Orient Express train in 1998.
- Nostalgia, where the farmer *Midlander* service from Rockhampton to Winton was relaunched as the *Spritit of the Outback* in 1993. An elimination of pensioner concessions on this service combined with a strong appeal to nostalgia characterised the marketing of this service.
- The youth-budget market, seeking to top Queensland's growing backpacker market which was estimated at 250,000 travellers in 1993. In 1994, the *Spirit of the Tropics* with its on-board disco was introduced on the Brisbane to Cairns route.
- Trains as tourist attractions as epitomised by the Kuranda Scenic Railway, with the *Gulflander* and *Savannahlander* also marketed in the same way. These utilise a range of heritage themes (e.g. mineral mining) and a strong emphasis on nostalgia.
- Rail-touring, using daytime travel along the Queensland coast between Brisbane and Cairns and overnight stays in motels along the lines of the 1962 Sunshine Rail Experience.

Following corporation, Queensland Rail only received state subsidies to operate services the state deemed were important from a public welfare perspective. The move towards profitability was underwritten by a 10-year A$4 billion capital works programme to assist with the corporatisation. Long-distance passenger services remain unviable, with a large network and high costs of operation. The *Sunlander* contributes

34 per cent of Traveltrain's gross revenue, followed by the Kuranda Scenic Rail service with 19 per cent. However, tourism ventures have not noticeably reduced operational losses on long-distance rail services due to what Prideaux considers to be Queensland Rail's inability to market its services. Until recently travel sales could only be made through railway offices and not through travel agents. However, recent alliances with tour wholesalers such as American Express and Jetset Tours are a major step forward.

Prideaux also points to the desire of Queensland Rail to reposition itself in the tourism sector, although its pricing structure continues to present a problem. For example, in 1995/96 only marginally more than 20 per cent of passengers on long-distance services paid the full fare (excluding the Kuranda service), with 50 per cent being pensioners paying a nominal charge or travelling free. Services often fail to reach 60 per cent cost recovery on operations, with some generating less than 25 per cent. In contrast, in New Zealand, organisations like Tranz Rail have developed successful tourist trains and perhaps such organisations may offer lessons for Queensland Rail with its privatised operation.

While Queensland Rail is still evolving its marketing of its services, opportunities to expand this role with packaging rail tours like Tranz Rail in New Zealand offer a new direction. The sale of a rail experience, moving Queensland Rail from a promotional to a more sales-oriented role will require new marketing strategies to enhance the marketing effect. Continued service improvements on-board trains combined with a higher degree of cost-recovery need to be a financial target for Queensland Rail. This can be achieved by increasing the profitability of its existing and forecast markets (e.g. tourists) and by developing a more sophisticated marketing philosophy, perhaps with a stronger emphasis on service quality.

As the case study of Queensland Rail has indicated, marketing has a certain degree of synergy with economics as an understanding of economic concepts and the way in which the marketplace works is fundamental to marketing. But the application of marketing principles to the tourist transport system requires one to recognise that one is dealing with a service and the tourist experience which is embodied in the concept of the service encounter.

Tourist Transport as a Service

Gilbert noted the growing importance of service quality and consumer satisfaction in tourism in the late 1980s. In the context of tourist transport, what is meant by a service? Defining the term 'service' is difficult due to the intangibility, perishability and inseparability of services. Kotler and Armstrong define these three terms as follows:

- *Service intangibility* - a service is something which cannot be seen, tasted, felt, heard or smelt before it is purchased.
- *Service perishability* - a service cannot be stored for sale or use at a later date.
- *Service inseparability* - a service is usually produced and consumed at the same time and cannot be separated from providers.

Van Dierdonck argues that the intangible nature of a service is determined by the fact that, unlike manufactured goods, a service is provided and consumed at the same time and same place, making it difficult to define and communicate its form to customers. Even so, it is possible to identify six core elements in a service if it is defined as a product, where each element affects customer perception of the service:

- the image of the service,
- the image of personnel with whom customers interact,
- image differences within the same sector as the service provider (e.g. how a service compares with those offered by its competitors),
- the customer group targeted,
- the influence of the physical environment in which the service is delivered (e.g. the building),
- the working atmospher in which the service is formulated, designed and delivered.

Source: Modified from Flipo; cited in Van Dierdonck (1992).

An alternative view of a service is that it constitutes a process rather than an end product, which actually disappears once it has been made. In the respect, a service can be conceptualised as a process which responds to the diverse needs of consumers. Since consumers are not homogeneous it is difficult to standardise a product to meet every need. The process of providing a service which tailors something to meet precise and varied needs is integral to the concept of responsive service provision.

Researchers such as Poon have argued that the challenge for tourism-related enterprises, such as transport providers, is to respond to the growing sophistication of tourists so that the entire tourism experience meets me expectations of the consumer. In this context, three key issues which emerge are service quality, customer care and the service encounter. From the consumer's perspective, the use of critical incidents in the service process (e.g. where the service delivery breaks down) has been used to analyse the consumer's service encounter and how they view it under adverse conditions. If we accept that there is a consensus among marketing researchers that service provision needs to be seen as an ongoing process, how does this process operate? examined this process as a four-stage system (see Figure 14.7) with the provider trying to offer a service in response to actual or perceived customer demand. The process is based on the following concepts: consumer benefit, the service concept, the service offer and the service delivery system.

The Consumer Benefit

At the outset, the supplier of a service tries to understand what the consumer wants and how they may benefit from the service. At this stage, a detailed understanding of consumer behaviour is required which recognised the relative importance of the factors influencing the purchase decision. These include social, economic, cultural, business and family influences and how they condition and affect the attitudes, motives, needs and perception of consumers. In the case of tourist transport service, a significant amount of research on the social psychology of tourists has examined what holidays tourists choose, the mode

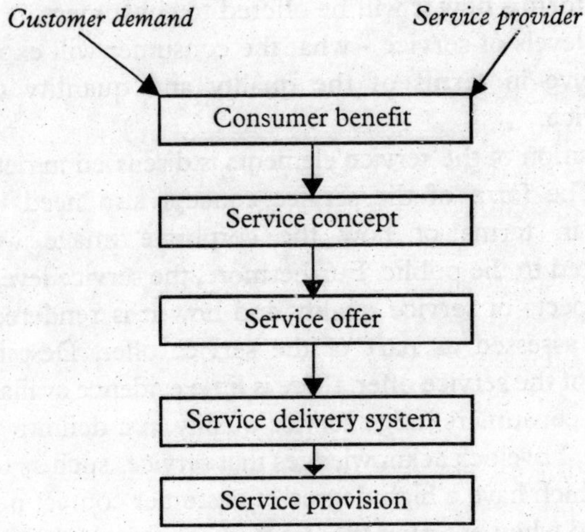

Figure 14.7: The service process.

of transport selected and the factors affecting their decision-making as consumers. Following the consumer benefit stage, the service provider translates the assessment of consumer demands into a service concept.

The Service Concept

At this point, the supplier examines the means of producing a service and how it will be distributed to consumers. Marketing research at both the consumer benefit and service concept stage is essential to assist in identifying the specific market segment to target and the nature of the consumer/producer relationship (e.g. is the service to be sold direct to the public or via a different distribution channel such as a travel agent?). lastly, the producer identifies and develops the image which is to be associated with the service. Having established what the service will comprise in concept form, it is developed further into the service offer.

The Service Offer

At this point, the service concept is given more shape and developed within precise terms set by managerial decisions which specify.

- the elements - the ingredients,

- the form - how it will be offered to consumers,
- the levels of service - what the consumer will expect to receive in terms of the quality and quantity of the service.

The composition of the service elements is discussed in detail by Gronroos. The form of the service concept also needs to be considered in terms of how the corporate image will be communicated to die public. Furthermore, the service levels, the technical aspects of service quality and how it is rendered also need to be assessed as part of the service offer. Despite the significance of the service offer, there is little evidence available to suggest that consumers judge service quality in a definitive way. For example, Lovelock acknowledges that services such as tourist transport, which have a high degree of customer contact need to be recognised when entering the last stage - service delivery.

The Service Delivery System

This is the system which is developed to deliver the service to the customer and will comprise both the people responsible for different aspects of the service experience and the physical evidence such as the transport and environment in which it is delivered. The tourist's experience of these components is embodied in the *service encounter*. It is in the service delivery system that barriers may occur in the provision of a satisfactory encounter and a great deal of marketing esearch has been directed to identifying deficiencies, critical incidents and ways of overcoming dissatisfaction in this area. The pursuit of excellence in service delivery has meant companies monitoring what the consumer wants and then providing it. In this context marketing assumes a critical role both in terms of research and communication with customers. By providing quality in service provision, it may help to develop customer loyalty in the patronage of tourist transport. As the competitive market for tourist transport intensifies, the demand for service delivery systems which are customer-centred is likely to be an important factor in affecting tourist use of transport services. The consumer is a key player in the service process, being as active participant and important judge of quality. It is, therefore, essential to consider how transport providers can integrate many of the perspectives discussed in the chapter so far, to meet customers' needs and to run a tourist transport business successfully. Attention now turns to the contribution which management can make.

Management Studies and Tourist Transport

Having examined the role of other disciplines and their contribution to the analysis of transport, it is useful to consider one area which draws the others together and harnesses their skills. That area is management. For this reason, it is pertinent to examine what management is, its rationale, the principles which guide managers and the factors which can impact upon the need to manage. This is followed by a case study of airline management. In a purely abstract academic context, management is concerned with the ability of individuals to conduct, control, take charge of, or manipulate the world to achieve a desired outcome. In a practical business setting, management occurs in the contact of a formal environment - the organisation. Within organisations (small businesses through to multinational enterprises), people are among the elements which are managed. As a result, Inkson and Kolb define management as 'getting things done in organisations through other people'. In a business context, organisations exist as a complex interaction of people, goals and money to create and distribute the goods and services which people and other businesses consume or require.

Organisations are characterised by their ability to work towards a set of common objectives (e.g. the sale of holidays to tourists for a profit). To achieve their objectives, organisations are often organised into specialised groupings to achieve particular functions (e.g. sales, human resources management, accounts and finance) as departments. In addition, a hierarchy usually exists where the organisation is horizontally divided into different levels of authority and status, and a manager often occupies a position in a particular department or division at a specific point in the hierarchy. Within organisations managers are grouped by level in the organisation from the:

- *Chief Executive Officer* (CEO or) *General Manager* at the top who exercises responsibility over the entire organisation and is accountable to a Board of Directors of other representatives for the ultimate performance of the organisation.
- *Top managers* are one level down from the CEO and their role is usually confined to a specific function, such as marketing or sales. They may act as part of an executive team who work with other top managers and the CEO to provide advice on the relationship between different parts of the organisation and contribute to corporate goals.
- *Middle managers* fill a niche in the middle of the hierarchy with a more specialised role than the top managers. Typically they may head sections or divisions and be responsible for performance in their area. In recent years, corporate restructuring has removed a large number of middle managers to cut costs and placed more responsibility on top managers or the level below - first line managers.
- *First line managers* are the lowest level of manager in an organisation, but arguably perform one of the most critical roles - the supervision of other staff who have non-managerial roles and who affect the day-to-day running of the organisation.

Managers can also be classified according to the function they perform (i.e. the activity for which they are reponsible). As a result, three types can be discerned:

- *Functional managers* manage specialised functions such as accounting, research, sales and personnel. These functions may also be split up even further where the organisation is large and there is scope to specialise even further.
- *Business unit, divisional, or area managers* exercise management responsibilities at a general level lower down in an organisation. Their responsibilities may cover a group of products or diverse geographical areas

and combine a range of management tasks, requiring the coordination of various functions.

- *Project managers* manage specific projects which are typically short-term undertakings, and may require a team of staff to compete them. This requires the coordination of a range of different functions within a set time frame.

The goals of managers within organisations are usually seen as profit-driven, but as the following list suggests, they are more diverse:

- Profitability, which can be achieved through higher output, better service, attracting new customers and by cost minimisation.
- In the public sector, other goals (e.g. coordination, liaison, raising public awareness and undertaking activities for the wider public good) dominate the agenda in organisations. Yet in many government departments in developed countries, private sector, profit-driven motives and greater accountability for the spending of public funds now feature high on the agenda.
- Efficiency, to reduce expenditure and inputs to a minimum to achieve more cost-effective outputs.
- Effectiveness, achieving the desired outcome; this is not necessarily a profit-driven motive.

In practical terms, however, the main tasks of managers are based on the management process, which aims to achieve these goals. Whilst management theorists differ in the emphasis they place on different aspects of the management process, there are four commonly agreed sets tasks. McLennan describe these as:

- *Planning* - so that goals are set out and the means of achieving the goals are recognised.
- *Organising* - whereby the work functions are broken down into a series of tasks and linked to some form of structure. These tasks then have to be assigned to individuals.
- *Leading* - which is the method of motivating and influencing staff so that they perform their tasks

effectively. This is essential if organisational goals are to be achieved.

- *Controlling* - which is the method by which information is gathered about what has to be done.

Managing requires a comparison of the information gathered with the organisational goals and, if necessary, taking action to correct any deviations from the overall goals.

Fundamental to the management process is the need for managers to make decisions. This is an ongoing process. In terms of the levels of management, CEOs make major decisions which can affect everyone in the organisation, whereas junior managers often have to make many routine and mundane decisions on a daily basis. Yet in each case, decisions made have consequences for the organisation. To make decisions, managers often have to balance the ability to use technical skills within their own particular area with the need to relate to people and to use 'human skills' to interact and manage people within the oganisation, and clients, suppliers and other people external to the organisation. Managers also need these skills to communicate effectively to motivate and lead others. They also need cognitive and conceptual skills. Cognitive skills are those which enable managers to formulate solutions to problems. In contrast, conceptual skills are those which allow them to take a broader view, often characterised as 'being able to see the wood for the trees', whereby the manager can understand the organisation's activities, the interrelationships and goals and can develop an appropriate strategic response.

In recent years, there has been a growing recognition that to perform a managerial task successfully, a range of competencies are needed. A competency, according to Inkson and Kolb is 'an underlying trait of an individual–for example, a motive pattern, a skill, a characteristic behaviour, a value, or a set of knowledge - which enables that person to perform successfully in his or her job'. The main motivation for organisational interest in competency is the desire to improve management through education and training. As Table 14.6 shows, competencies can be divided into three groups:

- understanding what needs to be done,
- getting the job done,
- taking people with you.

Table 14.6
The McBar Management Competencies Model

Competency	*Components of the model*
Understanding what needs to be done	• Critical reasoning • Strategic visioning • Business know-how
Getting the job done	• Achievement drive • Proactivity • Confidence • Control • Flexibility • Concern for effectiveness • Direction
Taking people with you	• Motivation • Interpersonal skills • Concern for impact • Persuasion • Influence

Source: C. Page *et al* (1994 : 26).

While the concern with competencies questions the traditional planning, organising, leading and control model as a description of the management Process, an overriding emphasis on the skills managers need to perform tasks also has inherent problems. Research has shown that the view that such skills are generic and can be generalised to all situations is incorrect. In fact, human skills are very much related to personality and individual style and conceptual skills are based on the natural abilities of individuals. However, a certain degree of training and development as well as everyday learning may assist managers to improve their effectiveness. What is critical is the manager's ability to be adaptable and flexible to change, particularly in fast-moving areas such as tourism.

Change is a feature of modern-day management and any manager needs to be aware of, and able to respond to changes in the organisational environment. For example, general changes in society, such as the decision of a new ruling political party to deregulate the economy, have a bearing on the operation of organisations. More specific factors can also influence the organisational environment including:

- *Socio-cultural factors* - which include the behaviour, beliefs and norms of the population in a specific area.
- *Demographic factors* - which are related to the changing composition of the population (e.g. birth rates, mortality rates and the growing burden of dependency where the increasing number of ageing population will have to be supported by a declining number of economically active people in the workforce).
- *Economic factors* - which include the type of captialism at work in a given country and the degree of state control of business. The economic system is also important since it may have a bearing on the level of prosperity and factors which influence the system's ability to produce, distribute and consume wealth.
- *Political and legal factors* - that are the framework in which organisations must work (e.g. laws and practices).
- *Technological factors* - where advances in technology can be used to create products more efficiently. The use of information technology and its application to business practices is a case in point.
- *Competitive factors* - which illustrate that businesses operate in markets and other producers may seek to offer superior services or products at a lower price. Businesses also compete for finance, sources of labour and other resources.
- *International factors* - where businesses operate in a global environment and factors which obtain in other countries may impact on the local business environment. For example, in December 1997 the unexpected financial crisis in South Korea led Air New Zealand to cease its four-times-a-week service to Seoul and from 1st February, 1998, Qantas also withdrew services.
- *Change and uncertainty* are unpredictable in free market economies, and managers have to ensure that organisations can adapt to ensure continued survival and prosperity, as exemplified by the rapid response of Air New Zealand and Qantas to the financlia crisis in South Korea to offset potential losses. Change

continually challenges all organisations and change in any one factor within an organisation can impact upon how it functions. Various techniques can be used to help to overcome internal resistance to change within organisations. As Kotter and Schlesinger observe, these include:

- education and communication,
- participation and involvement,
- facilitation and support,
- negotiation and agreement,
- manipulation and co-optation,
- explicit and implicit coercion.

Change may be vital for organisations to adapt and grow in new environments and the introduction of information technology is one example where initial resistance within businesses had to be overcome. Increasingly, managers are not only having to undertake the role of managing, but also the dynamic role of 'change agent'. Managers have to understand how systems and organisations work and function to create desirable outcomes. It is the ability to learn to manage in new situations where there are no guidelines or models to follow, which Handy views as the way people grow, especially in a managerial role.

CASE STUDY: Airline Management in the 1990s

The airline industry developed as a commercial enterprise during the 1930s as technological advances in aviation enabled companies to develop regular passenger services, cross-subsidised by the provision of freight and air postal services. In the postwar period, modern-day air transport emerged as an international business, providing services and products for a diverse group of users including scheduled and non-scheduled (charter) transport for air travellers and cargo transport for businesses. The airline industry is truly a global business and by the year 2002 commercial world passenger air transport is expected to generate 3,431.4 billion Revenue Passenger Kilometers (RPKs). The growth in global passenger travel by air has risen consistently, with the Boeing Commercial Airline Group anticipating an average annual rate of growth in air travel of 5.2 per cent through to the year 2013, led by growth in the Asia-Pacific region. This growth is 'equivalent to adding the capacity of one of the world's largest airlines, with a fleet of more than 600 airplanes, to the system, each and every year'. Such a rate of change is not new for the airline industry, sine it has a history of dramatic change over a short period of time dating back to the introduction of commercial aviation services in the 1920s and 1930s.

Airline Management as a Concept

Airline management is a concept which all commercial airline companies have taken seriously due to the rate and pace of change in the competitive global business environment in which they operate. It is also a volatile business where unpredictable external factors(for example, the gulf war) can dramatically affect their ability to attract customers and may threaten their profitability - 'the bottom line'. Consequently, airline management may loosely be defined as the process whereby individual (and groups of) airlines seek to organise, direct and harness their resources, personnel and their business activities to meet the needs of their organisation and customers in an effective and efficient manner. In the case of the airline industry, the ability to respond to change and to adapt is a key challenge for management. Profitability of the airline is the principal objective of privately owned airlines. Yet in reality, many airlines began life as state-owned enterprises, due to the capital-intensive nature of this business activity, which requires a steady and predictable long-term stream of revenue to absorb the high capital and operating costs. The airlines of many smaller countries are still subsidised and maintained for political reasons. For example, state ownership of airlines persists in order to ensure the prestige of the national carrier in international relations, to maintain a degree of control over tourist arrivals, and to provide competition with other carriers to prevent a monopoly or duopoly situation from arising. Therefore, airline management may, in some cases, be motivated by political factors that outweigh the forces of the free market system and normal competition.

To understand the scope and process of airline management, a focus upon the issues which all airlines have to deal with on a day-to-day basis (operational issues) and on a longer-term basis (strategic issues), together with the marketing of airlines, illustrates the wide range of issues and problems which require management to ensure the airline is functioning in an efficient and effective manner. In reality, the management process for airline companies is a continuous activity which requires a predetermined structure to ensure that all the business activities are adequately integrated to meet the needs of internal customers and external business needs (i.e. those of the customer or purchaser of services and products).

A typical management structure for one airline - Air New Zealand – is shown in Figure 14.8. It illustrates the scope and

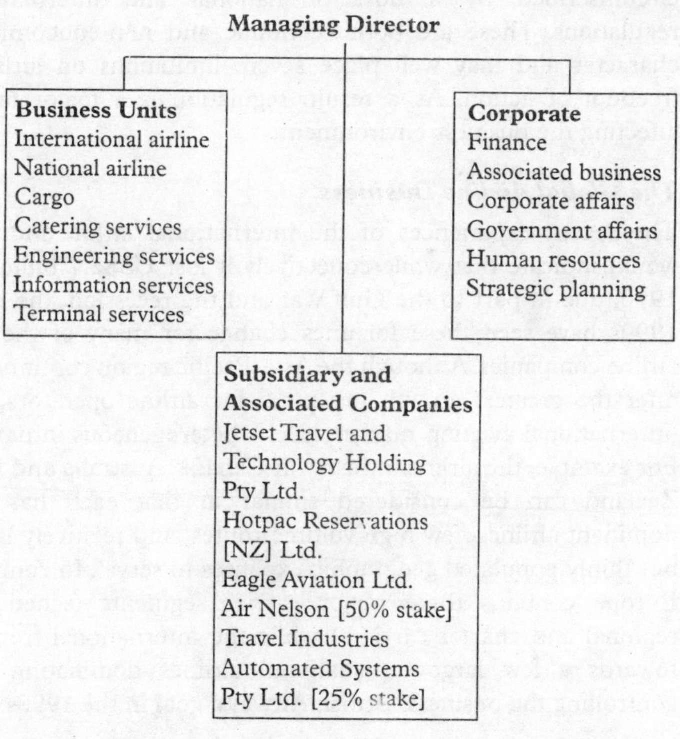

Figure 14.8: The management structure of Air New Zealand.

range of activities with which airline management is involved in this type of organisation. For example, airline managers not only have to oversee, coordinate and direct the activities of airline operations (domestic and international airline business), they also have to manage diverse activities which affect the organisation's main business (for example, ground handling, planning, human resource management and reservations). For the organisation to operate in an effective manner, airlines typically allow different elements to operate as separate business units, with a general manager reporting to a management board. This helps to achieve a degree of integration within the organisation while delegating responsibility for specialised functions to individual business units. However, before considering the management issues typically affecting international and domestic airlines, it is important to realise that 'airline managers are not free agents. Their actions are circumscribed by a host of national and international regulations. These are both economic and non-enocomic in character and may well place severe limitations on airlines' freedom of action. As a result, regulation is a major factor affecting the business environment.

The Global Airline Business

The recent experiences of the international airline industry would indicate that while collectively it lost US$2.7 billion in 1990, due in part to the Gulf War and the recession, the mid-1990s have seen these fortunes change for many of the top airline companies. Although the Asia-Pacific region continues to offer the greatest growth prospects for airline operators, the 'international aviation marketplace is heterogeneous in nature. For example, the airline industry in Canada, Australia and New Zealand can be considered similar in that each has few dominant airlines, few high volume routes, and relatively large, but thinly populated geographic expanses to serve'. In contrast, Europe contains three major carrier segments (scheduled, regional and charter carriers) while the international trend is towards a few large transnational airlines dominating and controlling the business. British Airways' goal in the 1990s is to become a global carrier and it has entered into strategic alliances to overcome competition by cooperating with other partners and by the purchase of airlines in other countries (for example, US Air). It has also purchased a stake in other airlines to gain access to the main airline markets in those regions and countries in which it does not operate in order to achieve a global mode of operation. Within Europe, strategic alliances have resulted from the prospect of the establishment of a single continental aviation market. Other airlines have pursued a strategy of vertical and horizontal integration to diversify their business interest in aviation so that they now operate subsidiary companies offering airport catering, passenger services, tour wholesaling, aviation maintenance facilities, pilot training, computer reservation systems, taxi services, property development and quality service training in addition to the core function of running an international airline. In this context, many airlines have adapted different management responses to the changing global environment for the airline industry in the 1990s. While technological developments in the 1980s assisted in the expansion and cost-reduction strategies of global airlines, the 1990s are being heralded as the decade of global aviation. The challenge for international and domestic airlines is to remain competitive and to develop the enhanced management and marketing skills acquired in the 1980s as the customer became the main focus of business activity, replacing the earlier focus on operational issues.

Airline Marketing and Management in the 1990s

One of the principal concerns of airline managers is the matching of the supply of services with the actual and forecast demand. Such a concern underpins all aspects of airline management and planning because without a fundamental understanding of marketing and planning. It is not possible to address issues such as aircraft selection, route planning, scheduling, product planning and pricing, advertising and long-term strategy, since each area requires an analysis of demand. The demand for airline services is also directly related to supply, since qualitative factors such as the quality of airline service (on the ground and in-flight) affect its supply features. Airline planning is therefore part of the management process. With supply adjusted to meet demand. The more competitive and unregulated the market, the greater the degree of planning and adjustment needed to match supply and demand. This is normally undertaken under the auspices of the marketing process. Such issues pose an even greater challenge for airline managers since the growing global competition for air travel has meant the 1990s are proving to be the decade of the air traveller as a consumer: not only have airlines been forced to reduce operating costs to compete for business, but they have been required to focus on the needs of their customers. If managers ignore the needs of their customers, their companies are unlikely to remain key players in the global airline business of the 1990s.

A common misconception in airline management during the 1970s was that marketing is simply about selling the final product. Airline marketing is now more complex than was recognised in the 1970s, since it is vital to the management process of deciding what to produce and how it should be sold. Thus, 'the role of airline marketing is to bring together the supply of air services, which each airline can largely control, with the demand, which it can influence but not control, and to do this in a way which is both profitable and meets the airline's corporate objectives'. If the essence of airline marketing is to satisfy customer needs, the airline needs to be market-oriented, as opposed to being dominated by an operational bias. For example, British Airways explained its financial turnaround from a loss of £544 million in 1981/82 to a profit of £272 million in 1983/84 in terms of its greater marketing orientation, based on recognising customers' needs and setting about satisfying them. Similar examples exist among other international airlines, such as Scandinavian Air Services (SAS) which has used marketing and a focus on service quality to retain a competitive edge.

The role of marketing in the management of airline services can be summarised as a four-stage process:

1. Identify markets and market segments using research methods and existing data sources and traffic forecasts.

2. Use the market analysis to assess which products to offer. This is known as product planning. At this stage, price becomes a critical factor. Therefore, product planning is related to:
   (a) market needs identified from market research;
   (b) the current and future product features of competing airlines and the cost of different product features.
   (c) assessing what price the customers can be expected to pay for the product.
3. Develop a marketing plan to plan and organise the selling of the products. Sales and distribution outlets need to be considered, together with a detailed programme of advertising and promotion.
4. Monitor and review the airline's ability to meet service standards, assessed through sales figures, customer surveys, analysis of complaints and long-term planning to develop new service and product features.

Retaining a Competitive Edge: New Marketing Techniques for Airline Managers

One area which international airlines have consistently targeted through advertising and the pursuit of service quality is business travel and the luxury market - first-class travel. This is because it is the most profitable segment of the market for scheduled airline, with premium pricing and high profit margins per seat, compared to lower yields in economy class, where profitability is attained by achieving high load factors. In the competitive airline business, the purchasing power of corporate business accounts, often in excess of US$100 million a year, has become the target for airline managers seeking to nurture this profitable segment. This is reflected in the estimated 150.6 million business trips undertaken in the USA in 1991. Airline managers have adopted aggressive marketing strategies, negotiating contracts and tying companies to one airline company. This is also reflected in the emergence of Frequent Flyer Programmes (FFPs)

Frequent Flyer Programmes

These programmes were orginally developed in the USA in May 1981 by American Airlines (AA) and nearly 30 million people in the USA have accumulated points for free travel. However, only 15 per cent of the participants ever redeem their points for flights. FFPs have, in part, been developed to attract business following deregulation. Aided by powerful Computer Reservation systems (CRSs), AA used its database of passengers to identify frequent flyers, who were enrolled into a 'Very Important Travellers Club'. The reward for loyalty was free air travel on a route which consistently had a high ration of unsold seats—Hawaii. While AA's Advantage FFP aimed to maximise revenue yield and its load factor, it also assisted in developing Dallas as a logical hub and capturing business from competing airlines. AA's Advantage scheme was closely followed by other companies launching similar schemes (united, TWA and Delta) with AA management recruiting British Airways to its FFP to add an international dimension. One consequence of FFPs was the greater utilisation of the 'hub and spoke' system.

To broaden the marketing appeal of FFPs, non-airline travel services (car rental companies, tour operators and hotel chains), airline-affiliated credit card purchases (mileage credits added according to the volume of spending) and other services now attract FFP points. It remains a fertile area for continued competition among airlines to offer the most attractive FFPs. While FFPs are a basic element of airline marketing strategy in the USA, they have also been introduced by European and other global carriers. In the Asia-Pacific region, Singapore Airlines, Malaysian Airlines and Cathay Pacific have agreed to establish a joint venture FFP to compete with the mega-carriers (that is, British Airways, United and AA). This appears to be the way forward for FFPs as carriers group together to broaden their scope and FFPs may be a basis for reinforcing the strategic alliances many airlines already operate.

Clearly, marketing is a key component of airline business strategies in the 1990s and a number of airlines have decided to withdraw from non-core activities, such as the hotel business, baggage handling, ground-support activities and catering. This has sometimes been a response to spiralling costs, which may be controlled through the use of contracted-in services. For example, in an attempt to reduce costs, the state-owned Irish airline, are Lingus, sold its holding in the Copthorne chain of airline hotels to reduce costs and to focus on core airline activities. Airline management has attracted very little attention from management researchers, probably because it remains a complex industry to understand fully unless one has worked closely with an airline organisation. Such organisations are wary of outsiders due to the highly competitive nature of their business and the prospect of 'insider knowledge' being used to the advantage of other airlines. A great deal of the available research data on airlines and their management remains confidential to the individual organisations and their employees, and only commissioned management consultants are usually privileged to consult it.

Despite these constraints, the airline industry is in a constant state of flux, adapting to changing trends. Computer reservation systems, controlled by the global airlines (for example, AA) now offer these organisations and unparalleled control over the passengers' choice of services, allowing them to become brokers of other travel services. This is transforming the airline business by offering a profitable business activity which may outstrip the actual profitability of individual airline operations. This has meant that airline managers need to be versatile, adaptable and more willing to view their business activities as part of a global travel and tourism industry. As customers' expectations increase, technological advances in aircraft design (for example, the new Boeing 777) may see the cost of air travel stabilise, if the cost of aviation fuel remains fairly constant. The future shape of the global aviation industry is likely to contain a limited number of global mega-carriers, with smaller airlines integrated into their operations by strategic alliances and other devices (for example, part-ownership by the larger carriers). A more hierarchical system of route provision is also likely to evolve and airlines will be forced to deal with greater volumes of passengers using a 'hub and spoke' system of provision to achieve efficient operations, with passenger volume tied to aircraft type. The major constraint on this rapidly evolving business activity for airline managers will be the availability of uncongested airspace and airports with sufficient capacity. This is already affecting air travel in Europe and the USA, while the environmental lobby regularly opposes airport expansion near to major urban centres. Airline managers will need to be increasingly focused on ensuring that their operational requirements can be fulfilled and their environmental impacts monitored and minimised to reduce local opposition to air transport. For example, many airports have introduced bans on aircraft which to not meet noise emission levels. These managerial issues have to be addressed and accommodated within the day-to-day operation and longer-term planning by airline managers so that passengers are not adversely affected by delays, congestion and inadequate planning.

15

THE ROLE OF GOVERNMENT POLICY AND TOURIST TRANSPORT

The development of tourism in specific countries is a function of the individual governments' predisposition towards this type of economic activity. In the case of outbound tourism, governments may curb the desire for mobility and travel by limiting the opportunities for travel through currency restrictions, such as in the case of South Korea in the 1980s, while still encouraging inbound travel. Similarly, in the USSR under the former communist rule, the opportunities for domestic tourism were controlled by limiting the supply of holiday infrastructure. However, such examples are not the norm because most governments seek to maximise the domestic population's opportunities for mobility and travel by the provision of various modes of transport to facilitate the efficient movement of goods and people at a national level. In fact, the development of transport to facilitate inbound tourism is often motivated by government's desire to increase earnings from tourist receipts.

To achieve the government's objectives for transport to facilitate tourist travel, policies are formulated to guide the organisation, management and development of tourist and non-tourist transport. This is normally followed by specific planning measures which seek to implement the policies. These will often require national governments to invest in - or encourage private sector organisations to invest in - new infrastructure which may be dedicated to tourist travel (and cargo) such as airports. Conversely, and more typically, governments may need to develop policies and planning measures which expand and develop national, regional and local infrastructure to accommodate tourist and recreational travel alongside the use for commuting and non-tourist travel. D. R. Hall rightly highlights the conceptual problem of distinguishing between what is tourist transport and what is not. Government policies often highlight this problem since while specialised, dedicated forms of tourist transport exist (e.g. tourist coaches, package flights and cruise liners), there are other forms of transport shared by hosts and tourists to varying extents. For example, urban buses and metro systems may be used by tourists, but their *raison d'etre* is primarily for local transport and this is reflected in generalised transport policies which often do not accommodate use by tourists. In Singapore, the state-subsidised mass rapid transport system is integrated with local bus services to provide the population with an efficient public transport system. Yet like many other metro systems it offers incentives for tourist use through the provision of 'tourist explorer tickets'. Indeed, there are few forms of transport which tourists are unlikely to use but the separation of tourist and non-tourist use is not usually an issue for policy makers. In a theoretical and more abstract context, research by sociologists interested in tourism, such as Urry and his work on the *tourist gaze* invokes notions of post-tourism, where all transport is potentially for and of tourism as the tourist gaze.

The transport policies developed by national governments are influenced by their changing attitudes, outlook and political ideology. This often manifests itself in terms of the level of expenditure on capital investment, infrastructure provison and policies to *facilitate* (Department of Employment/English Tourist Board 1991) or *constrain* tourist travel. Griffith discusses the effect of international airways sanctions as an example of government policies formulated to achieve a political goal against South Africa.

Likewise, when governments fail to acknowledge that policies and action are required to facilitate the development of tourist transport systems, capacity problems and bottlenecks may develop where tourism is imposed on inadequate national infrastructure. Gormsen documents the situation in China where 'serious capacity problems can be observed, not only for the airline companies, but also for railways, road traffic and river navigation, despite the fact that since the establishment of the PRC [People's Republic of China] all of these systems have been improved to a large extent'. As Table 15.1 shows, while the railway network, asphalt roads and air capacity have been expanded under government direction, the growth in patronage has outstripped supply as 'undercapacity at all levels of the transportation system remains a problem. Foreign tourists who must pay higher prices than citizens of China . . . receive preferential travel on the public transportation lines'. In an attempt to improve the efficiency of domestic air travel, the state airline, Air China, was divided into seven regional airlines after 1985. A further five Air China-related airlines and sixteen private airline companies are now in operation. By increasing the price of domestic air travel, airlines have managed to suppress demand to address capacity constraints. In the case of China, it is evident that even when policies are put in place to expand infrastructure, demand can often outstrip supply.

As Banister observes, forecasting the demand for transport planning is an Achilles' heel which has not improved even with growing technical sophistication in the methods used. Whitelegg may have highlighted one of the problems that needs to be recognised in a European context: 'leisure, recreation and tourism trips. . . are major growth areas in travel behaviour'. Page also argues that from a spatial perspective, tourist and recreational travel cannot be modelled and explained using conventional models and principles in transport geography. This it because is does not conform to principles of distance optimisation and least-distance patterns of travel. Therefore, government policy cannot necessarily assume that tourists will seek to use infrastructure developed for national economic goals. The car may be the principal agent driving tourist and recreational trips. The UK's Department of Transport observed,

> tourism and leisure depend heavily on travel and transport. In Britain, travelling by road represents the dominant mode for visitors to get to and from their final destinations or to see places of interest. . . [and] . . .

Table 15.1. The Development of China's Transport System 1949–87

Year	Number of public vehicles					Number of passengers (millions)				
	Trains (1,000)	*Buses (1,000)*	*Aircraft*	*Rail (1,000 km)*	*Road (1,000 km)*	*Rail*	*Road*	*Water*	*Air*	*Total*
1949	3	17	-	30	32	103	18	15	0.27	137
1952	5	19	45	35	55	163	45	36	0.02	245
1957	8	34	105	43	121	312	237	87	0.07	638
1962	10	47	245	55	263	741	307	163	0.17	1,221
1965	10	60	287	58	304	412	436	113	0.27	963
1970	11	75	293	70	411	524	618	157	0.22	1,300
1975	14	173	357	77	511	704	1,013	210	1.39	1,929
1978	15	257	382	85	647	815	1,492	230	2.31	2,539
1980	16	351	393	86	662	921	2,227	264	3.43	3,417
1985	21	795	390	95	750	1,121	4,764	308	7.47	6,200
1987	23	1,115	402	99	982	1,124	5,936	389	13.10	7,464

Source: Modified from Gormsen (1995) based on the National Statistics Bureau, China's Statistics Publishing House, 1989 and Historical Statistics by Provinces, China 1949–90, National Statistics Bureau, China's Statistics Publishing House, 1990.

> the tourism industry, in common with many other industries, also depends heavily on roads for the transport of the goods and services people need.

In fact, with over 21 million cars licensed in the UK, roads are assuming an even greater role in the patterns of tourist activity, despite problems associated with congestion in urban areas.

In the Republic of Ireland, the Department of Transport and Tourism recognises that:

> the development of an enhanced internal transport network fully integrated with appropriate access infrastructure and services is a fundamental requirement for the future development of the tourism industry. This requires the provision of good quality access transport services and facilities together with a satisfactory internal transport infrastructure and services.

Although the UK's Department of Transport and Government of Ireland highlight the interrelated nature of transport and tourism, in practice the responsibility for transport and tourism is often fragmented. It is frequently dispersed across different government departments, and where little interdepartmental liaison occurs, there is poor coordination of policies affecting tourist transport if they exist at all.

Public sector involvement in the tourist transport system at national government level is designed to facilitate, control and in some cases regulate or deregulate the activities of private sector transport operators with a view to 'looking after the public's interests and providing goods whose costs cannot readily be attributed to groups or individual's. Since the private sector's primary role is revenue generation and profit maximisation from the tourist transport system, the government's role is to promote and protect the interest of the consumer against unfair business practices, and to ensure that safety standards are maintained to protect the interests of employees in large- and small-scale transport operations. Oum argues that in the case of Asian airlines 'government policy makers and bureaucrats regulating the airline industry would agree that their long-run objectives are essentially two-fold: to attend to the needs of consumers (the travelling public and air cargo shippers) and to ensure a strong and viable airline industry within the country.'

This chapter examines the role of government policy in relation to tourist transport provision and how it can impact upon various modes of transport. The concept of transport policy is introduced and its meaning is discussed in relation to political variants of transport policy in free market economies. Emphasis is placed upon different political ideologies and how these have affected transport policies for tourism with the rising tide of privatisation in many societies. The significance of transnational organisations such as the EU and progress towards transport policies in aviation and rail travel are discussed.

The Role of Government Policy and Tourist Transport

The term 'policy' is frequently used to denote the direction and objectives an organisation wishes to pursue over a set period of time. According to Turner, the policy process is a function of three interrelated issues:

- the intentions of political and other key actors;
- the way in which decisions and non-decisions are made;
- the implications of these decisions.

Policy making is a continuous process and Figure 15.1 outlines a simplified, model of the policy process which is applicable to the way tourism transport issues are considered by government bodies. Hall and Jenkins examine the issue of policy making in a tourism context. The journal *Transport Policy* offers many relevant articles on this issue with regard to different aspects of transport, including tourist and recreational use. National policy is normally formulated by government organisations with economic and social factors in mind, without an explicit concern for tourism, even though transport networks are used for tourist and non-tourist travel. The development and shape of transport policy is partly affected by the existing infrastructure which has resulted from manor public and private serctor investment to achieve general and specific transport objectives. It may also be the case that other government policies (e.g. defence) impact upon transport. For example, many innovations in civil aviation have been developed as a spin-off from defence policy, particularly military research and

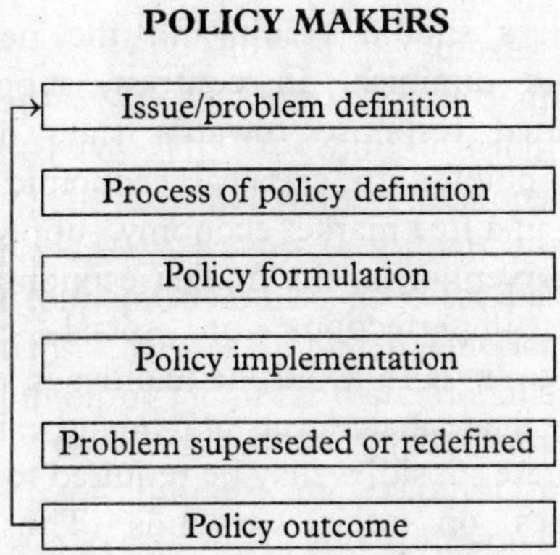

Figure 15.1: The policy making process.

development. In addition, defence infrastructure is sometimes used for civilian purposes, as in the case of the former Eastern Europe. Changes to the underlying infrastructure cannot be executed quickly because of the major capital costs, planning procedures and the time delay in responding to the demand for new infrastructure. For example, the expansion of an airport to accommodate a forecast growth in tourist arrivals may take between five and ten years from its inception to the completion stage. Such developments also have to be set against the increased environmental impact (e.g. noise, pollution, waste and greater numbers of tourists resulting from additional flights. Transport policy is a reactive element of government activity as changes in society and the demand for tourist and non-tourist travel require a certain degree of continuity and change in policy to meet new trends and activity patterns among the population. What political and ideological principles affect transport policy?

National transport policies have been characterised by a range of approaches which span a spectrum from a free market orientation to those based on planned resource allocation. The market-oriented view has been pursued on the premise that centralised state control of transport produces an unwieldy and often unresponsive service requiring unnecessarily high subsidies from state taxation. By introducing a greater degree of private sector involvement and competition, it is argued that improved services should result and the need for public subsidies should diminish. In contrast, supporters of the regulated planned response towards state involvement in transport have pointed to classical economic theory which recognises that, in a free market economy, supply imperfections result. State intervention in the market economy is justified to rectify supply imperfections on social efficiency and environmental grounds to avoid inequalities in accessibility. In situations where inadequate levels of demand exist to support a viable service, state subsidies may be required to provide access for communities on social grounds. Thus, government intervention in transport activities, either directly or through other agencies to coordinate different parts of the transport system, is essential to bring order to the different components of the system so that they operate in harmony. The level of intervention needed to achieve this coordinating function depends on the political views of the government and its policy objectives, which are subject to changing attitudes and external influences upon policy formulation. How have these principles been applied to transport policy in the past and what effect have they had on the tourist transport system?

Interpreting Transport Policy: Implications for Tourist Travel

According to Button and Gillingwater, in Europe and North America transport policy has affected the tourist transport system in a number of ways although it is based on two underlying economic principles:

- allocative efficiency (the use of resources and the price mechanism to achieve efficient access to transport and travel),
- political obligations (the need for the state to protect the public interest in transport provision).

These principles have had an important effect on the provision of transport for tourist travel in terms of the development, expansion and regulation of different modes of transport to facilitate access to tourism resources. Modes of transport which enable mass travel developed at different times in Europe and

North America but the effects were similar in terms of making tourist travel more available. Technological innovations and their commercial exploitation (e.g. the motor car), and their diffusion to different social groups during the late nineteenth and twentieth centuries, have been shaped by transport policy to achieve the twin goals of allocative efficiency and political obligations.

In historical terms, the principles of allocative efficiency and political obligations have been interpreted in different ways by governments and Button and Gillingwater identify four distinct phases in transport policy:

- *The Railway Age* - which, in the UK, led to heavy investment in the provision of infrastructure that made seaside resorts accessible to the working classes after the 1870s. Government promotion of railways in the private sector diminated the period, except during the wartime period (1914–18) when state control emerged to coordinate and manage the railways in the 'national interest' of efficiency.
- *The Age of Protection* - which characterised the 1920s and 1930s, saw the emergence of road transport, particularly the rise of the private car and coach travel in an unplanned manner. This led governments to intervene in the marketplace to avoid massive cost-cutting among private operators as competition intensified due to the growing number of small transport operators. Such intervention was justified on the basis that the effects of major competition might have led to a reduction in the number of operators, following a price war to secure passengers and market share. It was expected that this would be followed by a much reduced route network and poorer level of service. In the USA, this was characterised by the 1935 Motor Carriage Act which protected the Greyhound Bus Operations, providing one major operator with a virtual monopoly on interurban bus travel.
- *The Age of Administrative Planning* - which emerged in the postwar period (i.e. after 1945) and superseded the Age of Protection, saw the private car emerge as a potent force

for tourist and recreational travel. One consequence was the growing financial weakness of railways, although urban growth continued to dictate the need for large, efficient urban passenger transport systems. The nationalisation of railway networks and other forms of public transport epitomise this era in transport policy. The 1960s saw a growing burden of state subsidies to support public transport and some attempts to radically restructure the transport network (e.g. the Beeching Report in the UK and subsequent rationalisation of the rail network). In the UK, the 1968 Transport Act sought to reorganise public transport and one consequence for tourist travel was the establishment of the National Bus Company with the responsibility for express coach travel. In the USA, the 1962 Urban Mass Transportation Act provided Federal Grants for two-thirds of public transport projects. Efficiency in provision was interpreted by government policy in terms of integration and coordination of transport planning which reduced wasteful competition.

- *The Age of Contestability* - has characterised the period since the early 1970s in the USA (and the 1980s in the UK), based on the pursuit of the principle of deregulation to achieve 'allocative efficiency in transport policy'. By creating efficient transport operations and reducing public subsidies, the private sector is seen as the main panacea for efficient transport operations. In the UK the sale of the state-owned airline, British Airways, and its emergence as a profitable private sector company is cited by supporters of this political philosophy as one of the main successes of privatisation and deregulation. It is interesting to note that the UK/North American experience in transport policy in the 1970s and 1980s has not been adopted and endorsed in many other European countries where the state remains committed to investment in tourist transport systems.

In the UK context, Banister identified the essential need to recognise that 'society is now in transition from one based on work and industry to one in which leisure pursuits dominate - the post industrial society'. The implication is that policy making needs to recognise the significance of meeting the transport needs of this society. In a detailed review of 'the age of contestability' and transport policy in the UK between 1979 and 1991, Banister highlighted a number of major features including privatisation and a growing move towards meeting the transport needs of the leisure society. He cites the following actions of the Conservative government as instrumental in this, with the underlying premise of reducing public expenditure in transport:

- Transport Act, 1980 - deregulation Part 1
- Transport Act, 1981
- Transport Act, 1982
- Transport Act, 1983
- Transport Act, 1985 - deregulation Part 2
- Channel Tunnel Project launched - February 1986
- Terminal 4 opened at Heathrow Airport in 1986 and Piccadilly line underground extension to Heathrow Airport completed to Terminal 4
- British Airways privatised - January 1987
- British Airport Authority privatised - June 1987
- Docklands Light Railway opened - July 1987
- London City Airport opened - October 1987
- British Airways/ British Caledonian merger - November 1987
- National Bus Company privatisation - April 1988
- New terminal at Stansted Airport opened - Spring 1991.

As Banister explains, 'many of the policies have been justified on. . . criteria, such as ideology (for example, deregulation), democracy (for example, widening share ownership), efficiency (for example, private enterprises are more efficient than public ones), and accountability'. The Treasury was the prime mover in these new policy directions, constraining expenditure on investment and renewal of transport infrastructure by the state. The emphasis in policy was a shift from state investment in public transport to investment in roads to meet a demand for car use. While the government increasingly turned to the private section for capital and investment in the 1990s, it merely provided expenditure that was required in the 1980s to keep up with demand. Banister acknowledges that—

> In the early 1980s there was concern over the increasing levels of public support for bus and rail services with subsidy levels for each amounting to about £1,000 million. The market philosophy is to ensure that all services are provided at a level and a price which is determined competitively. Intervention should only take place when the market is seen to fail, for example, for social need, but even then the intervention should be specific... and that there should be no cross subsidisation between services.

The policy changes in the 1980s and up to the mid-1990s were characterised by:

- transferring transport from the public sector to the private sector through privatisation or denationalisation;
- the introduction of competition into public transport services and grater regulatory reform;
- the pursuit of greater levels of private capital in the large transport infrastructure projects such as the Channel Tunnel.

In fact, privatisation is not a process in government policy making which is confined to the UK and USA. For this reason, attention now turns to privatisation in the Asia-Pacific aviation sector.

Privatisation is Asia-Pacific Aviation

Oum indicates that the Asia-Pacific region is one of the fastest-growing regions of the world for scheduled air travel. In the period 1980–90, commercial air traffic expanded by 7.95 per cent per annum compared to 5.8 per cent growth per annum in North America. Forecasts from the International Air Transport Association (IATA) indicate that passenger traffic in Asia-Pacific will rise from 31 per cent of world scheduled traffic in 1990 to 41 per cent in the year 2000 and 51 per cent in 2010. While the currency crisis in Asia in 1997/98 may impact upon these forcasts, it is evident that the region will become the world's most important airline market. Oum, however, argues that 'even though the major airlines of Asia belong to the world's fastest growing airline market, they have remained relatively small in terms of network size, traffic volume and operating revenue, compared with major carriers in the United States and Europe'. Part of this is related to the restrictive bilateral agreements, which also protect the home market. There has been considerable research in the aviation sector which compares the productivity of airlines under government control with their subsequent performance as privately owned enterprises. Most of the studies indicate superior performance under conditions of privatisation although not in every case. Even the countries of Eastern Europe are privatising their national flag carriers as central state planning is removed.

Table 15.2 indicates that prior to 1985 there were isolated cases of privatisation but much of the privatisation occurred post-1985. For example, while the case of Singapore Airlines indicates that the government remains the majority shareholder, it is largely a private airline. In Oceania, the majority of airlines are privately owned, though many of the smaller airlines of the Pacific Island states remain state-owned to retain a degree of control over tourist arrivals and for strategic reasons related to accessibility and the independence of major carriers. In Pacific South American states, airlines have been privatised as well as those in North America, Canada and Mexico. In Asia, the situation is mixed. While some states have privatised their airlines and others intend to do so, a considerable number remain state-owned. Most of the privatised companies are the large successful airlines. As Forsyth observes, 'there is a strong correlation between per capita income levels and private ownership. In the richer countries in the region, such as Japan, Korea, Singapore, Taiwan, Malaysia, alongwith the colony of Hong Kong, all the airlines are privately owned. By contrast, there are few examples of private ownership of airlines in the poorer countries', while a number of governments have allowed the introduction of private airlines (e.g. Asiana in Korea, Sempati in Indonesia and Dragonair in Hong Kong) to compete on international routes.

Where privatisation has occurred, it can take a number of forms:

Table 15.2
Airline Privatisation in the Asia-Pacific Region 1985–95

Airline	*Country*	*1985 ownership*		*1995 ownership*	
		Private	*Public*	*Private*	*Public (%)*
American Airlines	USA	X		X	
Aeromexico	Mexico		X	X	
Aero Peru	Peru		X		20
Air Canada	Canada		X	X	
Air China	China		X		100
Air Lanka	Sri Lanka		X		100
Air New Zealand	New Zealand	X	X		
Air Nugini	Papua New Guinea		X		100
Air Pacific	Fiji		X		79.6
Air India	India		X		100
All Nippon Airways	Japan	X		X	
Anset Australia	Australia	X		X	
Avianco	Colombia	X		X	
Biman Bangladesh	Bangladesh		X		100
Canadian Air International	Canada	X		X	
Cathay Pacific Airways	Hong Kong	X		X	
China Airways	Taiwan	X		X	
Continental Airways	USA	X		X	
Delta Airlines	USA	X		X	
Garuda	Indonesia		X		100
HAL (Hawaiian)	USA	X		X	
Indian Airlines	India		X		100
Japan Air Systems	Japan	X		X	
Japan Airlines	Japan		X	X	
Korean Air	South Korea	X		X	
Ladeco	Chile	X		X	
Lan Chile	Chile			X	
Malaysia Airlines	Malaysia		X		30
Merpati	Indonesia		X		30
Mexicana	Mexico		X		35
Northwest Airlines	USA	X		X	
Pakistan International	Pakistan		X		57.4
Philippine Airlines	Philippines		X		33
Qantas	Australia		X		75
Royal Brunei	Brunei		X		100
Saeta Air Ecuador	Ecuador	X		X	
Singapore Airlines	Singapore		X		54
Thai International	Thailand		X		93.7
United Airlines	USA	X		X	
Vietnam Airlines	Vietnam		X		100

Source: Modified from Forsyth (1977).

- listing on the stock market (JAL and Singapore Airlines);
- sale of the airline to other companies in the same country;
- sale of the airline to strategic shareholders.

Privatisation also allows overseas investment in airlines through direct investment by shareholders and equity holdings through strategic alliances. In contrast, there has been less interest in the privatisation of airports in Asia, with only Australia taking Britain's lead in privatising all of its airports. The argument advanced to justify privatisation of airlines is the efficiency gains which will result. In the case of airports, it is widely recognised that the greatest proportion of costs are capital as opposed to operating costs. Therefore, the potential for efficiency gains is limited. However, some of the aspects of airport operation which private firms may perform efficiently include:

- terminal operation;
- retail outlet operation;
- building and operating runways;
- contracted-out services.

However, Forsyth maintains that 'investment policy, and ownership of the main facilities may best be left to the public sector'. In an Asia-Pacific context, privatisation has certainly opened up the opportunities for the region's airlines to become part of a global aviation industry through foreign investment, alliances and cooperation motivated by commercial motives in the absence of state policies to protect state airlines. As Wheatcroft argues, 'in the long-term, the privatisation of airlines seems certain to contribute to a reduction in protectionism in international aviation policies'.

Given that many of the airlines in developing countries within Asia-Pacific have remained under state control to assist with the development of the tourism industry, the following case study is introduced of a developing country outside of the region - Zimbabwe. The case study highlights some of the principles developed in the discussion of government policy and tourist transport to illustrate how the state carrier can be used to protect and then develop tourism. The case study also addresses a neglected aspect of tourism and transport within the literature, namely the situation in less developed countries, particularly those in Africa. It also provides an interesting counterbalance to the situation in Asia-Pacific and an opportunity to assess the extent to which the state has adopted different policy responses for tourist transport operations.

CASE STUDY: Air Transport and Tourism in Zimbabwe

Simon's innovative study *Transport on Development in the Third World* highlights the relationship of transport to the development process. It also illustrates the comparative neglect of the less developed world by transport researchers and a lack of critical debate on policy directions. This is also the case in relation to tourism and transport. In the case of Zimbabwe, the national government has identified tourism as a central theme in the plans for economic development. In 1990, some 10 years after independence, tourism was the fourth-largest earner of foreign revenue for Zimbabwe. In global terms, however, Africa attracts less than 3.5 per cent of world arrivals and Zimbabwe ranks seventh in terms of earnings from tourism in Africa, with less than 25 per cent of those in Kenya. De Kadt and Britton identified the significance of tourist transport in expanding tourism in developing countries. Turton and Mutambirwa rightly argue that 'air transport is essential to this process of tourism expansion in Zimbabwe, both in respect of long-haul flights from overseas and the provision of adequate domestic services'. Both international arrivals and domestic travel require appropriate policies to facilitate the development of tourist activity and travel. Visitor arrival in Zimbabwe have increased since 1980 (Figure 15.2), although the length of stay has decreased from 9.3 days in 1985 to 5.3 days in 1993. While a proportion of arrivals crossing the South Africa-Zimbabwe border are classified as visiting friends and relatives, over 90 per cent of arrivals are classified as tourists. A marked seasonality in arrivals is evident, with arrivals peaking in July-September and over Christmas, closely corresponding to peak vacation periods is the northern hemisphere.

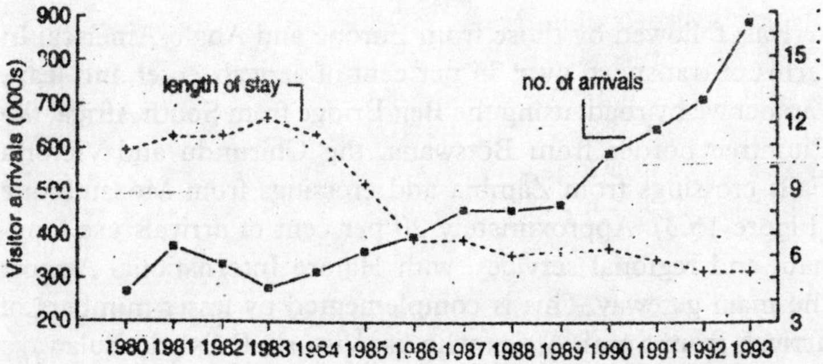

Figure 15.2: Visitor arrivals in Zimbabwe and the average length of stay 1980 - 93 .

As Table 15.3 shows, a significant number of tourist arrivals who stay one night or more are from South Africa and Zambia. Turton and Mutambirwa argue that if the day-trippers crossing the South Africa and Zambia border are removed from arrivals (Figure 15.3), 76 per cent of arrivals are from these two adjacent countries. Between 1985 and 1993 arrivals from these tow countries increased by 190 per cent and 116 per cent respectively. Aside from African arrivals, Table 15.4 shows that united Kingdom (UK) arrivals are the largest non-African source market. But they only represent 5.5 per cent of all

Table 15.3
Tourist Arrivals in Zimbabwe (Jan-March 1994) by Mode of Transport

Method of arrival	*Noumber of visitors*
Air transport	
Harare	34,646
Bulawayo	1,958
Rail transport	1,446
Road transport	
Beit Bridge	14,782
Victoria Falls	56,996
Plumtree Border Post	8,141
Chirunda	20,630
Total	138,599

Source: Based on Turton and Mutambirwa (1996).

arrivals followed by those from Europe and Anglo-America. In terms of transport, over 75 per cent of arrivals enter and leave Zimbabwe by road, using the Beit Bridge from South Africa, the Plumtree border from Botswana, the Chirundu and Victoria Falls crossings from Zambia and crossings from Mozambique (Figure 15.3). Approximately 20 per cent of arrivals use long-haul and regional services, with Harare International Airport the main gateway. This is complemented by lesser numbers of arrivals from South Africa who use Vistoria Falls and Bulawayo airports (Figure 15.3). In the period 1987 - 94, arrivals at Harare increased from 537,348 to 769,777.

Within Zimbabwe, Air Zimbabwe is subject to a high degree of government control through the Ministry of Transport under

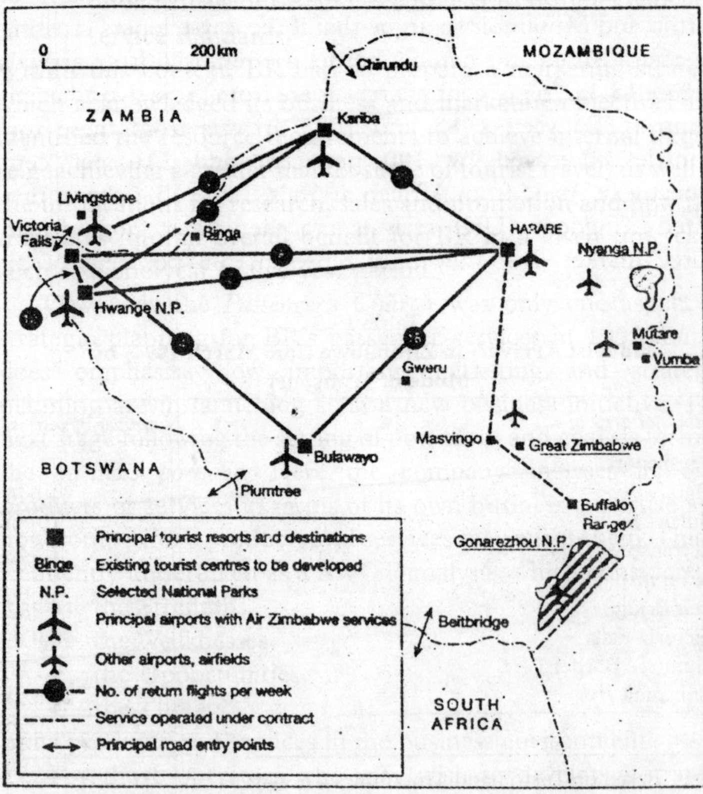

Figure 15.3: The air transport system in Zimbabwe.

the provisions of the Air Zimbabwe Act (1989). All decisions on the purchase of aircraft, marketing investment and the structure of air fares are subject to ministerial approval. Prior to the economic structural adjustment programme in 1991, which weakened the Zimbabwe dollar and increased air fares, 40 per cent of the foreign revenue earned by Air Zimbabwe was placed in government reserves. The result was a lack of funds for the airline to market itself effectively in a global environment. While Turton and Mutambirwa examine the development of air services in Zimbabwe prior to and after independence, they highlight the early problems the airline faced, including a lossmaking tour-operating business (Flame Lily Tours). In particular, the reluctance of government to allow the airline to raise prices in relation to market conditions led to infrequent but major price increases which advarsely affected inbound operators using Air Zimbabwe services in 1986 and again in 1992.

Table 15.4
Visitor Arrivals in Zimbabwe 1985–33

	Arrivals (000s)				
Region	**1985**	**1987**	**1989**	**1991**	**1993**
Africa	260	262	338	514	735
North and South America	16	15	17	15	25
Europe	48	53	68	64	99
Australia and New Zealand	6	8	13	13	15
Asia	3	3	3	4	6

Source: Besed on Turton and Mutambirwa (1996).

Turton and Mutambirwa highlight the limitations imposed by government on investment in tourism due to limited access to foreign exchange funds. The outcome prior to the 1990s was Air Zimbabwe's inability to 'provide an adequate fleet of aircraft for its internal routes and the supply of vehicles to transport visitors between airports and hotels and on game park tours'. In terms of the management and operating policies of Air Zimbabwe, long-haul services date to the former Air Rhodesia-British Airways service between London and Harare, a joint daily non-stop service. In the 1980s, Air Zimbabwe added other services between Harare and Frankfurt, Lisbon, Sofia and Athens highlighting the link to the European markets. A service to Perth, operated by Qantas using a seat-lease agreement, was also added.

Following the economic structural adjustment programme in 1991, government policy relaxed restrictions on foreign airlines. As a result, Air France launched a Paris-Luanda-Harare service in October 1992. This was followed by KLM's reintroduction of an Amsterdam-Johannesburg-Harare route. Both the Air France and KLM routes were suspended in the early years of independence to protect Air Zimbabwe. The explanation for the suspension given in the Annual Report of the Air Zimbabwe Corporation (1983) was that Air Zimbabwe's competitors operated larger aircraft on the European routes and so it was at a competitive disadvantage. Both Swissair and Lufthansa have also added flights to Johannesburg which then terminate in Harare. However, as Turton and Mutambirwa observe, 'current load factors on these routes suggest that long-haul capacity is in excess of market demand and vigorous fares discounting in taking place'. If transport policy has been characterised by a loosening of state control in aviation, Simon examines the effect of government policy on Harare's bus services between 1988 and 1993, which have moved from private to mixed ownership with government participation in stage bus operations and then moved back to private ownership in 1993. If this experience offers lessons for tourism and aviation, it is that government policy formulation is in a constant state of evolution to meet changing circumstances and ideological shifts.

Air Zimbabwe maintains domestic air services for international tourists with 80 per cent of traffic tourist-oriented on the Harare-Victoria Falls-Hwange National Park-Harare circuit (Figure 15.3). In contrast, on the Harare-Bulawayo route, only 20 per cent of traffic is tourist-oriented. Air Zimbabwe operations on international and domestic routes have been severely constrained by terminal facilities at Harare and smaller airports. A lack of suitable aircraft has also hampered operations. Although a new terminal is planned for Harare, funding the development remains a problem. The Department of Civil Aviation, responsible for aviation services, raised landing fees in 1994 and 1995 by over 1,000 per cent to be in line with European landing fees, although the level of service is not comparable with that in Europe. As a result, these policies may affect the viability of certain foreign airline operations and may thereby affect future arrivals. Victoria Falls airport was upgraded (i.e. a new passenger terminal was added for the Commonwealth Heads of Government Conference in 1991), but it has no night-flying capability. Airports at Kariba and Mutare also have limited runway capability, unable to cater for Boeing 737s. As a result, it is only possible to operate one Air Zimbabwe BAE 146 and some Fokker 50s. The use of appropriate aircraft for the services remains a major operational dilemma for the airline.

After independence, Air Zimbabwe used Boeing 707 aircraft on long-haul flights and in 1983, a Canadian overseas airline consultancy recommended the use of a fleet of Boing 737s for domestic operations and 747s for long-haul flights. Turton and Mutambirwa examine the subsequent purchase of a limited number of aircraft and the problems resulting from operating F-50s on a hire-purchase agreement for domestic services. While Air Zimbabwe's revenue is largely generated from domestic services, some fares are below operating costs, which may sometimes lead to state subsidies for tourist services. However, inconsistent policies resulting from state control of the airline and provision of services which are in the public interest mean that Air Zimbabwe cannot effectively meet the competing demands for air services. The inflexible nature of management decision making at Air Zimbabwe was identified by Turton and Mutambirwa. A restructuring of the airline to operate on a commercial basis and a more enterprising approach was seen as vital in the late 1990s.

Competition on domestic routes has been introduced, with Zimbabwe Express leasing BAc 146 aircraft from the government on the Harare-Kariba-Victoria Falls and Harare-Bulawayo routes. While the introduction of competition has aided route capacity, domestic services cannot always cope with the inbound arrivals from Europe on the range of airlines now operating international services. As a result, arrivals often have to stay overnight in Harare, though this has added to the development of urban tourism in the capital. However, proposals for additional direct flights to Victoria Falls from other countries may impact on Harare's gateway status. South African Airways can use Victoria Falls for scheduled and charter flights in conjunction with Air Zimbabwe. Arrivals have increased from 8,370 to 59,000 between 1987 and 1994. There is also pressure from South African Airways to increase capacity on this route. Furthermore, Air Zimbabwe has lost market share by the introduction of long-haul services from rival airlines. This may be compounded by plans in South Africa to promote a South African tourism product of which Zimbabwe will be just one component. This could result in increased charter traffic to regional airports at Victoria Falls and Hwange. It could also mean Air Zimbabwe loses a proportion of its existing domestic tourism market as foreign carriers terminate services in Johannesburg instead of Harare.

The contribution which Air Zimbabwe 'has made to the promotion of tourism has been seriously restricted by the rigidity of state control over finance, aircraft acquisition, pricing and operational policies . . . The recent liberalisation of air transport within the country is seen as providing the opportunity for Air Zimbabwe to offer improved services between Harare and the major resorts and to develop routes to new tourist areas, all at competitive fares and no longer subject to ministerial approval . . . Air Zimbabwe will have to adjust to . . . the challenge to its domestic service monopoly by other airlines in their bid to link up major Zimbabwe resorts within an international southern African framework'. From a policy framework, this study highlights the ever-changing nature of tourist transport and the importance of flexibility in government policy to accommodate new business conditions and the difficult balance to be achieved between ideology and effective management to tourism development through transport.

Since changes in transport policy within individual countries have repercussions on both tourism and on other countries, attention now turns to the role of policy formulation and development among transnational organisations such as the European Union. The single European Act has sought to introduce greater competition and a reduction in state subsidies to achieve greater efficiency in transport provision (see the special issue of the *Journal of Air Transport Management 3/4* 1997 on this theme). Even this is not without problems as the example of the Common Transport Policy indicates.

Towards a Common Transport Policy for the European Union

In the case of aviation, the EU policy 'has changed dramatically over the last decade after a move from aviation markets being a series of heavily regulated, discrete bilateral cartels, dominated by nationally owned flag carriers, to a structure which promises by the end of the century to have become a liberalise multinational civil aviation market'. Accordingly, Button views this as evolving into an institutional structure similar to that which developed into the USA. Aviation was initially excluded from the EU's Common Transport Policy in 1957, with individual countries regulating their own domestic aviation markets. In the international arena, bilateral service agreements were used to regulate air travel. Policies existed which regulated scheduled fares, market entry and service provision.

Changes have Occurred in the EU Aviation Market

- Individual countries (e.g. the UK) did not free the market entirely; instead the procedure for allocating licences was more liberal. Other countries like France, Italy and Germany have been more reluctant to institute domestic liberalisation.
- Since the mid 1980s, bilateral agreements have been liberalised between member states (e.g. the UK-Netherlands agreement in 1984), which relaxed market entry restrictions. Changes on the UK-Ireland routes indicate that lower fares resulted.
- External changes, such as the USA's 'open skies' policy have assisted EU member states in developing more liberal bilateral agreements.

- In the late 1980s, the EU began to develop a common policy following court rulings which led European politicians to consider liberalisation measures.

Since 1998, competition rules have been applied to aviation. The EU's three air transport liberalisation packeges aimed at removing restrictions on access, price and capacity. The First Package in January 1988 was modest and agreed to a move towards a single market. The Second Package in June 1990 removed 'government to government capacity-sharing arrangements, introduced in stages the notion of double disapproval of fares and prevented governments discrimination against airlines, provided that they conformed with technical and safety standards'. It also made foreign participation easier, making fifth freedom rights more available (the right of an airline to carry traffic from one point in a foreign country to a point in another foreign country, when this service is linked from an airline's home country to the point in the first foreign country. The final element, the Third Package, launched in January 1993, led to a regulatory framework which emerged in 1997 that is similar to the US domestic market. In other words, since 1997, full cabotage has been permitted and fares are no longer regulated. Foreign ownership among EU carriers can occur although the EU has reserved the right to intervene in the market under certain circumstances: to freeze the market if it becomes unbalanced and to prevent downward spirals on air fares. Aviation, however, is not the only area for action by the EU as rail travel has also been considered.

Rail transport and rail networks are state-owned in all member states of the EU (despite changes in the UK), and they receive subsidies to assist with the operation of uneconomic services. Yet there are certain governments (e.g. the UK and Sweden) which have sought to introduce greater competition, aspects of privatisation and a more explicit market orientation for rail passenger transport after many years of state control. As Page notes, state ownership of rail transport has produced organisations managing national railway networks which are characterised by:

- a close relationship with central government due to state ownership and the provision of operating subsidies,
- periodic changes in the political will of national governments to subsidise rail,
- constraints on investment planning and a forward-looking approach to development,
- a lack of management freedom prior to the 1980s,
- an inability to prevent loss of market share in rail travel in the 1970s and early 1980s.

The close relationship between the management of railways and the interests of national governments has meant that policy making has been largely inward-looking and focused on national rather than EU-wide concerns. Gibb and Charlton have confirmed this view in their analysis of the EU's role as an organisation intended to foster cooperation in transport policy among its member states. They found that in the case of rail travel, the wider consideration of the EU have been undermined by the vested interests of national governments in their own rail networks. As a result, the EU has made little progress towards developing a common rail policy due to two principal objectives to EU transport policy, which consistently cause conflict:

- the desire to liberalise rail transport to achieve free trade policies in the move toward the Single European Market,
- the need to harmonise the conditions of competition in rail services in pursuit of social intervention policies.

The EU 'Proposal for a Council Directive on the Development of Community Railways', which was finalised in July 1991, embodied these principles. It proposed that railway operations and infrastructure should be the responsibility of two separate organizations, so that railway companies can make commercial decisions about long-distance passenger services. This is designed to facilitate an expansion in international rail passenger services where the user entering a national network pays a user fee, thereby reducing the possibility of cross-subsidisation of railway networks by national governments. While the EU aimed to introduce freedom of access to national railway networks across its member states, the changes required by national governments to achieve these objectives imply an end to the highly regulated environment in which state-managed railway enterprises operate. To date, there has been a failure to agree the principles necessary to develop a Common Transport Policy, and rail transport is no exception to this. The prospects for providing access to national railway networks and the introduction of competitive operations are remote, due to the challenge to existing national markets and services. In the absence of an EU Common Transport Policy what should be the main components of an effective state policy for tourist transport?

The Organisation for Economic Cooperation and Development (OECD) has argued that effective state policies for tourist transport should be integrated so that tourism and transport concerns work in harmony rather than in isolation. Transport policy needs to consider tourism as a related activity which is directly influenced by the objectives pursued in national and regional transport policy. In fact, Sinclair and Page examine the role of policy formulation in a transfrontier region (the Euroregion - in North East France and South East England) in relation to transport, tourism and regional development. This is an interesting example where cross-border cooperation and planning for transport may assist in coordinating the variety of bodies involved in implementing tourism and transport planning in two different countries. It also illustrates how a wider policy-making framework can assist in the recognition of the vital link between transport planning and tourism to promote economic development in local areas.

Yet translating policy objectives into a planning framework may pose particular problems for tourist transport systems since the political philosophy of national governments can lead to different approaches to funding and development of transport infrastructure projects. For example, many airports are now commercially operated enterprises, a principle established in the UK government's White Paper *Airports Policy* which was mirrored in many other European countries. In this respect, infrastructure provision is now based in the private sector, with the UK government's market-led philosophy also applying to complementary infrastructure provision. For example, this was demonstrated by the public/private sector partnership between BR and the BAA'S £300 million Heathrow Experess rail-link project to connect Heathrow and Paddington in London.

Where countries do formulate a tourist transport policy, the following issues should be taken into account in its implementation through planning measures:

- the management of tourist traffic in large urban areas (see the London Tourist Board 1987 : 61—3, on managing transport used by vistors, particularly the problems of coach parking which is also discussed by the Bus and Coach Council 1991) and small historic cities. In 1997, the English Historic Towns Forum established a Code of Practice for coach tourism to address the issue among its members in line with growing concerns about managing tourists and non-tourists and traffic in town centres;
- the management of tourist and recreational traffic in rural areas;
- the promotion of off-peak travel by tourists to spread the seasonal and geogaphical distribution of tourist travel and the resulting economic, social, cultural and economic impacts of tourism;
- maximising the use of existing transport infrastructure and the use of more novel forms of tourist transport together with the provision of new infrastructure on the basis of long-term traffic forecasts;
- integration of transport modes.

With these issues in mind, attention now turns to a case study of the state's role in tourist transport to assess which objectives are being pursued towards tourist rail travel in the UK.

CASE STUDY: The Organisation and Management of a Tourist Transport System: Tourist Rail Travel in the United Kingdom

In this case study, the organisation and management of a tourist transport service - rail travel - is examined to illustrate the direct and indirect impact of government transport policy on a tourist transport system. The case study examines the implications of government policy prior to and after privatisation in 1994. It highlights how a systems approach, government regulation and policy issues need to be viewed in relation to the provision and consumption of a service for tourists which operates as an integrated system. In this system, the main input comprises the supply of a service and the demand for tourist travel, which the principal output comprises the tourist travel experience as a service encounter (see Figure 15.4). The nature and organisation of this system of tourist travel is indicated in Figure 15.4 which identifies the interrelationships between the provider of the service and the purchaser (i.e. the tourist). As Figure 15.4 shows, a complex set of relationships affect the supply and demand for tourist travel by rail, with a variety of organisations directly affecting the supply *via* regulatory and financial controls (e.g the Department of Transport and the Treasury). However, prior to discussing the role to the state in policy formulation and its implementation, it is useful to establish the dimensions to the supply and demand for tourist rail travel in the UK.

Tourist Travel by Rail in the UK Pre-privatisation

Turton examines the role of rail passenger transport in the UK, providing a broad overview of the various factors which affect the organisation and management of passenger services, the impact of government policy and the relative importance of rail versus other modes of transport. The UK rail network comprises 16,585 route kms and some 719 million passenger journeys were undertaken in 1981/82 and 738 million journeys in 1996/97. Potter argues that the main determinants of the demand for rail travel are:

- speed
- cost
- comfort
- convenience
- access to stations
- the image of the service.

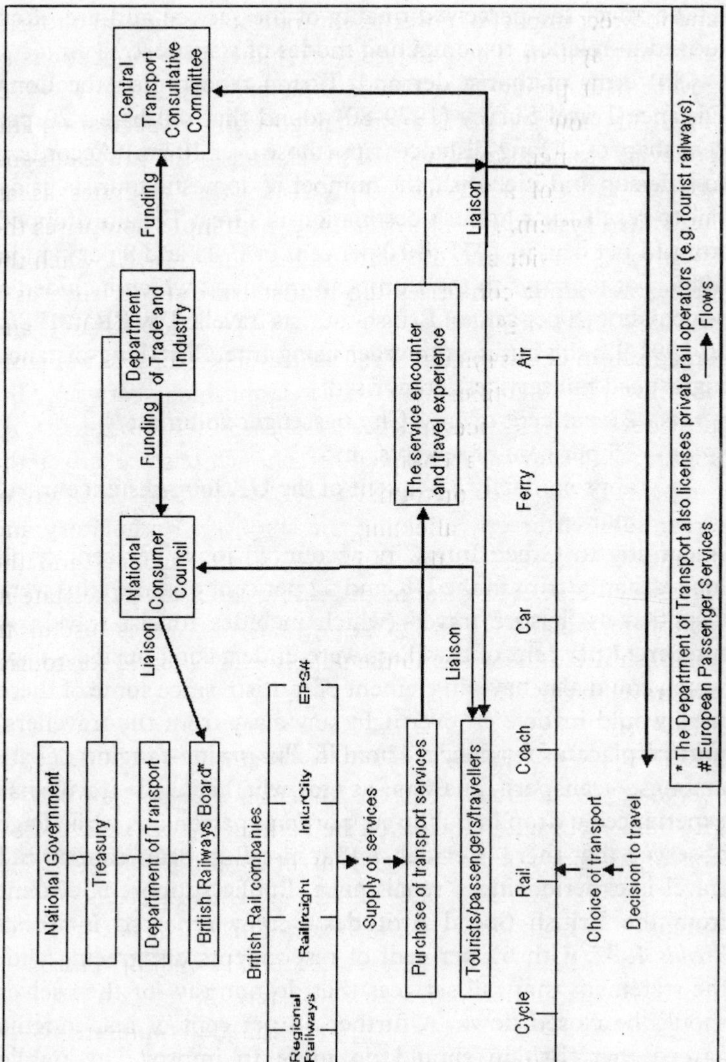

Figure 15.4: The tourist rail system in the UK prior to privatisation

These affect the perceived quality of the service and are often judged in relation to competing modes of transport.

In terms of tourist demand, Turton reports that the Long Distance Travel Survey (1979-80) found that rail had a 20 per cent share of all long-distance trips (those over 40 km). According to Jefferson and Lickorish, the number of domestic tourists using rail to reach their holiday destination in Great Britain dropped from 13 per cent in 1971 to 10 per cent in 1985 and 8 per cent in 1989. For journeys to the European mainland which included a sea crossing, 8 per cent of British tourists travelled by BR in 1986. In 1991/92, the business traveller using InterCity (long-distance high-speed rail services) comprised:

- 23 per cent of InterCity passenger volumes;
- 35 per cent of receipts; and
- approximately 8 per cent of the UK long-distance travel market.

According to Green InterCity accounted for 8 per cent of all long-distance trips in the UK and 52 per cent of these trips were classified as 'leisure travel' (which includes tourist travel). A further 27 per cent of travellers were undertaking business trips which could also have an element of tourism since some of these trips would involve an overnight stay away from the travellers' normal place of residence. There is also a wide-ranging debate amongst transport analysts as to whether rail travel has experienced a drop in public support and patronage, while Page observed that there is evidence that in a European context rail travel is experiencing a renaissance. Public support is evident from the British Social Attitudes Survey reported in *Social Trends 1997*, with 62 per cent of respondents disagreeing with the statement that rail services that do not pay for themselves should be closed down. A further 58 per cent of respondents agreed that 'Britain should do more to improve its public transport system even if its road system suffers'. However, the car still accounts for 88 pre cent of passenger traffic in Britain, compared to rail with a 4.5 per cent share in 1995.

Rail travel in the UK has seen a significant drop in public support and patronage since the 1970s as competition with other modes of transport (e.g. air, car and coach travel) have eroded

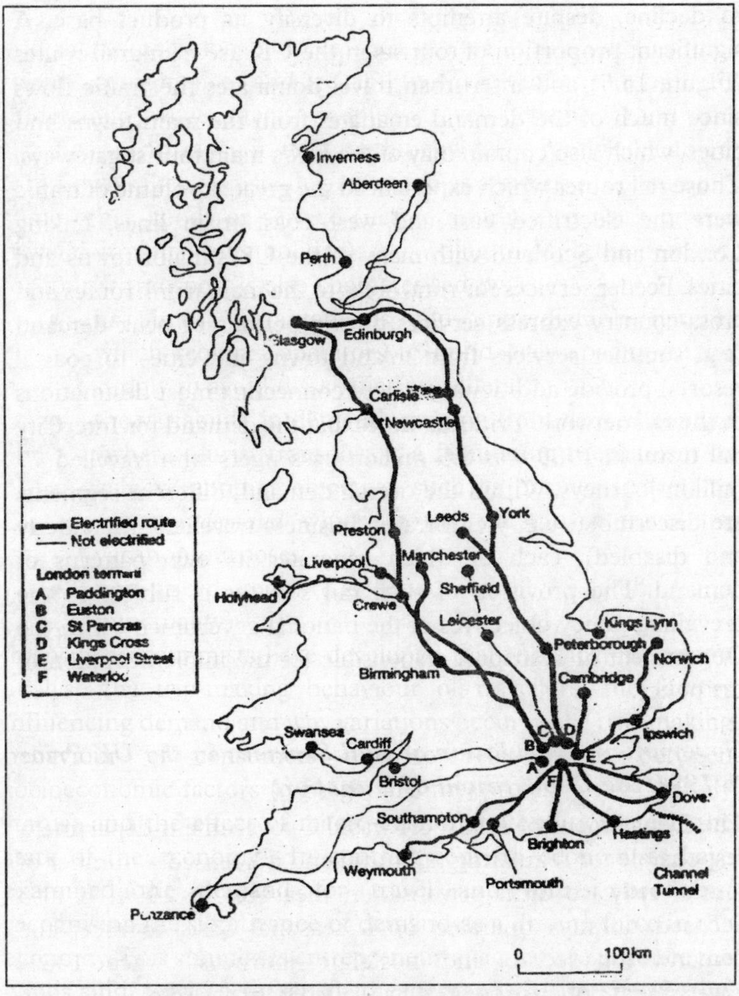

Figure 15.5: Trunk railway routes in the UK.

rail's market share. How far is this a result of government policy as opposed to changing attitudes and preferences among travellers, and to what extent is the decline in the use of rail for tourist trips a unique feature of the UK? For example, in the 1970s and early 1980s, BR penetrated the domestic long-distance holiday market, selling over 170,000 'Golden Rail Holidays' per annum in the late 1980s but its share of the long-distance travel market continued to decline, despite attempts to diversify its product base. A significant proportion of tourists in the UK use trunk rail routes (Figure 15.5) and interurban travel dominates the traffic flows since much of the demand emanates from the main towns and cities, which also contain may of the UK's main tourist gateways. Those rail routes which experienced the greatest volume of traffic were the electrified east and west coast main lines, linking London and Scotland with many of the UK's major towns and cities. Feeder services for rural areas to the main trunk routes and cross-country express services during periods of peak demand (e.g. summer services from inland towns and cities to coastal resorts) provide additional services connecting most destinations to the rail network. Prideaux notes that the demand for InterCity rail travel in 1989 was 8.5 million passengers who travelled 77 million journeys. Within the overall demand, different segments are discernible (e.g. youth travel, business travellers, the elderly and disabled), each of which generates its own patterns of demand. The provision of such rail services is subject to the prevailing policy objectives of the national government, with the Department of Transport responsible for the implementation of the policy.

Government Regulation of Rail Services in the UK Prior to 1994: the Department of Transport

The Department of Transport was the government department responsible for regulating rail travel and it licensed a number of tourist railways until privatisation measures in 1994. It also licensed railways operated on a seasonal basis to meet the demand for scenic and nostalgic journeys. Since 1981, government policy in the UK has rolled back the role of the state in the regulation of public transport through selective measures of privatisation as discussed earlier (e.g. the 1985 Transport Act, in an attempt to develop a greater degree of commercialism in service provision. For example, BR's government subsidy was cut by 60 per cent in the period 1983 - 89. For BR, this has meant that it has had to adopt a greater degree of market-led planning towards rail services.

Rail Privatisation in the UK

According to Gibb 'the process leading to the privatisation of British Rail (BR) actually started in the early 1980s and has been a more protracted process than most political commentators credit' and 'BR has been better prepared than most industries for privatisation as a result of a restructuring process that began well before the strategy and timetable for privatisation became clear'. Britain's Labour government has to launched a White Paper outlining the future for transport policy in the UK. However, in the case of privatisation the government's policy to privatise the railways after 1992 is clear: an 'underlying neoliberal philosophy - seeking to reduce government involvement and to encourage a free market driven by competition.' A number of commentators examine privatisation in detail and readers are directed to their lucid analyses. But it is also pertinent to outline some of the principal changes that have occurred and the implications for tourist rail travel.

In 1992, the Department of Transport announced its plans to implement government policy objectives by introducing further measures to privatise the railway system. Whilst seeking to reduce government subsidies for rail travel, a hybrid solution was sought to introduce private sector investment and involvement. Gibb show that 'up to 1982 the railways had been run as five geographical units. This was replaced with five business sectors - InterCity, Network South East, Regional Railways, Parcels and Freight.' Yet privatisation plans paradoxsically were not necessary on financial grounds by the early 1990s, since InterCity and Freight were operating without subsidy and the Department of Transport's *New Opportunities for thc Railways* acknowledged that BR was the most efficient of any European railway. At the time of privatisation, the existing business units were not selected as the best option for sale. Instead the Department of Transport's proposal intended to sell—

Table 15.5
Company Groups Within the Rail Industry According to Their Function

Function	*Description*
Central	Consultancies research and telecommunications services.
TOC	Train Operating Companies running passenger services
BRIS	British Rail Infrastructure Services (e.g. track renewal and maintenance).
BRML	British Rail Maintenance Limited (e.g. rolling stock maintenance and construction).
ROSLO	Rolling stock leasing companies.
GoCo	Railtrack, Union Railways and European Passenger Services (EPS). The ownership of these businesses as transferred to Central Government prior to privatisation. Union Railways was charged with planning the high-speed rail link from London to the Channel Tunnel. Union Railways and EPS were combined as part of the deal with LCR in 1996 to develop the high-speed rail link.

Source: Modified from Charlton et al (1997).

both freight and parcels to the private sector, the breaking up of passenger services into franschises to be operated by the private sector, the provision of rights of access to the rail network for private operators of freight and passenger services (overseen by a Regulator), the separation of track and train services with one part of BR becoming a track authority (Railtrack) with responsibility for running the track and infrastructure, and opportunities for the private sector to purchase or lease stations.

The Department of Transport's *Britain's Railways: A New Era* outlined the final structure of the privatised railway industry, where BR was compartmentalised into independent businesses, each cooperating on a commercial and contractual basis. As Charlton argue, the government's desire to break BR's monopoly was enacted using the concept of a *common carrier*, which avoided the provision of new infrastructure. By separating ownership of infrastructure from service provision, the common carrier could provide customers with access to its resources - the companies who compete to offer rail services to the public. In this case, Railtrack is the common carrier. The rail industry now comprises a series of companies which operate rail services or support services (Table 15.5) and Figure 15.6 summarises the interactions in this new system. Not only is this a complex operational structure, as a result of privatisation, 92 businesses emerged and 67 were offered for outright sale. The 25 train-operating companies (TOCs) were offered as regionally based franchises through a tendering process (Table 15.6). Railtrack is also responsible for central timetabling, train planning, signalling and the structural condition of the 2,500 stations leased to TOCs. Railtrack operates in 10 zones as illustrated in Figure 15.7. Charlton argue that government intervention and regulatory action have effectively prevented competition. Most TOCs are still supported by government subsidies to procure rolling stock and access to track. In fact, as Charlton indicates, 'in line with its [government] desire to break up BR's monopoly, the government also requires the Rail Regulator and Franchise Director . . . to promote competition in the provision of railway services. However, so long as TOCs are not financially viable, the goals of protecting passengers' interests and promoting competition are largely incompatible'. In other words, the first round of rail franchises (Table 15.6) have been protected from competition so that no new competition will be allowed before 31st March, 1999, and a wide range of restrictions will remain until 2002. Only in a few circumstances (e.g. where TOCs have separate routes between similar destinations or two or more operate the same route) does competition exist. Thus, 25 existing TOCs on balance have regional monopolies until 2002.

In a competitive context, Charlton observe that BR's monopoly has been replaced by an oligopoly due to horizontal and vertical integration where corporate interests have acquired TOCs, franchises and rail businesses. For example, the coach operator National Express integrated horizontally after obtaining the Midland Main Line and Gatwick Express franchises. It also integrated vertically by purchasing the rolling stock company from which it leases the trains. Other examples also exist which have reduced competition. In terms of the outlook for tourists and other travellers, both Cole and Gibb observe that the future is uncertain. However, in a policy context the 'philosophical desire to promote competition may be dangerous both for the railways and for public transport

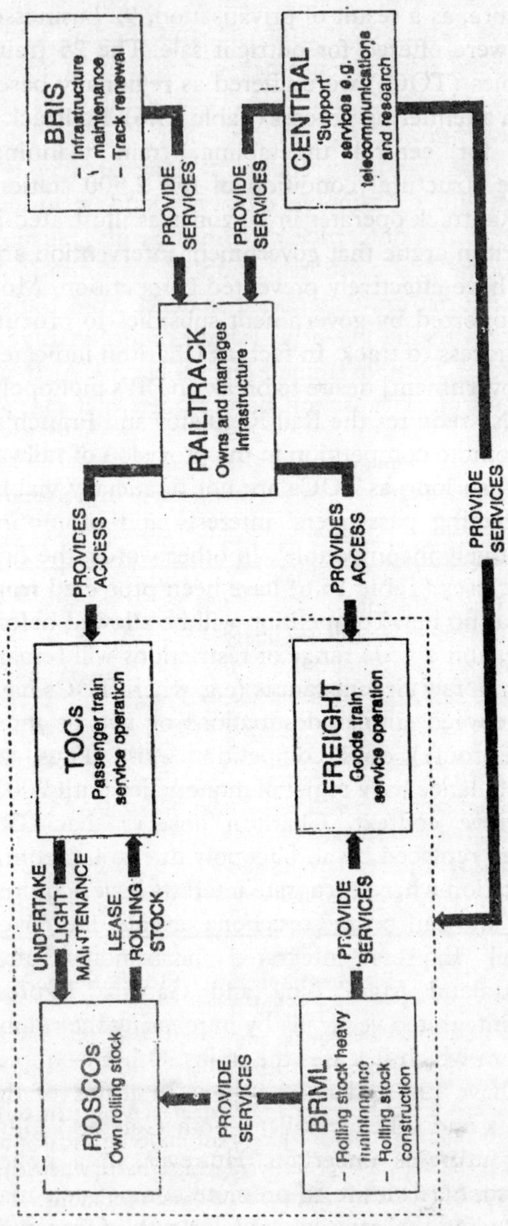

Figure 15.6: Interactions in the newly privatised railway industry in the UK post-privatisation.

more generally. Instead of a high-quality, responsive and affordable means of transport, the traveller may be left with a fragmented, confusing and expensive-to-use railway suffering fom under investment and decline'. The new climate for rail services has effectively ended BR's 44-year-old role as the main provider of rail services, and reflects a political ideology dominated by a desire to improve efficiency and introduce competition (European Conference of Ministers of Transport 1992). The outcome is a more complex organisational framework for the tourist rail experience as outlined in Figure 15.8 (compare this with the pre-privatisation model in Figure 15.4). Recent studies have examined the utility of such an approach and critics of privatisation have argued that lack of

Table 15.6
Rail Franchises Announced in 1993 by Former British Rail Sectors

Date	*InterCity*	*Network South East*	*Regional Railways*
Feb.1993	East Coast Main Line (ECML) Gatwick Express Great Western Main line	Isle of Wight Line[1] London-Tilbury-Southend South Western Division	ScortRail
May 1993	Anglia Cross Country Midland Mian Line West Coast Main Line (WCML).	Chiltern Great Eastern Kent Services Thames South Wales and Thameslink South London and Sussex Coast Northampton and North London West Anglia and Great Northern	CardiffValleys Line Central North East West North West Mersey Rail Electric Services

1. The Isle of Wight Line is a small railway and its management structure and operation are different from those which exist under privatisation. The franchise operates the line on a vertically integrated basis, where the operator is also responsible for track, infrastructure and operations.

Source: After Gibb et al (1996) based on the Department of Transport (1994).

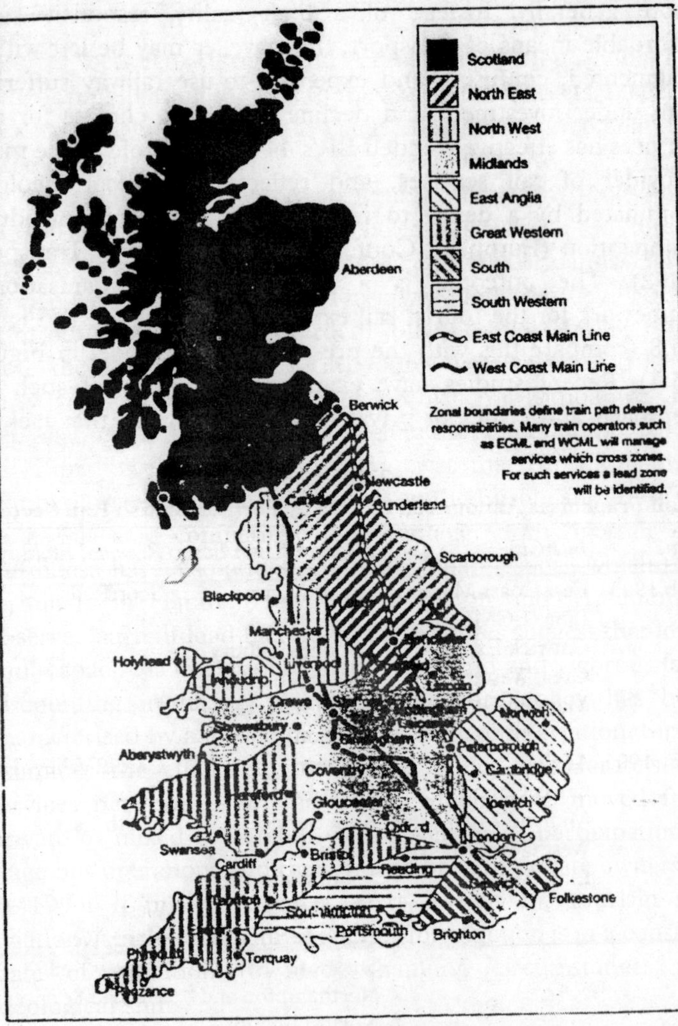

Figure 15.7: Railtrack Zones in the UK.

government investment is responsible for the poor performance of the nationalised railway company. Yet within the European railway industry, it is widely acknowledged that BR operated one of the most efficient railway networks in Europe, in view of the level of staffing and government subsidy provided per passenger kilometer travelled. Even so, the government

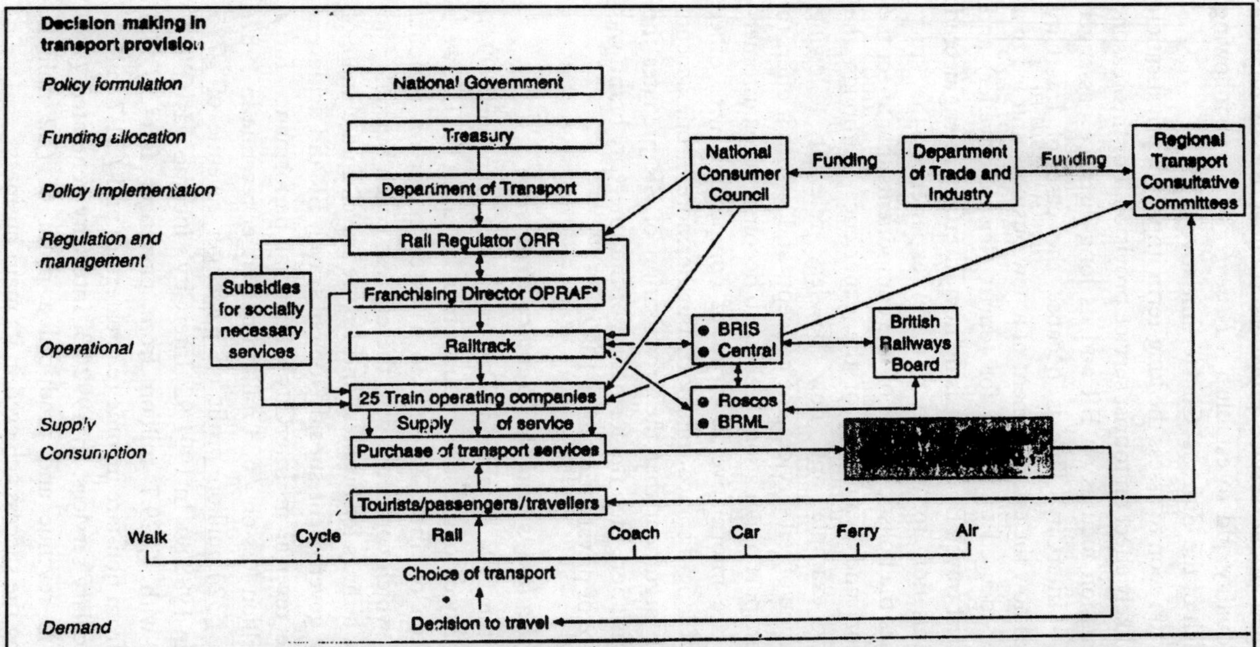

Figure 15.8: The tourist rail system in the UK post-privatisation.

**Note:* In July 1998, a government White Paper proposed the abolishing of OPRAF and the establishment of a strategic Rail Authority to create a more integrated system.

encouraged public service providers such as BR to improve service quality and to establish a *Passenger's Charter* following the launch of the Citizens' Charter initiative in 1991.

It is too soon to assess the long-term impact of privatisation and the likely effect on tourist service provision. For this reason, the discussion focuses on BR and its long-distance passenger service – InterCity. This is because the case of InterCity illustrates how the establishment of a new business unit led to a customer-focused approach for tourist (leisure-traveller) and non-tourist travel. By emphasising how InterCity re-engineered its organisation to provide a travel experience, the study recognises the holistic nature of the components that affect the perception and evaluation of the experience. Although the InterCity example any now be less relevant following privatisation of rail services, the concepts and lessons it offers to other transport organiations seeking to become more customer-focused are informative in terms of competition with other modes of long-distance transport. Furthermore, if one accepts the Gibb argument that the privatisation of BR predates the 1994 legislation, then the formation of the InterCity brand was a measure of privatisation after 1982.

British Railways and Rail Service Provision

Prior to the 1994 legislation (Department of Transport 1994), the majority of long distance tourist trips by rail in the UK were undertaken on InterCity and to a lesser extent on regional railways, which competed with the express coach business and domestic airlines for business and leisure travel. In a climate of reducing government subsidy for rail travel, BR did achieve a complete reversal in InterCity's financial performance for a £157 million loss on £623 million passenger revenue in 1987/88 to a £324 million profit on passenger revenue of £725 million in 1988/89. In 1991/92, InterCity's income was £896.7 million, with £829.7 million from passenger fares, £45.3 million from non-fare income (e.g. catering) and £21.7 million from ancillary services. In 1992/93, InterCity generated £889 million in revenue and produced a profit of £82 million, indicating the success achieved in its main business.

Prior to privatisation, in the medium-to-long term, the real potential for BR long-distance tourist travel was to expand its market share of the European passenger services running from London to mainland Europe through the Channel Tunnel. Following privatisation, these services were awarded to a consortium — London and Continental Railways - in 1996. The consortium, led by National Express and Richard Brancons's Virgin Group, was to use the profits from the service to fund the 68-mile Channel Tunnel high-speed rail link. However, in January 1998, LCR announced it was unable to raise sufficient capital to fund the scheme, and requested the government to increase its share of the development to £3 billion. In the event of deadlock, the government has the authority to take back the 18 Euroster trains given to LCR to operate the service. This is because the agreement was that the assets were only transfrerred to LCR until it met its obligation to build the route. This is a further example of the problems associated with privatisation.

British Rail and the Customer: the Tourist Travel Experience and Service Encounter

For the tourist, the journey on a train represents the consumption of a travel service. From a tourism perspective, this is the culmination of the desire to travel and the selection of a mode of transport to fulfil that need. Researchers such as Poon acknowledge the growing sophistication of tourists and their higher expectations from travel and tourism services. For the supplier, it has led to a much greater focus on service quality. Within BR those sectors which deal with leisure and business travellers on a regular basis (e.g. InterCity) have recognised the need to provide a consistent level of service which meets the expectations of customers.

InterCity Rail Services: Delighting the Customer

In a retrospective review of the development of InterCity in the 1980s and early 1990s, Vincent and Burley reveal that—

> InterCity had to reorientate its thinking so that its activities reflected a market-led organisation. InterCity no longer sold train trips but aimed

to provide a total travel experience. This meant thinking about customers' needs, not just when they arrived at stations to buy tickets, but when they were sitting at home planning to make a rail journey.

Key questions this posed for senior management included:

- How did customers want to make their first contact with InterCity?
- Were the telephone information points of contact welcoming?
- Was the route to the station adequately signposted?
- Did the station provide sufficient secure parking spaces?

The limitations on InterCity making further investment after 1982 meant the company turned to other solutions to improve market share in long-distance travel. Having become a profitable entity in 1988, InterCity sought at a time of severe recession to develop a business strategy to build the business. The vision for the 1990s which the company devised was one called 'Delighting the Customer'. Customer service and the travel experience were selected as avenues for development.

A radical change of culture was required to move from a product-led and operationally driven monolithic state enterprise to an organisation which was customer-focused. Within a two-year time frame, it required retraining and re-engineering an organisation of 30,000 employees. A guiding principle from the central management of BR, 'Quality Through People', this was the basis upon which changes would be built. Two driving forces in the process of change were empowerment of staff and teamwork to deliver tangible changes. This is a key component of Total Quality Management (TQM). One example of the culture change was the introduction in 1989 of a senior conductor role on board interCity train services to replace the traditional guard function. Guards had been chiefly responsible for revenue protection and safety and they had not worked exclusively for InterCity. As senior conductors, retrained guards were empowered to deal with problems associated with delays (e.g. authorising customers to receive free refreshment if severe delays occurred) and to be more visible on board trains. They were selected to be ambassadors for the business. By listening to the problems experienced by the new senior conductors, senior managers were able to introduce innovations to keep them in contact with land-based service centres. This enabled conductors to pass problems to service centres for immediate resolution.

One major catalyst for change was the arrival of a new manager of InterCity in 1992. This led to the recognition of a hierarchy of customer needs modelled along the lines of Maslow's basic needs study. Figure 15.9 reveals three levels of needs which had to be addressed before the customer would be satisfied. The base of the pyramid illustrates the operational focus of most transport providers – to offer a safe and reliable service. In-house research conducted by Inter City in 1991 recognised that it had a good product which was inconsistently delivered. As a result, to achieve the pinnacle of delighting the customer, a systematic review of service delivery and presentation was undertaken.

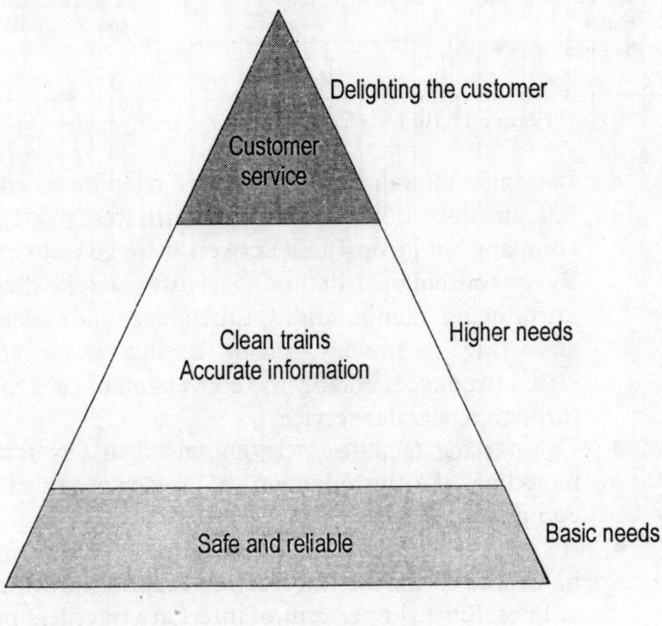

Figure 15.9: The hierarchy of rail travellers' needs.

InterCity develop the concept of the 'trail to the train' (Figure 15.10) to identify difficulties travellers experienced and where improvements could be made. Three monthly opinion polls were undertaken by external market research organisations to assess customer responses to service improvements and the ongoing problems. A number of practical responses to perceived problems included:

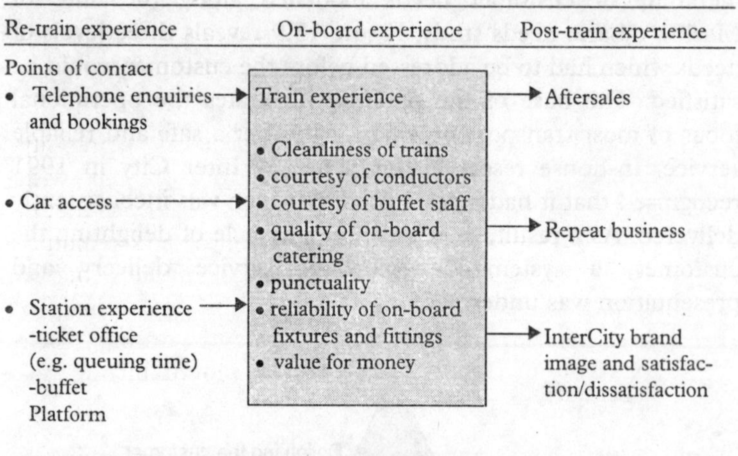

Figure 15.10: InterCitys' 'trail to the train' model.

- Rationalisation of Inter City's telephone enquiry bureaus since 1,800,000 calls a month were made to the company but inconsistent answers were given to callers. By establishing 20 dedicated centres across the UK, introducing computerised timetables and telephone answering technology, major service improvements were introduced, notably the conversion of calls to sales through a telesales service.
- Car parking facilities were enhanced at key stations, including the introduction of security surveillance equipment.
- A greater emphasis on customer welcome was pioneered to mirror the service reception provided by airlines. Since 90 per cent of interCity travellers passed through 20 stations, 'individuals were selected because

they wanted to work in a close customer environment' at key stations to give InterCity a heart and positive customer interaction. One tangible innovation was the introduction of claret uniforms which were seen as synonymous with friendly service.

- Platforms were zoned to ensure travellers could identify the positioning of First Class and Standard Class carriages, following best practice in Germany.
- Improvements to engineering workshops to reduce on-board defects to trains improved the reliability of the on-board travelling environment.
- On high-frequency, middle-distance routes an InterCity Shuttle service was introduced to compete with motorway travel. These services eliminated ticket checks at barriers and replaced them with a trainside welcome. Trains were available to board 20 minutes before departure and buffet cars were opened and remained open throughout the journey and during their turnaround. Catering trolleys also moved throughout the train during the journey.

Vincent and Burley summarise the business principles which characterised the InterCity culture by 1994:

- High-speed passenger rail business must be market-led and customer-driven.
- Operations and production are clearly vital to the efficient and safe running of a railway, but they must be subordinate to the customer and the market if they are to survive.
- Customers' needs have to be thoroughly understood and acted upon by all staff.
- Good customer service is a key concern for all those who work for InterCity.
- Consistent standards of customer service are essential to a national brand under pressure from competition.
- Giving customers added value is paramount for repeat business.

This service encounter begins at the point when the ticket is purchase and includes the time spent waiting at the station through to the completion of the journey. The experience on board the train is also deemed to be on of the most memorable aspects of the journey and an integral part of the service encounter. Shilton suggests that while it is difficult to quantify the quality aspects of InterCity services, factors such as the condition of the rolling stock, the image of the high speed trains and additional advertising, accounted for half of the increased patronage of the long-distance travel market in the early 1980s. InterCity has also been conscious of the need to expend its share of tourist and non-tourist high-speed rail travel in the long-distance travel market by introducing new products (e.g. Family Railcards), cultivating niche markets such as off-peak premium travel (e.g. 'Weekend First – discounted first-class travel) as well as budget advance purchase (Apex) tickets. As two-thirds of InterCity's business travellers chose second-class (standard) accommodation, InterCity introduced the 'Silver Standard' service for full-fare standard-class passengers. This included free seat reservations, complimentary airline-style meals and steward service; it was a deliberate attempt to offer a competitive service equivalent to what was currently provided by domestic airlines.

The demand amoung more discerning travellers for enhanced service quality on InterCity services meant that new services were also provided for different market segments. In addition, the quality and ease of interchange facilities at major rail termini in the UK (e.g. at the ports, airports and in major cities are important factors affecting the tourist travel experience and may influence the decision to travel by train.

Interchanges need to be integrated, with easy access to other modes of transport of onward travel, so that the commencement and completion of the journey are not marred by difficulties in making connections. One further development which has had a wide-ranging impact on the service quality of tourist use of rail, was the introduction of BR's *Passenger's Charter* which has now been a key feature post-privatisation for TOCs.

British Rail's Passenger's Charter: New Standards for Tourist Rail Travel?

It is widely acknowledged that BR was perceived by passengers in the 1970s and early 1980s as an archetypal state-owned enterprise, with a negative image in relation to service provision. Although there is no simple explanation for this image, factors such as limited public funding by successive governments since the 1960s and operational difficulties (e.g service interruptions) have contributed to the poor public perception. For example, the 'Consumer Concerns 1990' survey by the National Consumer Council (NCC) found that only 40 per cent of BR users were very satisfied to fairly satisfied with the service provided. This was confirmed by BR's acquisition of the Consumers' Association's 'Captive Consumer Award' in January 1992 for failing to adequately compensate consumers for poor service.

BR stated that some £7 million was paid to its customers in 1991 as cash refunds and travel vouchers through its Discretionary Compensation Scheme. However, to place service and performance on a more prominent footing, BR launched its *Passenger's Charter* in May 1992, with a view to having it fully operational by 1993. The funding of this new scheme was expected to cost £10 - 15 million and it aimed to ensure that rail travel for tourists and commuters meets certain standards. The charter set out to provide:

- a safe, punctual and reliable train service;
- clean station and clean trains;
- friendly and efficient service;
- clear and up-to-date information;
- a fair and satisfacto4y response if things go wrong.

This required BR to establish standards for services and the most publicised aspect of the charter was the provision of compensation for delayed or cancelled rail services. From BR's point of view, it has meant publicising its internal procedure for measuring performance. This process required data generated through its Management Information Systems to monitor and evaluate different aspects of its business. The main features of the *Passenger's Charter* are set out in Table 15.7 which shows that performance indicators and clear targets had to be met in terms of service provision. These were reviewed and published on a regular basis. In managerial terms, the process of producing a charter may have the advantage of encouraging the development of a corporate culture based on service quality, but staff training and commitment are required if this service ethos is to permeate staff consciousness in an organisation employing over 138,000 staff. Since the privatisation bill, the new TOCs have each introduced their own passenger charter and the Office of the Rail Regulator now has the power to imposc fines on companies

Table 15.7
The Main Features of the British Rail's Passenger's Charter

- Establishing performance standards and targets for groups of routes.
- Setting punctuality standards (e.g. 90 per cent of InterCity trains should arrive within 10 minutes of their scheduled time).
- Setting reliability standards (e.g. 99 per cent of InterCity services should run).
- Waiting time at ticker offices should be a maximum of 5 minutes in peak periods and 3 minutes at other times.
- The quality of staff communication is to be improved through training, particularly at retail outlets (e.g. ticket offices and enquiry bureaux).
- Managerial staff are to be placed on a performance-related pay scheme to ensure they reach predetermined targets.
- Passengers should be kept informed prior to and during their journey of any delays.
- Engineering work is to take place, wherever possible, at times which minimise inconvenience to passengers.
- Those with special needs (e.g. the disabled) are to be given assistance.
- Refunds are to be made for delayed or cancelled journeys within the confines of the new compensation scheme.

Source: Based on the British Railways Board (1992) *The British Rail Passenger's Charter,* British Railways Board, London.

for non-compliance. TOCs are expected to maintain an operational environment as prescribed by the National Conditions of Carriage (British Railways Board 1996) and each must produce a passenger charter which is user-friendly and as favourable as that of its BR predecessor. In some cases, TOCs have sought to aspire to higher standards than their BR predecessor. Table 15.8 outlines the key features of one passenger charter for Great Eastern Railway Limited which operates services east of Liverpool Street station in Central London. Gibb observe that new passenger charters also have to set out TOC's commitment to operating reliable and punctual train services, fares and facilities, to meeting the needs of disabled travellers and to putting measures in place to deal with delay. A useful comparison with the UK situation can be found in the Singapore Mass Rapid Transit Ltd. *Customer Charter – At Your Service: SMRT's Commitment to Passengers;* it pledges:

- 94 per cent of trains to arrive within two minutes of schedule,
- 96 per cent of trains to depart within two minutes of schedule,
- train service availability to be at least 98 per cent,
- a maximum of 6.7 failures per 100,000 uses of ticket vending machines,
- a maximum of 5 failures per 100,000 uses of ticket gates.

In contrast to the UK, each MRT station has customer feedback forms readily accessible, a World Wide Web page, a toll-free hotline and a voice-mail message system for out-of-hours contacts.

Critics, such as the Consumers' Assocation, have argued that passenger charters are a glossy public relations exercise with only a limited amount of finance devoted to the scheme which may be better deployed on improving services rather than compensating travellers for poor service. Sceptics have also argued that the targets set by different rail services are too low. Nevertheless, such charters have publicised the importance of service quality and provided tourists and other travellers with clearer information on their role as consumers, and the standards and attributes to expect from a rail journey. However, the NCC is still seeking further improvements to the process of producing charters for public services to achieve long-terms benefits for consumers.

So what does the case study tell us about the tourist transport system?

- Marketing research is an important part of the strategic planning process for a tourist transport service, particularly when attempting to assess what tourist and non-tourist travellers require from a rail journey. This has a critical role in establishing a benchmark for service quality to ensure minimum standards of provision are met.
- Government policy has adopted a long-term policy favouring privatisation under the guise of improving consumer choice and service quality, citing the transformation in former stateowned enterprises which have been privatised and are more customer-led. Yet as Charlton indicate, turning policy into reality has been problematic due to internal contradictions associated with the logic of inducing effective competition in rail travel.

Table 15.8
The Main Features of Great Eastern Railway's Passenger Charter, January 1998

The purpose of the Charter

- Conditions of carriage
- Our standards. How are we doing?
  - monthly reports of reliability to be published at key stations
  - publication of consumer surveys about the service
- Being on time
  Train times (actual arrival times) are measured against the advertised timetable on Monday to Friday departures between 0700-0959 and 1600–1859 (peak times arriving at Liverpool Street Station. The targets for services are:
  - Up to December 1997: 88 per cent of trains will arrive at their destination within 5 minutes of their scheduled time
  - January to December 1998 : 89 per cent of all trains will arrive at their destination within 5 minutes of their scheduled time
  - After January 1999: 90 per cent of all trains will arrive at their destination within 5 minutes of their scheduled time.
- Reliability (the percentage of trains that run instead of those cancelled). A target of 99 per cent of all published services to run between Monday and Saturday.
- Planning your journey
  - details on a dedicated customer service centre
  - details on buying a ticket

  - how to make a national rail enquiry
  - timetables, posters and leaflets provided to show how to contact Great Eastern Railway on its services
  - train services and engineering works
  - fares
  - bicycles on trains
  - policy on smoking on trains.
- Looking after you
  - sources of information which update the travel situation
  - staffed and unstaffed stations
  - train service updates
  - on-board service announcements
  - weather-related delays
  - refreshments
  - safety.
- Customers with special needs
- Asking your views
  - At the station
  - During the journey
  - Contacting the Customer Relations Team
  - Reviewing your comments.
- Paying compensation for providing a poor service
  - Season ticket holders
  - All ticket holders
  - Journeys you do not make.
- Penalty fares
- Our commitment to customer service
- Other commitments
- Summary of customer contacts
- Route maps.

Source: Great Eastern Railways Limited (1997).

- Since the 1970s, tourist use of railways in the UK has declined but there is potential for increasing the number of journeys involving air and rail for distances of 500 - 1,000 km now the Channel Tunnel has opened. In 1995, 1.9 million outbound. UK residents used the Channel Tunnel as a travel mode and 1.7 million inbound tourists chose it as a means of transit.
- Further investment is needed in the UK's aged railway rolling stock and infrastructure to improve journey times. This is likely to be limited within the context of

existing policy which favours a greater role for the private sector. It is unlikely to yield major investment in new rolling stock as the franchises available to private operators are only offered on a short-term basis, though some TOCs such as Richard Branson's Virgin Railways have made massive investments on the west coast main line.

- The introduction of the passenger charter is a direct consequence of government policy towards public service provision and it has led to a greater emphasis on service quality in the tourist transport system.
- Since privatisation, the unified InterCity brand and image built up since 1982 has been supplanted by the TOCs with their narrow focus on their own services rather than a broader rail travel perspective.
- For international tourists visiting the UK, the changes since privatisation are complex, confusing and not visitor-friendly. Even long-distance booking through services which cross several TOCs is a deterrent to tourists' choice of rail if it is not simple to make and readily available at local rail stations rather than at regional centres.
- The long-term implications for rail service provision outside of the main conurbations are less clear. The integrity of the existing network is in question as many of the TOCs operate under a subsidised regime and a series of privately owned monopolies have replaced BR's monopoly. Even with the new government White Paper of mid-1998, the situation has changed dramatically. However, it is worth considering Whitelegg's comment on the London Underground which received no government subsidy operating grant. It is an indication of what can happen if a private sector ideology dominates public transport as 'two and a half million journeys are made. . . every day. . . Travelling on it is also a very unpleasant experience. . . A poor-quality public transport system sends out strong signals to those seeking work, tourists and inward investors. They

are less likely to choose London as a destination if their experience of moving around, is one of delay, overcrowding, inconvenience and misery.'

- Government policy can radically affect the way in which transport services are delivered to tourists and non-tourists as well as ensuring a simplistic or complex operational structure exists.
- The degree of privatisation and model chosen in transport policy determine the style of competition and likely benefits which will result for consumers. It is too soon to assess the long-term competition which will result for rail travel, with many franchises protected from competition and receiving subsidies. If effective competition were to arise even in a modified form akin to bus deregulation in the UK, tourist and leisure travel would assume an even more complex form that might exacerbate the role of the car as a preferred mode of transport.
- Speakman argues that 'the current process of rail privatisation is. . . a serious threat to UK tourism. The recent controversy about the proposed withdrawal of the West Highland Sleeper Service focuses on the degree to which rail travel is still... a vital part of the region's tourism product.' The privatisation process may also mean a loss of discounted travel and accommodation arrangements for tour operators. This is serious for rail companies since Speakman estimates that 40 per cent of rail travel is leisure-based. One welcome sing in that one of the former elements of BR's regional railways division – ScotRail – has launched a short breaks brochure and discounted rail tickets and a Freedom of Scotland Travel pass (with discounts on other forms of public transport) and discounted entry to local tourist attractions. In fact, now some rail companies (TOCs) are owned by bus companies, such ventures should be a natural development. This will assume an even greater significance as inbound rail travellers from mainland Europe choose to use services

Beyond London to the UK regions. Speakman is optimistic that 'a more entrepreneurial approach. . . [by TOCs]. . . together with a trend towards more environmentally sustainable forms of tourism... could open the way to some exciting and creative partnerships with local authorities and tour operators to rediscover the country railways'.

APPENDICES

Appendix 1: How to Organise a Tourism Planning Project

The first step in organising a tourism project is to conduct a tourism assessment of the country or region. This assessment reviews the resources for tourism, its potential tourist markets, and the major development opportunities and constraints. Based on the assessment, the terms of reference (TOR) of the study can be written specifically to suit area's planning needs.

As was emphasised in Chapter 2, the TOR should be carefully formulated so that the study considers all the relevant factors and achieves the intended results. If the local understanding of tourism planning is limited, an outside specialist should be brought in to conduct the assessment and write the TOR.

Preparation of a comprehensive national or regional tourism plan requires a team of various specialists. The exact composition of the team will depend on the specific TOR of the study, and the extent to which some team members can perform more than one function. The core team members are typically as follows:

- Tourism development planner
- Tourism marketing specialist
- Tourism economist
- Tourism transportation/infrastructure planner.

The additional specialists who are often required include:

- Tourism development ecologist or environmental planner
- Tourism development sociologist or anthropologist
- Air transportation planner
- Tourism manpower planning specialist
- Tourism organization specialist
- Tourist legislation and regulations specialist
- Hotel and tourist facility specialist
- Tourist facility architect/development standards specialist.

If some detailed planning, project feasibility analysis or special studies are included in the project, additional types of team members will be required. These may include, for example, specialists on land use planning, project feasibility analysis, cultural heritage planning and ecotourism.

In organising the planning team, it is important that a team leader be appointed for coordination of project activities and with the government and project steering committee. Usually this position is filled by the tourism development planner who assumes both administrative and technical functions. Typically, an international team is contracted to carry out the project because of the specialised knowledge needed. To the extent possible, the team should include local experts from the country so that they can provide their specific knowledge of the area, as well as technical capabilities. Counterparts from the tourism office and other agencies should be appointed to work with the team, so that team members can transfer their knowledge to local staff. Also, if local officials understand how and why the plan recommendations were made, they will be better able to help implement them.

A detailed project work programme should be prepared. This programme specifies when each work activity should take place and shows the interrelationships and sequence of the activities. It also indicates when each project report should be completed. By following the work programme, the work activities are well coordinated and the study remains on schedule.

Several types of planning reports are necessary, as follows:

- *Inception report* - After assessment of field conditions, the project team leader prepares the inception report. This report includes the detailed work programme and schedule, when the various team members should commence and complete their work, and any other pertinent information.
- *Interim report* - This report presents the preliminary objectives and results of the survey and analysis steps of the planning process alongwith any particular conclusion, opportunities and constraints which have been identified. The interim report is useful to prepare for a large project but can often be combined with the draft report for smaller studies.
- *Draft report* - This report presents the objectives, results of the survey and analysis, conclusions and preliminary tourism development policy, structure plan and other types of recommendations.

- *Draft final report* - This report presents the final policy, structure plan and other recommendations and implementation programme as prepared by the planning team, alongwith all the background survey and analysis.
- *Final report* - The final report presents all the final recommendations and implementation programme agreed to between the planning team and steering committee, alongwith all the background material. It includes the final plan maps and other graphic information.

When each of the first four reports referred to above is ready, it is presented to an reviewed by the project steering committee and other interested parties, in order to obtain their feedback. Any differences are reconciled and agreement reached on the conclusions and recommendations. These are incorporated into, progressively, the draft, the draft final and final reports.

Appendix 2: Projecting Accommodation Needs

The formula for projecting accommodation needs, and an example for determining average annual and high season demand, are set forth below. This example is only for one type of tourist market and accommodation. The formula should be applied to each of the tourist markets and related type of accommodation to determine the total accommodation for the country or region. Calculating high season demand is important because that season determines the maximum needs.

Demand for beds

The formula is:

$$\frac{\text{No of tourists (per time period)} \times \text{average length of stay (in nights)}}{\text{No of nights (per time period)} \times \text{accommodation occupancy factor}}$$

For example, to calculate annual beds demand:

$$\frac{150{,}000 \text{ tourists per year} \times 10 \text{ nights}}{365 \text{ nights} \times 75\% \text{ occupancy}} = \frac{1{,}500{,}000}{274} = 5{,}475 \text{ beds}$$

For example, the calculate high season beds demand.

$$\frac{75{,}000 \text{ tourists per 4 months} \times 10 \text{ nights}}{120 \text{ nights} \times 95\% \text{ occupancy}} = \frac{750{,}000}{114} = 6{,}580 \text{ beds}$$

Demand for rooms

The formula is :

$$\frac{\text{No. of beds demand}}{\text{Average room occupancy (persons per rooms)}}$$

For example, to calculate annual rooms demand:

$$\frac{\text{5,475 beds}}{\text{1.7 persons per room}} = \text{3,220 rooms}$$

For example, to calculate high season rooms demand:

$$\frac{\text{6,580 beds}}{\text{1.7 persons per room}} = \text{3,870 rooms}$$

Allowance should be made for the percentage of tourists who stay in non-commercial accommodation such as with friends and relatives. If this factor is, for example, 5 per cent, that percentage should be deducted from the calculated bed and room demand.

Appendix 3: Establishing Carrying Capacities

Establishing tourism carrying capacities is based on the concept of maintaining a level of development and use that will not results in serious environmental deterioration, socio-cultural or economic problems, or be perceived by tourists as depreciating their enjoyment and appreciation of the area. Any development engenders some changes. Carrying capacity analysis typically is based on not exceeding the levels of acceptable changes. It is now a basic technique being widely applied in tourism and recreation plannings to systematically determine the upper limits of development and visitor use, and optimum utilisation of tourism resources. Numerous tourism areas in the world show evidence of having exceeded their carrying capacities. This has resulted in environmental, social and sometimes economic problems, with a decrease in visitor satisfaction and consequent marketing problems.

In practice, determining carrying capacities is often not easy or precise. It depends considerably on the assumptions that are made carrying capacities may also change through time. However, it remains a very useful technique in guiding planning for a sustainable level of development.

Carrying capacities can be established for both undeveloped tourism areas and those that are already developed, and perhaps even reaching or exceeding their saturation levels. It is often the developed destinations, which are experiencing some problems of overdevelopment, which have become concerned about their capacity levels. Carrying capacities can best be calculated for specific development regions or areas based on environmental and socio-economic analysis. At the national and regional levels, they must be considered more generally. At these levels, carrying capacities are often based on the total of capacities calculated for specific major attractions, such as national parks and archaeological sites, and development areas such as resorts.

The measurement criteria presented here are for establishing carrying capacities primarily for tourist destinations. The capacities of the transportation facilities and services used by tourists travelling to their destinations are also important to analyse. Each area and its type of tourism is unique and must be specifically defined for the area, but some common criteria exist for virtually all places. Some criteria are quantifiable while others must be evaluated qualitatively. In determining capacities, the two major factors to be considers are described as follows.

The Indigenous Physical and Socio-economic Environment

This refers to the capacity of development and visitor use that can be achieved without resulting in damage to the physical (natural and man-made) environment and generating socio-cultural economic problems to the local community, which still benefiting the community and maintaining a proper balance between development and conservation. Exceeding saturation levels will lead to permanent damage of the physical environment or socio-economic problems, or both. The criteria for determining optimum capacities include:

Physical

- acceptable levels of visual impact and congestion;
- point at which ecological systems are maintained before damage occurs;
- conservation of wildlife and natural vegetation of both the land and marine environments;
- acceptable levels of air, water and noise pollution.

Economic

- extent of tourism that provides optimum overall economic benefits without economic distortions or inflation;
- level of tourism employment suited to the local community.

Socio-cultural

- extent of tourism development that can be absorbed without detriment to the life styles and activities of the local community;

- level of tourism that will help maintain historic and cultural monuments, arts, crafts, belief systems, customs and traditions without detrimental effects.

Infrastructure

- adequate availability of transportation facilities and services;
- adequate availability of utility facilities and services of water supply, electric power, sewage and solid waste disposal and telecommunications;
- adequate availability of other community facilities and services such as those related to health and safety, and of housing for employees in tourism.

The Tourism Image and Product

This refers to the levels of development and numbers of tourists that are compatible with the image of the tourism product, and the types of environmental and cultural experiences that the visitors are seeking. If the area exceeds saturation levels, the development environment and attractions which visitors come to experience with the destroyed or degraded, tourist satisfaction will decrease, and the destination will decline in quality and popularity. The criteria for determining optimum capacities include.

Physical

- overall cleanliness and lack of pollution of the destination;
- lack of undue congestion of the destination including attractions;
- attractiveness of the landscape or townscape including quality and character of architectural design;
- maintenance of the ecological systems and flora and fauna of natural attraction features.

Economic

- cost of the holiday and 'value for money'.

Socio-cultural

- intrinsic interest of the indigenous community and culture;
- quality of local arts, crafts, cultural performances and cuisine;
- maintenance of archaeological, historic and cultural monuments;
- friendliness of residents.

Infrastructure

- acceptable standards of transportation facilities and services;
- acceptable standards of utility services;
- acceptable standards of other facilities and services.

For each of the factors, measurement standards must be decided for each particular area. For example, a measurement standard for the amount of sandy beach area and frontage for each tourist coming to a beach resort can be established based on various assumptions of what is acceptable environmentally and necessary to maintain visitor satisfaction.

Seasonality is a major consideration in the concept of carrying capacity. The saturation level of visitor use of a destination is often reached during the peak periods of use, and not during the low season or on an average annual basis. Therefore, carrying capacity must be calculated for the peak period of use. As was discussed in the text, various approaches can be applied to reduce the peak period use and even out seasonality during the year. This achieves more optimum use of attractions, facilities, services and infrastructure. For some types of natural attraction features, visitor use may need to be controlled or prohibited during an ecologically critical period, such as the bird or turtle breeding season.

Appendix 4: Checklist of the Major Elements of a National or Regional Tourism Plan

The list specifies the elements that typically should be included in a comprehensive national or regional plan. These are listed according to their general sequence in the tourism planning process, but feedback takes place among the various elements as explained in Chapter 3.

Tourism Development Objectives

- Economic, environmental, socio-cultural and other objectives.

General Background Analysis

- Brief historical background of the country or region, especially as related to possible tourist attractions.
- Brief geographical description of geology, land forms and hydrography of rivers, lakes and coastal areas, with identification of areas geographically suitable for tourism development. Any susceptibility to natural disasters, such as volcanic eruptions and earthquakes or other problems such as coastal erosion, should be noted.

- Climatic patterns, with identification of climatically suitable areas for tourism development and activities. Any susceptibility to high winds, rainfall and flooding should be noted.
- Natural resource areas, and existing land use and land tenure patterns, with identification of areas that should not or cannot be developed with tourism.
- Environmental quality generally and especially in existing and potential tourism areas, with identification of any particular problems of pollution or environmental damage taking place.
- Existing national and regional development policies, plans and programmes, with evaluation of their influence on tourism development.
- Demographic patterns of the number and distribution of the population, age-sex profiles, population growth rates and trends, migration patterns and any other relevant characteristics.
- Economic patterns of the existing economic sectors and growth trends, Gross National/Domestic Product (GNP and GDP), per capita income, employment/unemployment patterns, and other economic characteristics, with identification of any particular problems such as location of economically depressed areas.
- Cultural patterns of traditions, religious and social values and other relevant characteristics, and the effects of development on cultural traditions and values.

Infrastructure Analysis Recommendations

- Analysis of access to the country or region by air, land and water related transportation, including capacities and convenience of facilities and services for tourists.
- Analysis of the internal transportation system of facilities and services as related to tourism use.
- Analysis of other infrastructure of water supply, electric power, sewage and solid waste disposal and telecommunications, as related to present and potential tourism areas.
- Review of any already approved plans and programmes for improvements to infrastructure.
- Identification of any particular infrastructure constraints on developing tourism and recommendations on improvements required to the infrastructure for tourism development.

Tourist Attractions and Activities and their Improvements

- Survey and inventory of existing and potential attractions and activities, with categorization into a logical system such as natural, cultural and special types of attractions.
- Evaluation of the tourist attractions, with identification of primary and secondary attractions and any particular problems of existing attractions such as overuse or misuse.
- Recommended improvements (and conservation) required of the attractions.
- Identification of any particular positive or negative influences on attracting tourists such as strong or weak image in the market countries, recent political instability or natural disasters, extent of crime in the area and travel time, distance and cost from the major market countries.

Tourist Facilities and Services and Their Improvements

- Survey of existing and already planned accommodation by number, type, location and quality level.
- Survey of existing an already planned other tourist facilities, including (tour and travel operations, restaurants, banking and money exchange, handicraft, speciality and convenience shopping, medical and postal facilities and services, public safety and tourist information services.
- Evaluation of tourist facilities and services, with recommendations on improvements required.

Recommended Extent and Form of Tourism

- Determination of tourism carrying capacities of various potential tourism areas and the entire country or region, based on environmental socio-cultural, infrastructure and tourist satisfaction considerations.
- Determination of the most appropriate forms of tourism, by location, based on the inventory and evaluation of tourist attractions and activities, carrying capacity and market analysis and other considerations.
- Determination of the most suitable amount or extent of tourism (by type of tourism), based on the carrying capacity and market analysis, importance of tourist attractions and other considerations.

Market Analysis and Projections

- Review of global and inter-country regional tourism patterns and trends.

- Analysis of tourist arrival patterns and trends in the country or region being planned, including both international and domestic tourists, and of the specific characteristics of tourists visiting the country or region; special tourist surveys may need to be conducted.
- Evaluation of the effect of existing or potential competing tourist destinations.
- Determination of the major influencing factors on the types and extent of future tourist arrivals, and determination of the primary and secondary markets.
- Establishment of market targets by number, type and country or region of origin, socio-economic group, touristic interest groupings, length of stay and other relevant characteristics.
- Consideration of local residents' use of tourist attractions, facilities and services.
- Projection of the number, type and quality level of accommodation, other tourist facilities and services and infrastructure required based on the market targets.

Recommended Tourism Development Policy and Structure Plan

- Recommended policy statement including economic, environmental and socio-cultural factors.
- Recommended structure plan including type and location of tourist attractions, designated tourism development regions or areas (tourism zones) and the transportation linkages.
- Recommended staging of development by time periods.
- Recommended tour patterns and programmes indicating tourist excursion routes or circuits.

Economic Analysis and Recommendations

- Determination of the present and projected tourist expenditures by amount and type.
- Calculation of the present and projected economic impact of tourism by the standard measurements of contribution to GNP or GDP (or contribution to the regional economy), gross and net foreign exchange earnings, extent and types of national or regional economic leakages, income generated, the multiplier effect, direct, indirect and induced employment generated and contribution to government revenues.
- Recommendations on ways to enhance the economic benefits of tourism at the community regional and national levels.

Environmental Considerations and Recommendations

- Identification of any present environmental problems generated by tourism and recommendations on ways to lessen them.
- Recommendations on measures to prevent future negative environmental impacts and reinforce positive ones.
- Recommendations on ways to improve the overall environmental quality of tourism areas.
- Recommendations on environmental protection and conservation policies and programmes needed, and application of environmental impact assessment procedures to specific tourism projects.

Socio-cultural Considerations and Recommendations

- Evaluation of any existing and potential positive and negative socio-cultural impacts resulting from tourism.
- Recommendations on ways to lessen negatives impacts and reinforce positive ones.
- Recommended public awareness programme on tourism and a tourist information brochure to inform tourists about local cultural traditions and expected tourist behaviour.
- Recommendations on ways to achieve community involvement in all aspects of tourism at the local level.

Institutional Considerations and Recommendations

- Review and evaluation of present public and private organisational structures for tourism, with recommendations on changes or new structures required for the effective management of tourism, including how to achieve close coordination on tourism among public agencies and between the public and private sectors.
- Review and evaluation of present legislation and regulation related to tourism, with recommendations on modifications or new regulations required.
- Review and evaluation of financial capital resources available for investment in tourism, with recommendations on ways to provide more financial resources if needed, including development incentives.
- Manpower planning analysis for tourism, with recommendations for education and training programmes required in the public and private sectors to provide the requisite manpower.
- Evaluation of present travel facilitation procedures, with recommendations for any improvements needed.

Marketing and Promotion Recommendations

- Specification of the marketing objectives and strategy.
- Recommended specific promotion programme with cost estimates and possible sources of funding.
- Recommendations on respective and joint roles of the public and private sectors in promotion.
- Recommendations on overseas promotion representation.
- Recommendations on provision of tourist information services.

Plan Implementation and Monitoring

- Recommended development or action programme, with cost estimates and identification of responsible parties.
- Specification of implementation procedures including the respective roles of government and other agencies and the private sector.
- Specification of tourist facility development and design standards, and how these should be applied.
- Specification of zoning and other land use regulations.
- Recommended use of incentives or disincentives to encourage development according to the plan.
- Recommendations on establishing a tourism information system, or improving an existing system.
- Preparation of detailed area plans and project feasibility studies for the first stage of development, including demonstration projects.
- Identification of possible sources of funding for project development.
- Specification of the techniques and procedures to monitor plan implementation and the progress of tourism generally.

Appendix 5: Model Tourism Action Programme

This model tourism action programme presents a typical five-year programme for projects and other actions required to implement the first stage of a national or regional tourism development plan. It exemplifies the principles that should be applied in preparing such a programme.

Explanation of the Model

The model programme is shown in Table A.1. It is for a hypothetical medium size country or region which has had a modest level of business tourism in the past, but now wants to embark on development of controlled holiday tourism. The model is assumed to be based on a comprehensive tourism planning study, including the institutional elements. The development plan is focused on a combination of beach and manne attractions, mountain and nature attractions and some archaeological, historic and cultural features. The plan applies the gateway and staging area concept, with designation of zones for coastal and mountain tourism development. The plan also shows excursion roads for general sightseeing and to provide access to the tourism zones and attraction features.

The action programme is organised for a five-year period, representing the first development stage of the plan. The programme is focused on further developing the gateway city as a staging area, one of the coastal tourism zones (a beach resort) and two of the mountain zones, each based on a national park. Although this model is only for the first five-year development period, preparatory activities are indicated for projects which will be undertaken or completed in the next five-year period, including the opening up of new tourism zones. This overlapping of activities reflect the need to have continuity from one programme to the next. The model represents an idealised situation in which there is rapid execution of projects. In reality, most countries or regions would take longer to accomplish the projects and actions.

The programme is organised based on project categories—tourist facilities; tourist attractions; major infrastructure; and other projects and actions. Although organised into categories, all components of the programme are scheduled for development in a coordinated manner. This coordination of projects and actions is the basic principle or successful development programming. For example, infrastructure improvements must be available at the appropriate time in order for tourist attractions, facilities and services to be developed and start functioning. Some tourist attractions need to be available by the time that accommodation and other facilities are developed.

The model programme shows tourist facilities and services being improved in the gateway city/staging area first because some facilities already exist and can easily be expanded. Thus, a small amount of holiday tourism can be encouraged in the city even before the beach resort and mountain tourism facilities are opened. Also, the staging area will need to be reasonably well developed by the time other tourism areas are open. Within the tourism zones, development is shown to take place on a phased basis. This approach is important because capital resources and construction capability can be severely strained if too many facilities are developed at one time. Also, it is usually not possible for marketing to attract the sudden major increases

Table A.1
Model Tourism Action Programme

Project/action	*Year 1*	*Year 2*	*Year 3*	*Year 4*	*Year 5*
Tourist facilities					
Gateway city					
Historic district with commercial tourist facilities	Prepare and adopt plan	Apply historic preservation regulations and tourist facility investment incentives on a continuous basis			
Historic urban hotel restoration	Design	Restore	Open		
Urban hotel expansion	Design	Construst	Open		
New urban hotel 1		Design	Construct	Open	
New urban hotel 2 (to be opened in second programme period)				Design	Construct
Tourist information centre	Design	Construct	Open		Expand
Tour and travel agency 1		Organise	Open		Expand
Tour and travel agency 2		Organise	Open		
Duty-free shop	Design	Construct		Open	Expand
Beach resort					
Overall resort plan	Prepare and adopt plan				
Infrastructure		Design	Construct		Expand
Recreation facilities		Design	Construct		Expand
Resort hotel 1		Design	Construct	Open	
Resort hotel 2			Design	Construct	Open
Resort hotel 3 (to be opened in second programme period)				Design	Construct
Employee community		Design	Construct	Open	Expand
Mountain tourism					
Mountain lodge 1 (near national park 1)		Design	Construct	Open	
Mountain lodge 2 (near national park 2)		Design	Construct	Open	
Tourist stopover 1		Design	Construct	Open	
Tourist stopover 2			Design	Construct	Open
Village tourism project 1	Prepare programme	Organise community	Develop facilities	Open	
Village tourism project 2 (to be opened in second programme period)			Prepare programme	Organise community	Develop facilities
Tourist attraction					
National park 1	Prepare plan	Design facilities	Construct facilities	Open	

Project/action	*Year 1*	*Year 2*	*Year 3*	*Year 4*	*Year 5*
National park 2		Prepare plan	Design facilities	Construct facilities	Open
Marine park (near beach resort)	Prepare plan	Design facilities	Construct facilities	Open	
Archaeological site	Prepare plan	Design facilities	Construct facilities	Open	
Historic site		Prepare plan	Design facilities	Construct facilities	Open
Cultural centre (in gateway city)	Select site	Design facilities	Construct facilities	Open	
Museum expansion (in gateway city)			Design	Construct	Open
Infrastructure					
Airport expansion	Design	Construct	Construct	Open	
Excursion road improvements	Design	Implement on phased basis during three-year period			
Electric power extensions	Design	Implement on phased basis during three-year period			
Urban water supply improvements	Design	Implement on phased basis during three-year period			
Urban waste disposal improvements	Design	Implement on phased basis during three-year period			
Telecommunications improvements	Design	Implement on phased basis during three-year period			
Other projects and actions					
Tourism law and regulations	Review and adopt	Apply on a continuous basis			
Facility development and design standards	Review and adopt	Apply on a continuous basis			
Tourism office	Organise	Train staff	Train staff		Expand
Marketing	Request funding	Improve image	Implement annual promotion programmes		
Investment incentive	Review and adopt	Apply incentives and adjust as needed			
Tourism training school	Design facilities	Construct facilities	Implement training programme		Expand
Public awareness programme on tourism	Prepare programme	Implement programme on continuous basis			
Tourist education		Prepare brochure	Distribute brochure on continuous basis		
Detailed planning for new tourism areas (to be developed in second programme period)				Conduct planning	Adopt plans

of tourists required to occupy a large new supply of accommodation rooms.

As shown in the model, development is programmed so that complementary facilities are available in a balanced manner. Some accommodation is shown being opened in the gateway city, beach resort and mountain areas in the same years. By the time this accommodation is open, the excursion roads (which also function as access roads), alongwith tourist stopovers and some attraction features, are scheduled to have been improved. This coordination of development will provide alternative destinations and rapidly broaden tourist markets, and allow for efficient organisation of circuit touring with overnight stops.

The other major infrastructure improvements required are programmed to be available when needed. Airport expansion is scheduled to be completed by Year 4, when there is expected to be an increase in tourist arrivals using the new beach and mountain resorts. Electric power extensions to those places will have been completed by then. Urban infrastructure will have been improved for use by both tourism and general development. The national/regional telecommunications system, important for both tourism and general development, will also have been improved by Year 4.

As shown in the model, the institutional elements must be programmed alongwith physical development. The tourism law and regulations and any other necessary legislation should be adopted in Year 1, so that these can be applied to tourism development. The tourism office also must be organised - or perhaps reorganised if an office already exists - early on. Funding for marketing needs to be budgeted. Image building of the destination is often the first step in marketing, and that can be commenced before many facilities are available. Then the specific promotion programme can be started, with its timing coordinated with the development of attractions and facilities. Investment incentives, if needed, should be adopted during the first year in order to attract the private investment required. The public awareness programme on tourism should also be commenced early so that people are informed about the anticipated tourism development and can prepare for it.

Having personnel trained to work effectively in tourism is essential. Training must be coordinated with the development of tourist facilities and services. The tourism training school or other type of training must be started early in the development programme, with phasing of training, so that trained personnel are available as the facilities are opened.

In addition to listing of projects and actions by year, a complete action programme will also include general cost estimates for projects, where relevant, and the agencies (or private sector) responsible for implementing the projects or actions. In some cases, project profiles including a calculation of costs and benefits will be attached to the programme. In order to maintain its viability, an action programme needs to be adjusted as it proceeds, taking into account unexpected delays or changing circumstances.

Appendix 6: Checklist for Monitoring Plan Implementation

This checklist identifies factors that should be periodically monitored to determine if the tourism plan and programme are being implemented properly and on schedule. Some different or additional factors might also be monitored, depending on the particular characteristic of the tourism area and its plan.

Development Factors

- Improvement of existing and development of new tourist attractions and activities, including tour programmes.
- Upgrading of existing accommodation, by number and type of units.
- New accommodation development by number and type of units.
- Location of upgraded and new accommodation.
- Occupancy levels of accommodation by type and month.
- Upgrading and expansion of other tourist facilities and services including tour and travel agencies, tourist restaurants, shopping, banking and money exchange and medical and postal facilities and services.
- New development of other tourist facilities and services.
- Improvement of existing and development of new tourism-related infrastructure, including access to the country or region, the internal transportation system, water supply, electric power, sewage and solid waste disposal and telecommunications.
- Extent that location criteria and development and design standards of tourist facilities are being applied to new development.
- Tourism projects that have been planned and approved but are not yet developed.

Marketing Factors

- Number of tourist arrivals, by month, and their characteristics-place of origin, socio-economic group, age-sex profile, etc.
- Average length of stay of tourists by type.
- Tourist satisfaction levels and attitudes toward attractions, facilities and services.
- Promotion activities by the public and private sectors.
- Effectiveness of the different types of promotion activities.
- Improvements in tourist information services.
- Number of visitors at the various tourist attraction features.

Economic Impact

- Expenditure patterns of tourists.
- Economic impact of tourism by the various standard measurements, including direct and indirect employment.
- Type and extent of economic leakages from tourism, and reduction of leakages.
- Extent that economic benefits of tourism are being received by local communities, including local development of tourism enterprises and employment of local residents in tourism.

Environmental and Socio-cultural Impact

- Improvement of any environmental problems of existing tourism development, including air, water, noise and visual pollution and ecological disruption.
- Improvement in overall environmental quality of tourism areas.
- Application of environmental quality protection policies and programmes and impact assessment procedures to proposed tourism projects.
- Identification of any specific environmental problems such as congestion at tourist attraction features or degradation of these features.
- Maintenance of authenticity of traditional arts, crafts and dance and music performances.
- Involvement of local communities in tourism, and any complaints from residents about tourism.
- Progress of the public awareness programme on tourism, and informing tourists about the local environment and society.
- Extent of crime, drugs and other social problems being generated by tourism.